I AM NOT MY BODY

I Am Not My Body

A Study of the International Hare Krishna Sect

Angela Burr

VIKAS PUBLISHING HOUSE PVT LTD

VIKAS PUBLISHING HOUSE PVT LTD
Regd. Office: 5 Ansari Road, New Delhi 110002
H.O. Vikas House, 20/4 Industrial Area, Sahibabad 201010
Distt. Ghaziabad, U.P. (India)

COPYRIGHT © ANGELA BURR, 1984

ISBN 07069-2296-4

To
Auntie Nell

Printed at The Central Electric Press, 80-D, Kamla Nagar, Delhi-110007 (India)

Acknowledgements

Thanks are due to the Social Science Research Council of Great Britain who made possible this research by awarding me a Post-doctoral Fellowship which was held at the School of Oriental and African Studies (London University) between October 1976 and April 1979. Dr Alan Entwhistle, Dr Anne Grinter Mr Donald Sheridan and Mr Richard Mcfie also receive my gratitude for their useful comments on my manuscript as does Mrs Pat Davis for typing it out.

But, most importantly, I would like to acknowledge my debt and express my sincere thanks to the International Society for Krishna Consciousness (ISKCON) and all the other new Eastern religious movements that I visited during my study for allowing me to participate in their activities. ISKCON in particular showed me great kindness during my visits to their temples in London, India and the U.S.A. between 1976 and 1979.

This book was written in 1979-80. Since then ISKON in Britain has naturally undergone changes. For example, to house the increasing number of devotees it has bought a country house in Worcestershire which it has named "Chaitanya College". But the hypothesis put forward is this study still applies.

A standard academic form of Hindi and Sanskrit transliteration has been used throughout this study. But it has been modified to fit in with printing needs and conventionally accepted anglicised spellings of major terms such as "Krishna". To protect devotees' privacy many of their names have been changed.

In passing, I would like to stress that this study in no way attempts to question the validity of the beliefs and practices associated with the worship of the God Krishna or any other Hindu belief or practice for that matter. Such an evaluation is outside the scope of this analysis and the author does not feel qualified to do so. Indeed it would be inappropriate for a foreigner to question religious beliefs and practices that have existed for so long in India. Instead, this study seeks only to look at the way Western devotees of Krishna have themselves made use of these beliefs and practices in the ordering of their daily lives and in the solving of their problems.

ANGELA BURR

Contents

Chapter One: Introduction — 1

Chapter Two: 'Srilaprabhupad Picks up Those Who are Down': The Background to ISKCON in America and Britain — 10

Chapter Three: The Science of Self Realisation and the Bliss of Surrender to Krishna — 41

Chapter Four: 'All Glories to Srilaprabhupad' : The Role of the Guru in ISKCON — 66

Chapter Five: Bhakti Yoga and the 'Personal Trip': The Individual Versus the Group in ISKCON — 77

Chapter Six: Preaching Krishna Consciousness and the Economics of Bhakti Yoga — 89

Chapter Seven: Power and the Politics of Asceticism — 115

Chapter Eight: 'I Am Not My Body, I Am Spirit-Soul' — 133

Chapter Nine: The Role of the Body in Western Society Today — 149

Chapter Ten: Soul as a Symbol of Self—Body as a Symbol of Society — 160

Chapter Eleven: Bodily Ritual in ISKCON and Devotees' Attitudes to the Body, its Boundaries and Orifices — 172

Chapter Twelve: Appearance: ISKCON Dress and its Relationship to Internal and External Relations — 185

Chapter Thirteen: The Sexual Rites of ISKCON—Devotees' Attitudes to Sexuality and Their Use of Sexuality as a Means of Social Protest — 191

Chapter Fourteen : Hair Symbolism in ISKCON — 214

Chapter Fifteen: Bodily Movement and Dance in ISKCON — 222

Chapter Sixteen: West Meets East: ISKCON and India   231

Chapter Seventeen: East Meets West: ISKCON and the Asian Community in Britain   239

Chapter Eighteen: Brainwashing: Fact or Fiction—Conversion or Subversion?   257

Chapter Nineteen: Conclusion   276

Bibliography   291
Index   297

CHAPTER ONE

Introduction

> Around the world misfortune reigns
> As people acting whimsically
> Create a hellish atmosphere
> Where no one can live peacefully.
> It's getting most impossible
> To know what's right and what is wrong.
> Great sinful deeds are being done!
> The future sings a gloomy song
> —Jagadisa dasa adhikari SVPB 1976 : 35

'I am not my body, I am spirit-soul' claim the shaven-headed, saffron robed men and sari clad women of ISKCON (the International Society for Krishna Consciousness) or the Hare Krishna sect as they are more commonly called by the public. Processions of ISKCON devotees, dancing and chanting 'Hare Krishna' to the accompaniment of cymbals and drums have become a familiar sight in the last decade, particularly in Central London and Oxford Street. Being accosted by them on the streets and given a voucher for a 'free lunch' in their temple, or to be offered magazines, books or records in return for a donation, has become an everyday occurrence for Londoners too.

The Swinging Sixties saw the blossoming of many bizarre groups and esoteric mystic religions and cults in Britain: Hippies, the advocates of 'make love not war' and 'Flower Power,' Hell's Angels, Mods and Rockers, Skinheads and so on. It also saw the mushrooming of many new religious sects emanating from the East, including not only ISKCON, but Transcendental Meditation and the Divine Light Mission which focuses around the boy god Guru Maharaj Ji; as well as a whole plethora of other gurus all offering different paths to salvation.

It would be very easy to dismiss ISKCON out of hand, as do many of the public, as just one of the numerous exotic groups which arose during the sixties and to characterise them as hippies, layabouts dropouts, escapists, weirdos and so forth. But it is precisely because of ISKCON's marginality and overtly bizarre behaviour that they are of interest to the student of society. It is often said metaphorically that 'society bleeds at its margins', that society's problems are reflected in microcosm in marginal groups and this appears to be the case with ISKCON. ISKCON is clearly an outstanding example of a social protest group which uses religion as its medium. An examination of its belief system, social structure and, in particular, the claim made by devotees that they are not their bodies but spirit-soul, reveals a great deal about the social problems of western society, especially in Britain and America.

Precisely because of its members' strange clothes and eccentric behaviour, the movement, perhaps bette than the other groups that arose during the 1960s, throws into relief more clearly some of the basic problems and contradictions that nowadays confront individuals in our society, particularly modern youth. One may cite, for example, the dehumanising nature of modern scientific technologicla society, its lack of clear-cut values, the poverty of modern Christianity, the boredom and routine of everyday life, the frustration felt by people in dead-end jobs, the gap between what is desired and what is practically obtainable in an individual's everyday life, the realisation that their high expectations cannot be fulfilled, as well as contradictions in the relationship between men and women. ISKCON also appears to be a genuine attempton the patr of its members to resolve and come to terms with the basic fundamentals of human existence, namely the relationship between spirit and matter and the individual and society.

ISKCON is a religious movement originating in India. The movement was founded in America in 1966 by A.C. Bhaktivedanta Swami Prabhupada or 'Prabhupad' as he is affectionately known to his followers. He was born Abbe Charan De in 1892 in Calcutta, a Bengali *vaishya* belonging to a merchant jeweller caste. Before his retirement he worked as a commission agent for a chemical company. Early in his working life, whilst still married and a householder, he joined the Gaudiya Matha, a reformist mission of the Vaishnava Gaudiya sect, founded by Bhaktisiddhanta Sarasvati Thakura in 1918. Prabhupad finally gave up secular life and took sannyasa which is the fourth and final stage, and one of total renunciation in the Hindu religious system, in 1959 at Mathura, Uttar Pradesh, the supposed birthplace of Lord Krishna.

Prabhupad's teachings and ISKCON's philosophy are based on Gaudiya philosophy which has a long history in India. Gaudiya philosophy focuses around *bhakti yoga* (selfless and loving devotion to God), the worship and teachings of Lord Krishna and Chaitanya Mahaprabhu, a fifteenth century Bengali mystic who is worshipped as an incarnation (*avatara*) of Krishna in the form of a saintly devotee.

Prabhupad, who died in November 1977, always maintained that he had been ordered by his own guru, Bhaktisiddhanta Sarasvati Thakura, to bring 'Krishna Consciousness' (as his teachings are known in the movement) to the West. This he did when he went to the United States in 1965, setting up the movement in a store-front in the Bowery in New York in July 1966. The movement found very fertile ground amongst disaffected American youth and rapidly spread throughout America. Three American couples, who were numbered amongst Prabhupad's earliest disciples, brought the movement to England in 1969. It quickly attracted a small following, including pop star George Harrison of the Beatles.

ISKCON's original preaching centre in London was at Bury Place, W.C. 1. It is a three-storied narrow Georgian-style house, squashed between a pub on one side and a block of renovated ex-artisan flats on the other, and situated in a side street near the British Museum. But in 1979, ISKCON moved to larger premises to, Soho Street, W. 1., in the heart of the West End. The ground floor of the three-storied Victorian terraced house in Soho Street they have converted into a vegetarian health food restaurant named 'Healthy, Wealthy and Wise.' They have also been loaned a terraced house in Clapham and rent a number of houses in Watford which they use for accommodation purposes. ISKCON also owns a mansion, Bhaktivedanta Manor. The manor is situated in the village of Letchmore Heath (near Watford) some thirty minutes by car from the centre of London, it was donated by George Harrison. It is the movement's main centre in Britain and houses the majority of the devotees. ISKCON has also recently opened a small temple in a private house in Dublin. The movement in 1978 had just over 200 full-time adult members in Britain and some 4,500 members in all scattered in some hundred temples throughout the world.

ISKCON in both Britain and the States, where it originated, is clearly a social protest group par excellence. Most of the religious groups that mushroomed in the 1960s are critical of the establishment and society in general to some degree. But in its social protest, ISKCON appears to be the most extreme of them all and as such is of special interest. When you first come into contact with the devotees, one of the most noticeable features is their extremism and antagonistic attitude towards the 'karmi' world, as they refer to the outside society. Devotees' attitudes to western society are summed up in a remark made by Swami Satsvarup, a leading devotee, in *Back to Godhead*, the movement's magazine:

"Srila Bhaktisiddhanta Sarasvati Thakura, the spiritual master of his Divine Grace A.C. Bhaktivedanta Swami Prabhupad, once described materialistic civilisation as 'a society of the cheaters and the cheated.' Looking at our modern world we can easily see why: massive advertising campaigns for cigarettes and liquor that promise pleasure but deliver disease: widespread gambling rackets of all kinds, some government sponsored, that milk the public of billions each year: high level corruption of many leaders in industry and government that reveals a nearly total disregard for the public's welfare. From all this, and much more, the only conclusion to draw is that the vast majority of people, out of ignorance of a meaningful goal of life, actually desire to be cheated—actually feel the need for the false promises and outright lies of the hucksters to provide some hope of happiness from day to day. Thus a few clear aggressive professionals take advantage of the ignorance of the masses and engage in large scale cheating for their own selfish interests.

"Whilst cheating goes on in all fields of endeavour, one of the most outstanding is modern science. Scientists can make useful contributions to material life, but they become cheaters when they say that science is (or some day will be) independent of the laws of nature. Theories such as 'Life originates from matter and can be created in the laboratory', or 'Since there is no supreme intelligence directing the universe, we [the scientists] are the only ones who can explain existence', are all bluffs perpetrated without a shred of scientific proof."

Reflecting this attitude, ISKCON has totally rejected western society and has attempted to cut itself off from it completely. Further, the whole institutional structure of ISKCON is an inverted mirror image of the outside world. It is based on an all-out rejection, not only of western religious forms, but of the liberal, permissive, materialist society with its scientific technological base in which devotees have been brought up. ISKCON is a total 'Indian trip' since 'devotees' as Prabhupad's followers call themselves, rejecting western culture totally, have attempted to create a new and alternative lifestyle based on a version of Indian culture.

Prabhupad had a very sensitive ear to the needs of modern western youth. He did not teach a modernised version of Hinduism that would fit in with the needs, orientation and framework of the modern technological society. Rather he had a very traditional fundamentalist conservative view, typical of the religious-minded of his generation in India. He totally rejected modern society as bad and corrupt. A view that found fertile ground amongst the disaffected youth who became his devotees. Instead he harked back for his ideal society to a supposed Hindu golden age of 5000 years ago when, according to traditional Vaishnavism, Lord Krishna, the 'Supreme Personality of Godhead' actually lived. He used the supposed culture of this period, an essentially pre-industrial rural 'back to nature' society which focused around the keeping of cows, as the blue-print and model of ISKCON. In this 'Vedic' society, as he called it, asceticism is the ideal. Its members are expected to renounce the material world and all its pleasures in order to attain salvation and oneness with Krishna. It is essentially a contemplative society based on loving devotion (*bhakti*) to Krishna. 'Simple living and high thinking' is the basis of Prabhupad's philosophy.

Devotees reject their own culture so completely that they even go as far as to reject western lavatory paper—they use water instead. Following Prabhupad's teaching, they totally renounce the luxuries and commodities of material life and all their possessions, as well as their emotional life, personal opinions and freedom of action, for a life of asceticism and austerity, including sleeping on the floor and getting up in the early hours of the morning.

Devotees are highly puritanical. They do not drink, smoke, gamble, eat meat or take drugs. They stress premarital chastity, and regard celibacy as the ideal. They are against abortion and homosexuality. They are extremely right-wing in outlook, conservative, anticommunist and authoritarian. They accept as the norm a social structure organised on hierarchal principles; a form of the Indian caste system. Men and women are not considered social equals. Men are held to be superior and are expected to be the decision makers. Women's functions are only to have children and look after their families. Science, the traditional educational system, and knowledge for its own sake are all rejected, and replaced with the philosophy of Krishna Consciousness. This includes fabulous and mythical stories of the exploits of Krishna. The traditional Indian Swastika symbol, generally despised by westerners, especially by Jews and the devotees' parents' generation for its unfortunate Nazi connotations, is also valued in ISKCON. So, too, is a liking for the kind of 'kitsch' art so scorned by the bourgeoisie which they display prominently in their literature. Far from being the drug-taking hippies that outsiders assume them to be, the devotees are, as they often jokingly remark, 'straighter than the straights.'

The devotees, both in Britain and in the States are the products of the permissive society. They have been brought up in a time of great social licence and freedom of choice. This is particularly true of the early American devotees who joined the San Francisco temple in the late 1960s. As a means of attracting more members to the movement Prabhupad moved from New York with some fifteen devotees in 1967 to set up a temple in the Haight Ashbury district of San Francisco, the notorious hippie ghetto and centre of the American 'counterculture'. It is the Haight Ashbury temple that functioned as the 'nursery' of ISKCON. It is around this temple that the movement developed and it is to this temple we must turn to understand the form of ISKCON's social protest. Significantly it drew its members from the hippies, the most extreme example of the permissive society, for whom the 'hang loose' and 'footloose' ethic was the norm.

But what makes products of the Permissive Society join a movement which totally rejects the Permissive Society and stands it on its head? Why do they, of their own free will, reject the Permissive Society and choose its opposite? Why do they choose to lead such an apparently spartan way of life which requires total obedience to the authority of the guru? Why are they willing to live in what can only be described as 'topsy turvy' land?

It is not without significance that devotees have inverted the beliefs of their own society and have sought answers in its opposite extreme. Inversion, as is clear from the structural study of myth, is a form of symbolic categorization frequently used by the human mind to emphasise and reconcile contradiction in the fabric of a culture and to stress the ideal. Inversion in fact provides the basis of ISKCON's belief system and institutional structure.

Moreover, although theoretically the movement has totally rejected western society and cut itself off from it, in practice this is not so, for ISKCON is closely integrated with 'karmi' society. Actually, the movement is both dependent and parasitic on it. Although farm life is the ideal, the majority of temples are in big cities in the West and have to be, for the movement is almost totally dependent on city life both economically and for recruitment. Most devotees too, particularly when distributing literature on the streets frequently come into contact with 'karmis', as outsiders are called. Even where farm communities have been set up, and they are few and far between (the most famous being New Vrindaban in West Virginia, named after Krishna's supposed dwelling-place on earth), they are not self-sufficient farm communities like those of the Amish Mennonites used to be. Rather they are generally close to a town and dependent on the outside infrastructure, their inhabitants too interact a great deal with the outside world.

The close integration of ISKCON into 'karmi' society indicates that the movement's rejection of western society is essentially symbolic rather than actual. The fact that although the movement's ideal is withdrawal from the outside world and it is anti-materialist in ethic, yet its temples are generally situated in towns, also suggests that it can be little more than a symbolic rejection. The fact that so few farm communities have been set up is indication too of the symbolic nature of ISKCON's rejection and of its being essentially an urban phenomenon.

ISKCON in Britain is a particularly good example of the essentially symbolic nature of the movement's 'back to nature' ethic. Far from withdrawing to the country, ISKCON temples in Britain are situated in cities and Bhaktivedanta Manor, the nearest they get to a rural retreat, in the suburbs of London. The manor is situated in 17 acres of land. Paying lip service to the movement's ideal, ISKCON keeps a few cows at the manor and grows a small amount of vegetables there. But reflecting the essentially symbolic nature of their interest in farming, the land is very under-utilised. ISKCON, if they choose, could grow a great deal more of their own produce. But few devotees are really interested in farming and even fewer would be willing to work full-time at it. Instead ISKCON buys the majority of its food from the outside 'karmi' world.

ISKCON is a passive and contemplative movement rather than a socially and politically active one. Whilst it is evangelical and foresees the day when the whole world will be Krishna Conscious, it does not advocate social involvement. It does not actively attempt to change society; but aims to achieve this goal by chanting 'Hare Krishna', the holy names of God, and thereby change people's hearts. It would be reasonable to assume that if members of ISKCON really aimed at changing the world, they would attempt to become heavily involved socially and reform society. Their passivity and lack of involvement further tends to indicate that theirs is an ideological and symbolic rejection rather than a real one. Indeed, it is a rejection on the level of belief and culture rather than on the social and economic plane.

How to explain this symbolic rejection of western culture and ISKCON's claim that 'I am not my body, I am spirit-soul'? It has often been pointed out, e.g. Hall and Jefferson *et al* (1975) that in modern western society, particularly amongst the youth culture, marginal groups have resorted to symbolism and ritual as a means of dealing with personal problems and as a form of social protest. ISKCON appears to be following this pattern, for its belief and institutional structure seems to be a symbolic attempt to come to terms with and control society and social relations.

There appear to be no social or ideological solutions to many of the existential and social problems confronting the individual in modern western society. But, ISKCON has attempted to find answers to them and transcend them, as will be demonstrated in the following chapters in an analysis of ISKCON's belief structure and social, economic and political institutions and process of conversion in Britain and, where relevant, in America and India too. The movement has done so by expressing, resolving and seeking solutions to such problems by projecting them onto the system of belief and concomitant ritual and manipulating them symbolically.

ISKCON's system of belief has developed so as to incorporate a symbolic model of the world and society through the medium of which devotees are able to deal with their personal problems and act out their social protest. This model focuses around their claim that 'I am not my body, I am spirit-soul', which is the movement's fundamental concept. This symbolic model of the world and social relations is not group-oriented, but is centred around the individual, as the devotees' claim ('I am not my body, I am spirit-soul') indicates. The relationship between the 'individual' and 'society' provides the symbolic conceptual framework for this individualistically oriented model; the latter also centres around the body and body symbolism. In fact, the body is the focus point of devotees' attention and that of the movement as a whole, for it is through the medium of the body, and the dichotomy between individual and society and soul and body, that the movement expresses and answers the social and existential problems faced by individuals in modern society. The soul in ISKCON is identified with the individual and a person's body with society. Devotees resolve the problems faced by individuals in modern society which are articulated in ISKCON by expressing and reconciling them in terms of bodily symbolism, by identifying themselves with their soul and by projecting their problems onto their bodies which function as a symbol of society.

Beliefs and practices related to the soul and body have become in ISKCON a substitute and surrogate for action. Not only do they provide devotees with a meaningful world view, but they also offer a satisfying answer to existential and social problems in the wider society which in practice, its members are unable to solve individually. The following analysis of ISKCON should also be of particular interest to the student of society, for it throws into relief and sheds light on an important new social variable that is developing in western society, namely the 'body' and bodily symbolism.

CHAPTER TWO

'Srilaprabhupad Picks up Those Who are Down':
the Background to ISKCON in
America and Britain

> Every living being in the world today is in darkness, forced to struggle hard for nonpermanent goals and for relief from the continual onslaught of the miseries of material life. You [Srilaprabhupad] have the power to free us from this oppressive bondage, and because you are a pure devotee of Lord Caitanya, you are imbued with the divine characteristic of unlimited mercy for the fallen souls. Your blessings have been received by hundreds of millions of people, and the entire course of history is being changed by your inconceivable powers and your pure love for Krishna. Generally, "in this iron age of Kali men have but short lives. They are quarrelsome, lazy, misguided, unlucky and, above all, always disturbed." (Bhag., 1.1.10). Their health and life-span is reduced because of irregular habits, overeating, indulgence in sense gratification, overdependence on another's mercy and artificial standards of living—all of which weaken and waste their vital energy. Their laziness especially refers to spiritual practices, due to illusory bodily misidentification. Because everyone's mind is victimized by many diversions of politics, cinema, sports, gambling, clubs, mundane libraries, bad association, smoking, drinking, cheating, pilfering, quarreling, etc., they are always disturbed and full of anxieties. The whole world atmosphere is surcharged with faithlessness, lying propaganda and the strain of competition for sense gratification, enmity and war. Despite external appearances, it is impossible for any person to independently achieve happiness, peace of mind, and freedom from the suffering inflicted by this distorted way of life.
> —Ramesvara Dasa Swami : SVPB. 1977 : 80

One of the most noticeable and striking features of western society in the 1960s was the re-awakening of interest in things religious, mystical and irrational, especially on the part of youth, and American youth in particular. Indeed, it witnessed an exploration and raising of consciousness on a scale hitherto unknown, and a renewal of interest in all things spiritual. Not only eastern religions, but subjects as varied as I Ching, Satanism, astrology, ESP, spiritualism, Tarot, witchcraft and magic, as well as flying saucers and space people, became the subjects of interest and often active participation, especially on the part of youth.

That this spiritual and mystical re-awakening took place in a decade when participation in the established religions declined rapidly, and secularization in all spheres of society increased by leaps and bounds, is of interest in itself. So, too, is the fact that youth's spiritual search often led them to turn their backs on Christianity altogether and to seek answers in foreign and exotic religions and in forms of mysticism which appear to have no relevance, and even to contradict the ethics, social structure and scientific foundations of modern western technological society. That it was the youth who showed a predominant interest in things religious and mystical is an interesting phenomenon in itself as well. Since it would tend to be assumed that this would be the age group least interested in religion and a spiritual way of life, particularly one such as is offered by ISKCON, with its ideals of asceticism and renunciation. It would be expected that young people would prefer to be out enjoying themselves and savouring the delights of materialism and the permissive society. That some do not is, in itself, a subject worth examining.

The belief structure and institutional forms of modern Christianity are often put forward as the cause of both the decline of the established Christian religions and the development of interest in the 1960s in eastern religions and spirituality and mysticism in general. Scientific thought and increasing secularization have undermined traditional Christian beliefs and practices, making them appear increasingly obsolete and irrelevant to the institutional forms which have developed as the basis of the West's modern scientific technological society. By the 1960s, itself a period of rapid social change and upheaval, these Churches could no longer give convincing answers to fundamental questions of existence confronting man in the Space Age society and people rejected Christianity in droves, especially the youth. Brought up in a totally modern milieu with modern life expectancies engendered by living in a technocratic society and educated to expect clear-cut scientific-type answers to their questions, modern youth found Christianity wanting and turned elsewhere for the answers to life.

Indeed, the decline of Christianity and the development of modern science has led to a collapse of traditional values. However, it has not resulted in the development of a similarly coherent and unitary one either. Much the opposite; modern science with its emphasis on theory rather than truth has effectively prevented any such development. Rather, it has legitimised contradictory and competing world views. The individual is confronted by a plethora of conflicting systems of belief. The credibility gap in modern society looms large. The man in the street does not know what to believe or whom to believe. For young people, and particularly those brought up in a liberal family atmosphere and in families in which expressive relationships are emphasised, this is often difficult to accept and represents a particularly acute problem.

The small nuclear family of today is inward looking and relationships within it tend to be intense and expressive and concomitantly modern parents, especially the more liberal amongst them, whilst they socialise their children to expect answers to everything, generally do not, as traditional parents did, provide their children with an explanation of the meaning and purpose of life and specific guidelines for behaviour. A not insignificant proportion of youth, and especially those from liberal families who have not been provided in childhood with definitive explanations and guidelines, find great difficulty coping, when they reach adulthood with the multiplicity of conflicting systems of belief nowadays and lack of clear-cut standards for behaviour. This is particularly true of ISKCON devotees, many of whom came from very liberal backgrounds. Significantly, what the great majority of eastern religious groups have to offer such people, and this is especially true of ISKCON, is a structured interpretation of the meaning and purpose of life which provides clear-cut guidelines for behaviour, and in this lies much of their attraction.

ISKCON devotees appear to be typical products of a modern liberal upbringing, particularly in America, where quite a high proportion (14.5 per cent in a survey Judah, [1974: 147,] carried out of Berkeley and Los Angeles Temples) of devotees came from middle-class Jewish backgrounds, noted for the liberalism of their child-rearing practices. In fact, in the early days of the movement, Prabhupad was nicknamed the 'Jewish guru' for this reason. The lack of guidance offered by devotee parents is reflected in their attitudes towards their children's future. Devotees frequently say that when they discussed their future with their parents they would simply say, 'all we want is for you to be happy.' For individuals who need the meaning and purpose of life to be explained, ISKCON provides the ideal answer. Devotees are quick to point out, 'ISCKON provides clear-cut answers to all questions'. Pointing to the Christian Church's inability to provide a clear and meaningful explanation of reality, devotees say derisively, 'Christians can't even tell you who God is'. This attitude is also evident from a remark made by Kulasekhara, the first English devotee, who joined the movement in 1969.

> I knew who Jesus Christ was, but no one could tell me who God was. I discussed it frequently with priests and even went to the White Friar monks. Some said he was a white-haired old man, others that it was 'hugging', whilst others said it was a feeling like when people helped each other. None of them could give you any answers. But the first time I went into a Krishna temple, I opened the *Srimad Bhagavatam*. The first line said Krishna is the Supreme Personality of Godhead. I read three pages immediately.

This view is reflected in devotees' attitude to the western educational system too which they despise and reject. Science and material knowledge for its own sake are seen as a major cause of society's ills, and devotees will not send their children to 'karmi' schools. Many devotees said they dropped out of college because they went there expecting to find the answers to life. Their teachers, they said, didn't know the answers and they felt cheated.

Another major function of Christianity, traditionally, was to satisfy, channel and provide an outlet for mankind's emotional, spiritual and mystical needs. But under the influence of secularisation, bureaucratisation and modernisation, its beliefs, rituals and symbols, have become atrophied. They have lost much of their emotional, mystical and spiritual content and no longer fulfil the emotional needs of man, performing as they do now, a primarily social function.

Superstition, too, which traditionally provided a channel for these needs, has largely died out under the onslaught of science. In general, modern society, with its impersonality, rationality, over-organisation, uniformity and bureaucratic orientation, does not cater well for man's emotional, psychic, mystic, experiential and spiritual needs. Indeed, it has led to the underemphasis and denial of the experiential and mystical level in modern society. No longer can man communicate to others his inner mystical experiences or feelings for fear of being considered mad. Understandably, people have sought other channels for expressing these needs. Eastern religions, most of which have a strong emotional, spiritual and mystical content, are, of course, highly appealing for this reason. ISKCON especially, as will be seen, offers perhaps the biggest mystical 'trip' of all the new Eastern religions which mushroomed in the 1960s. It offers instant ecstasy!

The whole basis and fabric of western society, its belief and institutional structure were questioned and found wanting during the 1960s, especially by the youth. Western society's obsessive rationalism, its bureaucratic basis, the gigantic scale of everything in it, its over-organisation and regimentation, its unresponsiveness to people's needs, its impersonalism and the alienation of urban life and lack of close ties between people, its obsessions with quantity rather than quality, are all dehumanising. This is also the effect of its obsessive materialism, continuous social crisis and chaos, mounting violence, the rape of the natural environment and its lethal pollution level, as well as the threat of nuclear war that permanently hangs over it. Its machine-like nature reduces individuals to cogs and robots and, viewed in terms of 'kill ratio', they are only taken into account as expendable resources. This has given rise to the feeling that if the present system continues on its present course, society is heading for disaster. In the 1960s, the dehumanising nature of western society and the basic incongruities between its ideals and actual reality became glaringly apparent and could no longer be avoided. It left people not only with a sense of inadequacy and impotence, but with a sense of a world devoid of meaning. It led to a search for meaning on a scale never before witnessed. This search for meaning clearly underlies the renewed spiritual quest and massive exploration of consciousness of the 1960s. One of the most important and most frequently recited prayers in ISKCON refers to Prabhupad as the deliverer of western society from 'voidism'. In the States it led to the rejection of American society by large sections of the youth.

It is no accident that ISKCON and the other eastern religious groups blossomed during this decade or that they tended to originate in the States rather than Europe. For America it was a period of great social upheaval. It witnessed the assassination of both John Kennedy and Martin Luther King, the horrors of the Vietnam war, as well as a successful landing on the moon and the emergence of Black Power, the Counterculture and the Hippies. It saw the development of a crisis of meaning and consciousness unique in United States history and the erosion and rejection of traditional mainstream society and the legitimacy of established institutions and the parental generation which was seen to embody them. Also, there arose the feeling that the materialism of a modern society, geared to the development of wealth and power for its own sake, was destroying the fabric and quality of life. It resulted in disenchantment with modern society among a wide section of its members, especially by youth and particularly those who were educated. It saw the development of total opposition to, and rejection of, the prevailing traditional culture and the parental generation which personified it. There evolved what has been referred to as the Counterculture, by which is usually meant an alternative way of life—a completely different set of beliefs and practices set up in opposition to the traditional culture. Moreover, as both Roszak (1969) and Slater (1970) have pointed out in their seminal works on the Counterculture, it was primarily middle-class and educated American youth who were in the vanguard of the Counterculture. It led to a conscious exploration of and experimentation with alternative life-styles, such as the human potential movements, communes and, of course, religious movements, especially eastern religious groups, of which ISKCON is but one of many.

Social protest and extremism in general have played an integral role in American history and have been frequently expressed in religious terms, to which the proliferation of small religious sects in the eighteenth and nineteenth centuries bears witness. But never before, until the Vietnam War demonstrated the total lunacy of modern American society, had the totality of society been questioned so deeply by so many. In such an environment, any worldview, religion or ideology which offered a philosophy fundamentally opposed to the belief structure of the prevailing society would, understandably, find fertile ground amongst the most disaffected, affluent American youth under the threat of being drafted to Vietnam and perhaps killed in a war to which they were fundamentally opposed. ISKCON, of course, offering a complete inversion of the prevailing life-style, was understandably attractive, found adherents easily and spread rapidly.

ISKCON appears initially to have attracted Countercultural youth, especially hippies. Although devotees in America, and this is true of Britain too, maintain they come from all walks of life, this was a more symbolic statement of the ideal than the actual in the early years of the movement. The composition of the Counterculture, white middle-class, affluent and educated youth, appears to be consistent with the background of the majority of ISKCON devotees in America during the movement's formative years in the late 1960s. The academic literature on ISKCON which has so far dealt with the movement in the States, namely, Stillson Judah (1974) in *Hare Krishna and the Counterculture*, Francine Daner (1976) in *The American Children of Krsna* and Gregory Johnson in *An Alternative Community in Microcosm* (1973) all agree that American devotees came from the middle and upper middle classes. A small proportion came from elite back grounds, for example, Alfred Ford the grandson of Henry Ford.

Nevertheless, a point under-emphasised by these writers, a small, but not insignificant minority came from the lower status groups, including, crucially, some of the most prominent devotees, such as the first female devotee, Yadurani. She is the daughter of a printer and functions as the informal leader of the women in the American movement. A sannyasin, the former Swami Govinda and one of the new gurus, Swami Hamsaduta, the son of a baker, also came from the lower status groups.

Moreover, since a large part of the American population because of their high standard of living would be considered middle-class, to say that most ISKCON devotees came from the middle and upper classes is to say little more than that they came from the mainstream of American society and this is reflected in their college education. Although most devotees have had some sort of college education, few had been to Ivy league or other elitist institutions. Most had had a mainstream college education of a not very high intellectual or cultural standard, similar to their mainstream and middle-of-the-road social background. Indeed, many had studied non-academic subjects and had attended college part-time.

But, broadly speaking, regardless of class and education, what the great majority of American devotees had in common, at least in the early years, was that they were not from economically deprived groups as is often the case with new religious sects. In fact, it is the material standard of devotees' former lives, their very affluence, which is seen as a major cause of their joining ISKCON and as the underlying basis of the counterculture as a whole too. It was the affluent children of the American dream, disenchanted with their society which they felt had failed them, who formed the Counterculture and joined ISKCON. Generally, ISKCON is characterised in the States as consisting of middle-class and upper-class college dropouts satiated with materialism, searching for meaning and seeking to overcome alienation and identity problems. Certainly there would seem to be some truth in this viewpoint. Despite the affluence of their homes devotees had, as they frequently remark, a feeling that something was missing—that there was more to life than this—and they have attempted to find it in ISKCON.

American society, too, provides few cultural channels for expression. The mainstream of American middle-class society with its basis in the small nuclear family centred as it is around materialism—two cars, television and Coca Cola—tends to be culturally impoverished, as is the American educational system which offers a low standard of education prior to the postgraduate level. Yet through television and other media, the American youth are made aware of wider horizons and exotic and distant places. Nor does their way of life offer any scope for their imagination. Movements such as ISKCON, however, not only give such scope, but provide people with a means of expressing their cultural impoverishment and overcoming it, as the following discussion of Krishna Consciousness philosophy will demonstrate.

Devotees' lack of sophistication and cultural impoverishment is reflected in their attitude to the movement. Although from an academic point of view ISKCON's philosophy is not intellectually sophisticated, devotees are greatly impressed by Prabhupad's intellectualism and Gaudiya philosophy and view ISKCON as a highly cultured intellectual movement. Devotees' attitudes would thus appear to fit in with what Glock (1964: 24-36), in his seminal study of the role of deprivation and the origin and evolution of religions, would describe as 'ethical deprivation', though perhaps 'ethical and cultural' deprivation would be a better description of ISKCON devotees.

The 1970s however saw the disappearance of overt social protest on the part of middle class educated youth and with it the decline of the counterculture and the Haight Ashbury scene—the hippy ghetto in San Francisco where ISKCON had its first West Coast temple—which, for many people, epitomised the Counterculture. This decline appears to be directly related to the ending of the Vietnam War in April 1975 and to the world-wide economic recession of the 1970s and is reflected in ISKCON, which has itself declined in numbers over the years.

The Vietnam War provided an impetus to social protest on the part of American youth and when it came to an end, middle-class youth were deprived of their major rallying symbol and main reason for protesting. It is no accident that in ISKCON in America numbers dropped radically in the year immediately after the ending of the Vietnam War. According to Johnson, by July 1974, ISKCON had reached its peak of approximately 5000 members throughout the world. But by 1976 however, according to statistics derived from *Sri Vyasa Puja* books, total world membership had declined to about 2000 and membership of American temples to about 900.

Also, the economic recession had a radical effect on middle-class college students. Worry about their futures contributed to their giving up social protest in the mid 1970s. They turned their attention to their careers and concentrated on their studies and getting a good job and this, too, clearly contributed to the decline in numbers in ISKCON. The American movement has always seen itself as being, to some extent, a college movement and views students as providing the pool of potential devotees. Generally, ISKCON has attempted to build their temples near university campuses in the hope of attracting students. Significantly, although ISKCON has temples near Harvard and Berkeley (which in its early days provided a significant proportion of devotees), they no longer recruit devotees from these institutions. 'They are too puffed up' say devotees derisively.

Since 1976, ISKCON has increased in numbers again somewhat. But it has never reached its former size. In 1977, there were about 2200 devotees all told throughout the world with about 1400 living in America and in 1978 there were about 1300 in America and 3500 throughout the world. This increase in numbers is a reflection of the effect of recession and unemployment on the lower status groups who have rapidly increased in numbers in American ISKCON in recent years.

As an indication of the change in status of devotees who join the movement nowadays, two people joined during the week I stayed in the New York temple in 1978. It is no accident that both were from lower status backgrounds. One was a divorced 42 year old Catholic Puerto Rican taxi driver and the other was a 19 year old waitress of Irish-American Catholic descent.

But ISKCON in Britain, although the age profile is somewhat similar to American ISKCON and is youth-focused too, there is a slight difference in emphasis in the social background and status of British devotees. ISKCON in Britain has been influenced by and has been adapted to fit in with the British milieu and social structure. Differences in traditional social organisation and history in Britain and America, particularly since the Second World War, have resulted in there being some variation and difference in emphasis in the social groups and categories that are recruited into British ISKCON, which have consequently affected the social structure and social organisation of the movement in Britain.

By comparison with America, the tradition of social protest in Britain, whilst always existing (Methodism and Non-Conformism in general are examples of such in the religious spheres), has been muted in comparison. British culture appears to operate more in terms of compromise than confrontation. Thus, an extreme form of social protest such as ISKCON's is, in itself, so unusual as to be worth examining. But, as elsewhere in the Western world, the 1960s in Britain was a time of rapid social change and saw the development of the youth phenomenon. But it was a time of less social upheaval and unrest than in America. Whilst British youth, like their American counterparts, were faced with a crisis of meaning and questioned and rejected the life-style of its parents, it did not take the form of extreme confrontation and did not lead to a generation split or the development of such a clear-cut Counterculture as it did in America. Partly, because British youth was not directly affected by the Vietnam War and did not live under the threat of being drafted and perhaps killed in a war it was opposed to on principle. Rather, as the terms 'Permissive Society' and 'Swinging Sixties' clearly reflect, there was in Britain a general opening up of society based on a more liberal and permissive attitude to which the older generation had the wit to adapt gracefully. Nevertheless, much of the American Countercultural superstructure including Eastern religious cults such as ISKCON, made their way to Britain in the Swinging Sixties and quickly found adherents.

ISKCON was brought to Britain in 1968 by three American couples who were amongst the first of Prabhupad's disciples. They included Malati, an ex-hippy with religious tattoos on her body who was a close confident of Prabhupad, and is famous throughout the movement for having shoplifted the first Krishna deity. Also her husband Shyamsundara, who has since 'blooped' (as leaving ISKCON is referred to in the movement) and is noted in the movement for having supposedly tried to sell a dud diamond mine to George Harrison. A small nucleus of Americans, usually between five to ten, live in the British temples. They all appear to come from affluent backgrounds and would seem to fit in with the general classification of American ISKCON.

In both Britain and America, ISKCON is essentially a male-dominated movement, orientated primarily towards satisfying male needs. This is reflected in the fact that in both countries men outnumber women by more than two to one, a common feature in fact in the new eastern religious cults. Although a small percentage of older people visit ISKCON temples in Britain, few of them join. As in America the movement attracts primarily the youth group. In both countries over 90 per cent of devotees are under the age of 30 and a great proportion of these in their late teens and early 20. In Britain, there are only three devotees over the age of 40.

But, in Britain, the majority of devotees do not come from such affluent backgrounds. Sons and daughters of professional parents are fairly rare, too, and they tend to be predominantly women devotees. One female devotee is the daughter of a director of a college another's father is an executive of a large garage concern, whilst another is the daughter of an architect. Only one of the British female devotees appears to have come from a very rich background, a daughter of a famous business family. The widowed mother of one male devotee is a mayor, another's grandfather is a famous Socialist Methodist leader, and another's father is reported to be a 'King of Porn'.

Public school educated male devotees appear to be few and far between too. In two years only four cases came to light, and none had been to any of the top schools. Unlike the American movement,

which boasts three science Ph.Ds., in Britain only about 20 per cent
have had higher education and those who have had higher education
attended state schools and predominantly non-university institutions.
Most attended technical colleges, polytechnics or art schools and
many dropped out before completing the course. In two years only
seven university graduates came to light, and a few who dropped
out before graduation. They have only one Oxbridge graduate,
Jnanadasa, a 31 year old former Zen monk who obtained a second
class degree in Physics and has become British ISKCON's leading
intellectual.

The majority of British devotees tend not to be well educated
and come from the working and lower middle-classes, with a few
from the middle-middle-classes and even fewer from the upper-
middle-classes. In fact, a typical devotee comes from an ordinary
'man in the street' background and this is particularly true of the
earliest British devotees. The majority of devotees previously held
manual jobs, e.g. plumber, mechanic, factory worker or ex-white
collar job, e.g. shop assistant, nurse, clerk, typist. The very first
British devotee, Kulasekhara was expelled from his South London
comprehensive school at fifteen for what he described as 'gang
fighting'. He became an 'acid-head' and involved in the pop music
scene and is an example of a typical British devotee. Another early
member, Deva Datta born in Cumbria, who has since 'blooped',
was a street hawker in Oxford Street before joining the movement.
George Harrison of the Beatles, who donated Bhaktivedanta
Manor, was an early convert. Indeed, George Harrison, in attitude
and background—Liverpool, suburban, semi-detached, working-
class, clean-cut, with social aspirations and a keen interest in pop
music—is very typical of British ISKCON and, to some extent, is
symbolic of the movement in Britain.

However, in Britain, over 80 per cent of the population belong
to the working-class and thus, the higher proportion of lower status
group devotees in British ISKCON might appear to be purely a
reflection of the higher proportion of lower class people in Britain.
But, in fact, there are other reasons why lower status group
people join British ISKCON in the numbers that they do. If
ISKCON had not satisfied their needs and motivations, no matter
how high their proportion of the population, they would not have
joined. They would have avoided ISKCON, as did the majority of
the working-class in America in the movement's early days.

There appears to be a number of social reasons why, unlike in America, ISKCON in Britain does not attract the upper echelons of society, the public school educated or the highly educated, or the children of the very rich, i.e. elite youth. Although some do have a mild flirtation with ISKCON, they do not tend to join. Class snobbery on the part of the upper-class, a sense of elitist superiority and conservatism and their traditional suspicion of unconventional behaviour, as well as devotees' lack of intellectualism, and their extremism and dogmatism which the British upper-classes tend to find particularly off-putting, are all factors which make ISKCON unattractive to the upper end of the British social scale. An example of such is Jack, a public school educated second-year student at London University. An enthusiastic hippie-type, bored with his studies and thinking of dropping out of college, he visited for several weeks and, on one occasion, turned up carrying the proverbial hippie rose. But after a while, the movement's attractiveness paled as he gained knowledge of the internal structure of the movement and the devotees and he became aware of their lack of education and predominantly lower status backgrounds, and came up against their dogmatism. He lost interest and stopped visiting.

ISKCON, too, is somewhat like a boarding school or a club and British males who have been to single sex boarding schools want to enjoy their freedom when they leave. Having been denied female company during their school days, they want to enjoy the companionship of and to have sexual relations with women. The last thing they normally want to do soon after leaving school, is to join a similar institution and to become celibate!

Also, in Britain, middle and upper middle-class youth, unaffected directly by the Vietnam War, were, in general, the least disaffected of all youth categories in the 1960s. They were still largely committed to establishment values such, as getting a good job when they left university or school. Thus they did not have the motivation to reject totally their parents' values and life-style as did their American peers, and thus did not see an attractive alternative in ISKCON and similar groups.

Lastly, British middle and upper middle-class children on the whole have never been materially indulged to the degree that middle and upper middle-class children in America are or been provided with a materially luxurious life-style. Much the opposite; middle-class parents and the public schools have made a virtue of strictness and austerity in the upbringing of their children. Thus, when middle-class Britons leave school, far from wishing to renounce all, they are generally motivated by a desire to sample the pleasures of life. As such, ISKCON asceticism has little appeal for them.

In order to understand the interest shown by lower status youth in eastern religions and ISKCON in particular, one must take into consideration the development of 'mass culture', the nature of the Swinging Sixties in England and the role played in it by lower status youth. In Britain, existential factors, a lack of meaningful values, are major reasons for joining ISKCON too, but, as will be seen, they are not so relevant as in America. In Britain, purely social factors are just as important.

In Britain, an interest in eastern religions has existed since the time of Schopenhauer and before. From the late nineteenth century, for example, Rosicrucianism and Theosophy, both rooted in eastern forms of mysticism have attracted western followers. In modern times, too, literary notables such as Aldous Huxley and Christopher Isherwood, as well as Alan Watts, the western doyen of Zen, in their quest for the mystical, have been led to the East. But this western interest in eastern religions until recently has been primarily a middle and upper-class phenomenon and of little concern to the masses. Never before the 1960s had forms of eastern religions had such wide appeal or percolated so far into mass culture.

The 'Swinging Sixties' in Britain was a time of optimism, economic boom, affluence and general prosperity, a time when, according to Tory election posters, people had 'never had it so good'. It heralded the permissive society, and witnessed a general opening up of, and, liberalisation of society. It was a much more positive decade than it was in America. The 1960s saw in Britain the development, culmination, legitimisation and coming of age of mass culture, and the mass society. Although it appeared to be a period when the British class structure was levelling out and the lines between the classes were becoming blurred, it did not witness the beginning of the end of the British class structure as many optimists had forecast. Each social class reacted to the 1960s differently. Each made a different contribution and had a different influence on its development.

It was the man in the street, the lower status groups and their youth in particular who spearheaded and developed the Swinging Sixties. Mass culture in the 1960s was essentially the culture of the people, namely the lower status groups. It was the product of a mass movement and reflected the political clout of the masses as the development of the power of the labour unions and their ability to control government policy bears witness.

In the last hundred years the British working classes have made rapid progress in the political arena owing to mass enfranchisement, the increased power of the unions and general economic prosperity. They have always had their own very distinct culture. But, prior to the late 1950s and 1960s, the standards, values and cultural norms in the wider society, especially in cultural spheres such as the arts, had been dictated by the elite—in the language sphere, for example, Oxford or BBC English was deemed the norm. Socially aspiring members of the working classes tended to emulate them and take on their values.

But the 1960s saw a reinterpretation of lower status group culture. Working-class culture was recognised as having a value in itself. As the power of the masses increased during the 1960s, the norms of mass lower status group culture started to provide and dictate the norms of the wider society, as is reflected in the acceptance of regional accents during this decade. Lower status groups also provided the leadership and cultural vanguard of the 1960s. The middle and upper-classes, however, did have something to contribute as their participation in politics such as CND and their denunciation of the Vietnam War and their involvement in the general hippie scene indicates. But, in general, they provided neither the stimulus nor the leadership, rather they jumped on the bandwagon.

The changes that took place in the arts in the 1960s clearly demonstrate the catalytic effect and prominent part played by the lower-status groups, and lower status group youth especially, in the development of mass culture in the 1960s. The doyens of middle-class drama, Terence Rattigan and Noel Coward, went out of fashion and 'kitchen sink' drama such as Osborne's *Look Back in Anger*, which depicted and romanticised working-class culture, and such working-class playwrights as Arnold Wesker became fashionable. Whilst in the cinema the box office attractions of the forties and fifties who projected an upper-class image, such as Gielgud, Guinness and Oliver, whilst retaining their status, lost their box office appeal to young actors who presented a working-class image, such as Michael Caine, Albert Finney, Tom Courtney and Billie

Whitelaw. Similarly in fashion modelling, the refined Barbara Goalen-type model of the fifties lost out to Twiggy, whose working-class image was considered a major part of her appeal. In photography, the elitist Cecil Beaton gave way to David Bailey, the cockney photographer and finally, of course, the dinner-suited dance bands of Joe Loss and Victor Sylvester lost out to mass pop music culture.

The youth phenomenon which emerged and swept throughout the world during the 1960s acted as a catalyst to the Permissive Society and the coming of age of mass culture in Britain. Yet, unlike in other countries, particularly America, where the Counterculture was led essentially by middle-class youth, in Britain, although middle-class youth took part in it, especially in the political sphere, it was essentially lower status group youth, as represented by the "likes" of the Beatles, who provided the leadership and dictated the norms.

Youth culture during this period developed in the West as a unique phenomenon in itself. The 1960s saw the emergence of a more dynamic and outward going younger generation with money to burn and time on its hands, which was willing to question the norms and standards set by its parents. Many factors have been put forward to explain the development of the youth phenomenon during the 1960s in Britain, such as the economic boom and general affluence which provided single young people with large incomes but little responsibility and increased leisure time. Urbanisation, a side effect of the 'Bulge'—the population explosion just after the war—and the desire on the part of young people who had grown up and fought in the last war, to create a better society which led them to rear their children in a more liberal and less authoritiarian way, have also been put forward as causes. Other reasons put forward include the influence of Dr. Spock, whose baby-rearing bible which emphasised the importance of fostering a child's individuality and personal growth, which influenced a whole generation of parents after the war, the result of mass enfranchisement and the development of the political power of the masses which was reflected in child-rearing practices and helped create a more progressive and liberal attitude in parents. Other factors suggested to explain the youth phenomenon include the massive increase in 'working mothers' and 'latch-key' children, the result of twenty years of a 'Welfare State', the effect of the 1944 Education Act which led to a progressive and questioning form of schooling and, lastly, the development of the media, and television in particular, which brought the world into everybody's sitting-room and allowed people to make their own evaluation and criticism of events as well as, of course, making them familiar with exotic cultures and eastern religions. It is no accident that it is modern youth who have been brought up on a diet of television who have taken to eastern religions, for it was 'the telly', the arbiter of their thought, which laid the ground for their interest.

Modern youth has been socialised to expect a great deal more out of life than their parents. Lower-status youth, particularly in the 1960s, unlike their middle and upper middle-class counterparts who still saw their future to some extent in class terms and were still committed in some degree to the established social system, had no commitment to their parents' way of life. Much the opposite, they wanted more out of life than the eternal round of 'the telly' and the pub. But whilst the Swinging Sixties in Britain created a more progressive, liberal and outgoing society, nevertheless for some groups and categories, including lower status group youth in particular, the 'swinging' side of the 1960s hid fundamental discrepancies between their desires and ideals and the reality of their social situation. The permissive society created frustration and problems for young people which they were unable to deal with and solve empirically. Whilst the desire to seek wider horizons and a more meaningful life than their parents had been inculcated in lower status youth, there was a massive gap between the desired and the obtainable, a gap which their major frame of reference, the 'telly', brought home to them all the time. Modern lower status youth have been socialised to expect a great deal out of life and, in theory, have more opportunity and a greater degree of choice and freedom in everyday life and social relations in general than their parents ever had. But in reality their daily lives and futures are just as bleak and dismal as their parents' were. Their lives are just as restricted as their parents' and outside the sphere of personal social relations they have little choice. The future they have to face is as humdrum and boring as was that of their parents, expecially in terms of job opportunities. They have to look forward to the frustration and boredom of dead-end skilled and semiskilled jobs. Nor is this to be compensated for by family and community life, as it had been in the past, particularly in traditional lower status group and working-class families. By the 1960s, large families had given way to the small nuclear family; family life was in the process of withering away and with it an individual's traditionally large network of kin relations. Urbanisation and massive rebuilding, particularly in lower status group areas, resulted in the breakdown of traditional closeknit neighbourhood community life which had been the basis of much lower-class city and suburban life before the 1960s. Nor had any substitute for family and neighbourhood social ties developed. Life in the provinces and suburbs was particularly boring and the gap there the greatest, for there was little for young people to do. For the majority of them, the life they had to enjoy now and in the future was dull, boring and routine, bearing little correspondence to the one portrayed on the television or in the cinema.

A major function of the Swinging Sixties' was to create a more meaningful life for young people by providing an outlet for their frustrations and social problems, by channelling them into cultural and ideological spheres such as pop music, the human potential movements, and by making a fetish of fashion. Teddy Boys in the 1950s, Mods and Rockers and Skinheads in the 1960s and latterly Punk Rockers too, are clearly forms of social protest and are attempts to find answers to the boring routine of modern youth's daily lives and dead-end existences. Eastern religions, too, such as ISKCON provide a similar outlet for modern youth and enables them to express themselves in ways which would not otherwise have been possible. The first signs of modern lower status youth's social rebellion against their humdrum existence was heard in pop music in the late 1950s, which Melly (1972) in *Revolt into Style*, a study of the history of Pop Music, sees essentially as a form of social protest by working-class youth.

Certainly the problems confronted by modern lower status group youth in Britain is reflected in microcosm in ISKCON and appear to be major reasons for joining the movement. Devotees are not generally 'nine-to-fivers'. They are people who appear to be unable to tolerate and cope with routine. The boring routine of the skilled and semi-skilled jobs open to them in the outside world is reflected in their pattern of behaviour before joining the movement.

Most devotees, prior to joining the movement, did not have steady jobs and when they did work, tended to change the type of job they did frequently. Generally, they tended to have been in and out of work and often to have had a period on the dole immediately prior to joining the movement. This pattern of behaviour appears to be true, too, even of devotees who were student dropouts prior to joining the movement. Few joined immediately they dropped out of college. This pattern of behaviour is found even among the earliest devotees who joined in the late 1960s, prior to the economic depression. The frequency with which they changed the type of job they did, when they did work, is an indicator, too, of their frustration and inability to cope with dull, boring jobs. Devotees frequently comment on the boredom and frustration of their former jobs.

The gap between the desired and obtainable and lack of career opportunities and meaningful life is particularly felt by those who have had a middle-range education, namely at technical college, polytechnic or art college and is also a reason why they appear in significant numbers in ISKCON. This type of education, while it educates people to be well aware of the possibilities of a more meaningful life, makes them realise that their own future is going to be mundane, that their second-rate education equips them only for second-rate jobs and to a life little different from that of their semi-skilled and unskilled peers. This is particularly true of art students, who find on reaching college that whilst they may have been much better than their class mates at art, they are really only second-rate and that their future lies only in art teaching or graphics.

The present economic recession and high level of unemployment appear to be an important factor in determining recruitment in British ISKCON too. In Britain, according to membership statistics recorded in the *Sri Vyasapuja* books, ISKCON has increased in numbers by a half between August 1976 and August 1978, including children, from about 86 to 203. The present high unemployment amongst school leavers is also reflected in the movement— devotees are getting younger and some are not long out of school.

Although routine jobs are something devotees find difficult to cope with, many are not institutionalised work-shy layabouts. Rather, prior to joining the movement, a lot just could not get work and this often triggered off their joining the movement. As Dave, a recently joined devotee remarked, he hadn't anything to lose by joining. Being on the dole acts as an important catalyst to joining the movement. Not only does it induce boredom, frustration and a sense of personal inadequacy but often the desire to do something about it by the more positive minded. It also provides the leisure time to indulge an interest and experiment in oriental religions.

It is no accident either that although a few devotees come from suburban London, the majority of devotees are not sophisticates from the capital and the home counties, but come from the provinces and the provincial suburbs in particular. Many come from the North, especially the Manchester area, Scotland, Ireland and Wales; places where unemployment is high, where there is little to do and dead-end existence is the norm. It is no accident that George Harrison of the Beatles came from one such depressing environment in Liverpool. As one devotee from Edinburgh said, 'There is nothing to do in Edinburgh but play football'.

The young are attracted by the strange and unusual and devotees often say it was the devotees themselves rather than the philosophy that first attracted them to the movement. The sophisticated London and the home counties youth, who are provided with more leisure-time activities and are more familiar with such movements as ISKCON which tend to congregate in London, look at them with jaundiced eyes and tend to deride them. Their less sophisticated provincial contemporaries, however, find the bizarre nature of ISKCON devotees and their appearance especially, particularly glamorous and attractive. Often provincial devotees join in the provinces or become members soon after they arrive in London, before the novelty and glamour of groups such as ISKCON wears off.

It is often argued that the youth phenomenon and the American Counterculture in particular, is the age-old generation conflict being enacted in a new guise. But generation difference and differences in attitude to progressiveness at least are not important reasons for devotees joining as they are often assumed to be, for devotees' parents in both the States and Britain, on the whole, appear to be trendy liberal types, not old-style 'squares'. This is particularly true of the parents of the younger devotees who have joined in recent years. As such, devotees have little to rebel against at home and to see their joining ISKCON as a form of rebellion against their parents' conservativeness and rigidity would be misleading.

However, conflict between devotees and their parents appears to be more acute in the States than in Britain and is a factor in their becoming members there. Frequently in the States antagonism between devotees and parents on their joining becomes so great that devotees break all ties with their parents. It is not unknown either for American parents to have their children abducted from the movement and 'deprogrammed'. Conflict between American devotees and their parents is not only due to a general tendency to extremism in American culture which is reflected in the family structure, but also devotees, and modern American youth in general, also blame the parental generation for the Vietnam War and America's social problems. Moreover, most American parents tend to be very opposed to the movement because they fear that if their children join, their middle-class career prospects will be ruined.

In Britain, however, whilst some devotees have broken all ties with their families, the majority of devotees and parents appear to visit each other as frequently as 'karmi' youth who live away from home. In fact, one mother visits her daughter twice a week! Relationships with parents tend to be less strained, partly because of the general tendency towards compromise in English culture. The whole idea of having their children deprogrammed would be anathema to the average English parent, nor do most English devotees have career prospects that their parents need worry about. As devotee Greg's mother, a very trendy 'Swinging Sixties' type in her mid-thirties said, when asked how she felt about her 17 year old son joining the movement, 'What is there for him outside?'.

Besides conflict within the family (e.g. between parents), dissatisfaction with school also acts as an inducement to join ISKCON, particularly in the case of devotees who join at the age of 18 or under. Many of the young boys hated school, felt they learnt nothing there and not infrequently skipped their last year at school.

It is generally assumed by outsiders that anybody who joins ISKCON, or some other similar esoteric group such as the Moonies or Divine Light, must suffer from psychological defects and have inadequate personalities. There is no doubt that ISKCON does attract people with psychological problems—often very overt and bizarre ones. Certainly, if cases cited by Judah (1974) and Daner (1976) are anything to go by, many of the early American devotees, prior to joining the movement, had severe psychological problems and were 'spaced out' through use of drugs. The devotees are well aware that they attract the disturbed. Most have stories to tell of 'weirdos' who have joined the movement.

The movement itself would much prefer to attract the more normal members of society to the movement, but to keep up the numbers because of the difficulty it has attracting followers, it operates a policy of tolerance to individual personality quirks, but the really disturbed who manifest very obvious and bizarre psychological defects and scruffy, 'down-and-out' types, are not allowed past the door. Anyone who is not willing to conform to the rules and regulations of temple life or who cannot fit in with the group, is soon asked to leave and those devotees who do manifest very overt psychological problems tend to be shunned by their more 'together' colleagues. But, people with very strong psychological problems are generally unable to cope with routine. Such people, when they join ISKCON, soon find that they cannot cope with the discipline and routine of temple life and soon leave.

The impression is created and, being an anthropologist and not a psychologist, it can only be an impression, that devotees in Britain represent a cross-section of personality types. Although about 20 per cent manifest overt psychological problems, the large majority, particularly those who have been in the movement a long time and hold positions of real power, appear to be either as normal as the average person in the outside world or to manifest only marginally more psychological problems. This is especially true and understandably so of those who joined through job frustration, since they joined for social reasons, not because of psychological problems. For those devotees who were emotionally disturbed, or, had had psychological problems when they joined the movement, ISKCON appears to have helped them 'get their heads together', as devotees put it.

Significantly, although psychological problems are found amongst devotees of all classes, the more upper-class devotees appear to have a proportionately higher rate of emotional disturbance. Radha, for instance, a devotee in her mid-twenties and the daughter of a college director, ended up in a mental hospital. Perhaps psychological factors are important reasons for the more upper-class devotees acting differently from their class peers and joining ISKCON in the first place.

Few married couples join the movement in Britain and those that do tend to be young and under the age of 25. Understandably so, since married people tend to have outside commitments and responsibilities, such as a mortgage, a steady job and children which make it difficult for them to foster an interest in or be predisposed to joining a movement such as ISKCON, where home comforts are sparse and facilities for children are minimal.

Few single people over the age of 30 join the movement either, though some do visit the temple. In 1979 there were 10 devotees who, when they joined the movement, had been between the age of 30 and 40 and two who had joined over the age of 40. People over the age of 30 rarely join the movemnt because, by this age, many of them have grown to like their creature-comforts and are unwilling to rough it as they would have to do if they joined the temple. Also, of course, and this is particularly true of couples, generally they have families, responsibilities and attachments in the outside world. Where older people join the movement as full-time devotees, they tend generally to be single, often have no dependents and frequently, though not always, have psychological problems. Devotees who join over the age of 35 tend to belong to the following categories: the lonely, divorcees, misfits, homosexuals, and single people who have looked after aged parents.

Older people who are believers in Krishna or interested in the movement usually just visit the temple. One such is a typical retired Anglican priest, Father James, who in manner and looks is very upper middle-class and rotund with rosy cheeks and a nice smile. As with many other devotees, he had experienced a crisis sometime prior to joining the movement. He had been very ill and almost died, which made him seriously rethink his values and life in general. It had led him not only to kick over the traces, but to be receptive to new ideas. He was impressed by the genuineness and sincerity of the devotees whom he had first met when walking past the Bury Place temple one day. He has become something of a devotee of Krishna himself and says he has found it easy to integrate his Christian beliefs with those of Krishna seeing the Christian God and Krishna as being essentially the same. He chants 'Hare Krishna' too and visits the temple not infrequently. He said that his family thought he was 'dotty' and had said to him, 'You're not still interested in those awful people?' The devotees for their part are only too happy to have him visit, for not only is he a very pleasant character, but he is good public relations for the movement and an excellent advertisement for their genuineness and sincerity.

Another important factor which puts off people over the age of

30 is the age gap—the youth of the devotees. A well dressed and well spoken lower middle-class taxi driver in his mid-thirties from Wembley was very keen on the movement. He and his wife had discussed joining ISKCON, but they felt that not only did they have too many commitments and were past the age when they could rough it, but also that they had little in common with young people and felt out of place amongst them. This attitude appears to be shared by many of the older people who become interested in the movement. As Emanuel, an eccentric Greek American in his early fifties and the oldest full-time member in Britain who appears to be in a category all on his own said, 'You have to adapt to them [the young devotees], they don't adapt to you'.

Some devotees just drifted into ISKCON and perhaps this is where Emanuel fits in. He claims to have been an office manager in New York earning 15,000 dollars a year prior to joining the movement at the beginning of the seventies though other devotees maintain he was a pool hustler. His son was a devotee and, after getting a divorce, he too joined and has spent several years in Britain where he has carved out a niche himself for in the movement. At one time he supervised in the kitchens, but latterly he has run a travel agency—Three Worlds Travel—set up by the movement to get devotees cheap fares, and opened a Sandwich Bar. He does not appear to have a very strong belief in Krishna, but goes his own way and holds his own by paying lip service to the movement's rules and regulations.

Pauline, too, is another example of a drifter, someone for whom the religious side of ISKCON was initially unimportant, who got caught up in the movement and stayed. Many drifters actually become converts after a time, and she appears to be one such. Sandra came to London having quit her job as a hotel chambermaid in Brighton. The first night, having nowhere to stay and virtually no money, she slept rough in a park. The next day, dirty and hungry, she visited Bury Place which she was familiar with, having visited there out of curiosity some months previously. In sheer desperation, hungry, having no money and nowhere to stay, she asked to become a member and was accepted. She donned a sari and within a few weeks she had become a convert. Not just Pauline, but for a number of devotees, particularly those who had been living rough or in squats, the prospect of free board and lodging in the temple was an important initial attraction.

A small proportion of foreigners have joined the movement in London. Most of whom, like the American devotees in Britain, are from a middle-class background. Generally they join the movement soon after they arrive in Britain, before they have had time to develop a friendship network, which tends to suggest that loneliness was a reason for their joining ISKCON.

In America, according to the literature, there is a high correlation between drug-taking, especially the use of hallucinogenic drugs like LSD and membership of eastern religious sects. Psychedelic drugs hit the Counterculture in the mid-1960s under the high-priesthood of the most famous 'head' of them all, Timothy Leary, the ex-Harvard mathematics teacher. LSD (lysergic acid diethylamide) or 'acid' as it is often called is an hallucinogenic drug that was seen in the early days by advocates such as Leary, as the 'religion of the twentyfirst century'. By penetrating, exploring, enlarging and liberating the consciousness, it was held to induce mystical and spiritual experiences and a kind of religious ecstasy. Its exponents maintained that it could produce in the mind visions of the intrinsic nature of things, including the ultimate and even God himself. Leary himself maintained that LSD turns you onto God and stated in *The Politics of Ecstasy* (1968: 113):

> The aim of all Eastern religions, like the aim of LSD, is basically to get high: that is, to expand your consciousness and find ecstasy and revelation within.

Certainly, according to Judah (1974), Daner (1976) and Johnson (1973), the majority of American devotees prior to joining the movement had been heavily into the Countercultural drug-taking scene. Many had been 'acid heads' prior to joining the movement, particularly devotees who had joined the San Francisco temple which was situated in the heart of the Haight Ashbury, the hippy ghetto, to which young people flocked from all over the States in the 1960s. According to Johnson (1973), the majority of devotees in the Haight Ashbury temple up to 1968 were upper middle-class migrants, and did not appear to be suffering from any kind of deprivation. He concluded that they had joined the movement not as a means of escaping from daily lives which they found unsatisfactory, but for positive reasons, it was an 'active construction of meaning on reality'. One reason was to help them to obtain spiritual insight and increase the sense of spiritual transcendence and enlightenment which they had tried to obtain through taking acid, but which had been inhibited by the nature of acid itself and the materialist drug culture of Haight Ashbury. After 1968, however, he concluded, life in Haight Ashbury began to disintegrate. Barbiturates took over from acid as the major drug taken in the Haight and this was reflected in the drug-taking habits of devotees prior to joining the movement. Barbiturate-takers, permanently 'on the nod', are unable to carry on a normal life; and their social life soon disintegrates. He concluded that devotees who joined the movement after 1968 had been heavily into 'barbs' and joined ISKCON as a means of personal transformation, as a means of breaking away from an unsatisfactory life and escaping from the social and emotional problems engendered by a 'barb' way of life.

It seems reasonable to see the taking of acid by early devotees, whom Johnson refers to as 'seekers', as a means of seeking a genuine religious experience and to view their joining ISKCON as a means of helping them on their journey to enlightenment, but it is difficult to believe that their life prior to joining the movement was in no way 'deprived'. As Johnson (1973) himself admits, life in Haight Ashbury was characterised by unrestrained individualism and unfettered egotism. There was a lack of close ties between people, no sense of community and people there led a footloose existence. Such a way of life alone is bound to engender both emotional and social problems. In the atmosphere of the free and easy sexual mores and drug haze of the Haight, many of the early devotees appear to have led very promiscuous lives which they eventually became ashamed of and found very unrewarding. A not insignificant proportion appear to have joined the movement, amongst other things, to escape their promiscuous past. For some of the very earliest devotees in the Haight, including those who had taken acid as a means of attaining a mystical experience, social and emotional problems engendered by the social infrastructure that went with the acid-head way of life, appear to have made them so unhappy that they were only too willing, as a means of getting away from their past, to renounce their hedonistic life for one of total renunciation.

Since the demise of the Counterculture in the early 1970s, fewer new devotees appear to have had such a heavy drug-using past.

The lower status groups in America seem to join the movement for reasons similar to their British counterparts (although fewer tend to have spent long periods on the dole). The use of drugs appears to be a less important factor contributing to their joining the movement too.

Among British devotees, however, the drug scene and the drug-use of devotees is very different from that of their counterparts in the States. British devotees, in general, do not have the heavy drug-taking background of the majority of the early American devotees. Moreover, the Counterculture and hippy scene never developed as such a distinct alternative life-style as it did in the States. Drug-taking, particularly cannabis, found its way to British youth in the 1960s too, but never to the same extent as it did in the States, nor was excessive use of the hallucinogenics (LSD, mescaline and psilocybin) so prevalent. Addiction, too, to hard drugs such as heroin, barbiturates and cocaine was minute compared with America, and this is reflected in ISKCON devotees' drug-taking patterns prior to joining the movement. Whilst quite a large proportion of devotees had experimented with drugs such as LSD and cannabis prior to joining the movement, a significant percentage had not, including nearly all the women. Although they number amongst them one or two ex-heroin addicts, the majority of devotees who took drugs prior to joining were not heavy users of LSD, cannabis or hard drugs. The number of ex-acid heads in the movement is really quite small, though since LSD is taken by such a small proportion of the population in Britain, the fact that acid-heads are in the movement would appear to be a significant factor.

Krishna Bhakti, a 20 year old working-class Londoner is a good example of the superficiality of a typical British devotee's hippy past. He boasted he had been a 'real hippie' before joining ISKCON at the age of 17. But it appeared that his former life consisted, as he put it, 'of the smoking of the occasional joint and Seven-Up' with a group of his mates.

Significantly, and this appears to hold for the majority of both British and American devotees (see Judah, 1974: 135), most of those devotees who had experimented with drugs had already become disenchanted with them prior to joining the movement. In the case of British devotees, they had given them up prior to joining the movement, indicating that the drug scene and the way of life that goes with it had already paled for them and they were looking for something else: for some new experience. But, of course, experimenting with drugs indicates a willingness to be unconventional. To join such an overtly bizarre movement such as ISKCON, this is a necessary prerequisite, particularly in Britain where to be unconventional is so frowned upon.

Lofland and Stark (1965) in their 'theory of conversion to a deviant perspective', point to tension of some sort as being a necessary prerequisite immediately prior to joining a sect. This would appear to be the case with many ISKCON devotees too, including Father James. Many young people live in dead-end existences, do boring jobs or are on the dole, but do not join movements such as ISKCON. A factor which appears to differentiate many ISKCON devotees from their peers in the outside world is a crisis or tension of some sort immediately prior to their joining ISKCON, which appears to have acted as a catalyst.

Those who join ISKCON tend to be individuals who have had a bad time in some way and feel frustrated and antagonistic towards society and fed up with the material world and are looking for an alternative. The Permissive Society, although it has given people freedom of choice, particularly in personal relations and in sexual and emotional spheres, has concomitantly increased their potential for getting hurt and being confused. Frequently, ISKCON devotees and especially the more upper-class and educated women in particular, suffered some emotional upheaval prior to joining the movement, such as feelings of inadequacy due to being on the dole fo long periods, an unhappy love affair, an abortion, the birth of ai illegitimate baby, family conflict or disturbance. One young middle-class male devotee's mother committed suicide.

Certainly, the devotees themselves are well aware that they recruit from those who have problems or who have lost out in the rat-race. They, themselves, stress deprivation as a reason for joining the movement. People come from 'distress' they say. As Citraketu, the British movement's court poet remarked, 'Srilaprabhupad picks up those who are down—drug-takers, etc. Those who think something of themselves aren't interested. You have to be really at the bottom to realise your state'. Indeed, the movement is rather proud that they turn 'rascals into gentlemen'.

In fact, devotees justify and rationalise the drawbacks of their previous life-style, the social problems and crises they faced in their daily lives prior to joining the movement in terms of 'Krishna's mercy'. It was Krishna's desire, they say, that they should have these things happen to them, so that their 'fallen state' should make them humble and receptive to Krishna Consciousness philosophy and thus bring them to Krishna.

To people who have been hurt and are fed up and frustrated by material life and as such implicitly antagonistic to society, an ideology such as Prabhupad's which views society as corrupt—'the society of the cheaters and the cheated'—and offers the possibility of renouncing the world that makes them unhappy, is understandably attractive; a point of view summed up by a former temple commander in charge of Bhaktivedanta Manor domestic organisation. A divorced ex-butcher in his early thirties and extremely alienated, he remarked 'it's all a con in the outside world, there is nothing in it. You want to get out'.

ISKCON ideology enables devotees to project their problems onto the outside society and to make the outside society the scapegoat. They can lay all the blame for their problems and crises into the outside world. It is the outside world that is corrupt—the 'society of the cheaters and the cheated'. It is the 'karmi' world that is the cause of all their problems. Thus, their problems are not their own fault, but the outside society's. By renouncing the outside society, they are renouncing their problems. Understandably, such an ideology provides a meaningful and satisfying world-view for the type of people who join ISKCON. It is not without significance and no accident that devotees frequently maintain that 'devotees don't have any problems'.

But why did modern youth, the products of the Permissive Society, seek to express themselves and utilise the specific forms of self-expression that they did, namely eastern religions, pop music, making a fetish of fashion and so forth? Why did they choose to express their frustrations and social protest predominantly on the cultural and ideological levels rather than the economic and political? The social climate in which modern youth grew up—the progressive postwar child socialization processes described previously—the withering away of the family, the breakdown of neighbourhood communities and concomitant networks of social relations, encouraged them not only to want a better and more meaningful way of life, but also provided them with the freedom of choice of action to do so.

But whilst modern youth is liberated to a great extent from the traditional constraints of social structure, the crisis in meaning and the social problems that face modern youth in Britain and America too are problems inherent in the belief system and structure of modern society, and can only be solved by a major reorganisation of society, not by the individual. Thus, modern youth, in both Britain and America, have had to find answers to their problems and seek forms of self-expression that are not encapsulated within and constrained by traditional social structural restrictions. This seeking by youth of forms of self-expression is an implicit recognition to the fundamental limitations and inability of the scientific and technological society to cater for individual needs. Modern youth realised that answers to their problems could not be found outside themselves in the wider society and they realised that the onus was on them, it was up to them and them alone to seek their own solutions. For some the answer lay in nihilism, vandalism, petty crime and soccer hooliganism and, for a small percentage in Britain, in political activity. The great majority, however, were inspired to focus on themselves and to resort to ideological and cultural forms of expression as a channel for the individual quest. They turned to such forms of expression because, whilst they are expressive of social structure, they are to some extent independent of it and less constrained socially. To a great extent culture and ideology are open to personal choice and, as such, can be focused around the individual and are open to individual manipulation. The last hundred years in the West has witnessed a gradual change from values and way of life being superimposed on the individual by society, to one where personal choice is emphasised and the individual self-consciously chooses his own life-style and values. Modern youth's use of culture and values to express social protest and as a means of coming to terms with their problems is clearly an expression of this trend. Moreover, the cultural and ideological levels have contained within them beliefs, rituals and symbols, which frequently are laden with emotional and mystical content and, as such, provide an ideal channel for the emotional and mystical outlets denied man by modern society.

From this perspective, modern youth's interest in new eastern religious groups such as ISKCON and the human potential movements, pop music and the fetish made of fashion become understandable. Being essentially cultural and ideological in orientation and centred on the individual, they are only minimally socially constrained and are thus open to individual forms of self-expression and manipulation. For this reason they make an excellent channel for self-expression and social protest and as such are very attractive to modern youth who have made them their own.

ISKCON has provided devotees with a cultural framework within which they can make sense of their problems and allows the individual devotee to attempt to work out, through a series of transformations on the level of belief and culture, basic problems and contradictions that confront them in their everyday lives.

It is clear that ISKCON devotees (like many of their more positive contemporaries who are interested in and committed to new eastern religious cults), have utilised ISKCON belief and concomitant ritual, dress, dance, music, drama etc. to articulate and resolve the problem of meaning and their everyday problems and focal concerns which they could not otherwise transcend. The active organisation of objects, patterns of behaviour and attitudes in ISKCON has provided devotees with an organised individual and group identity in the form and shape of a coherent and distinctive way of 'being' in the world. In so doing, ISKCON has provided devotees with the means of organising and controlling the world which, for them, would otherwise tend to be both chaotic and extremely frustrating. Also the way ISKCON has used Vaishnava symbols, beliefs, objects and rituals to express or signify things about themselves, the way they have taken them over, reinterpreted, structured and ordered them, reveals a great deal about the problems and contradictions faced by Western society and particularly lower status group youth in Britain.

CHAPTER THREE

The Science of Self Realisation and the Bliss of Surrender to Krishna

Namas te sarasvate deve gaura-vani-pracarine nirvisesa-sunyavadi-pascatya-desa-tarine

Our respectful obeisances are unto you (Srila Prabhupad) O servant of Sarasvati Goswami. You are kindly preaching the message of Lord Chaitanya-deva and are delivering the Western countries, which are filled with impersonalism and voidism.

People usually look to the West and the ills of its society, rather than to the East, in order to find reasons why westerners have taken with such alacrity to the new eastern religions. But eastern religions are in themselves highly attractive to westerners because they offer an ideal framework for dealing with the existential and social problems which confront them personally in their daily lives.

Realising that it is up to them to find meaning in their lives and solve their everyday problems, people have turned to themselves, to their internal worlds for answers. They have concentrated on their inner psyches in order to discover meaning and a deeper understanding of the nature of things. They have attempted to explore and transcend their consciousness and so achieve a radical transformation of self; a self better able to cope with the problems of life. In essence, as an answer to their problems rather than try and change society, they have decided to alter themselves. The exploration and raising of consciousness which flourished in the 1960s, to a degree hitherto unknown, is an expression and reflection of this attempt to transform themselves rather than change society as is youth's experimentation with hallucinogenic drugs during this decade.

Significantly the new eastern religions parallel this developing focus of westerners. For such an exploration of consciousness the new eastern religions are ideal for they focus on the individual and his personal liberation, his inner experience, self and consciousness. They consider altered states of consciousness such as are achieved by meditation, mind control and various forms of yoga, as the primary means of attaining understanding, knowledge and salvation.

It is no accident that ISKCON refers to Krishna Consciousness as 'The Science of Self Realization' or that it too focuses on altered states of consciousness as the means to salvation. The goal of Krishna Consciousness is to attain one's original 'God Consciousness' through *bhakti yoga*; personal loving devotion to God.

> The revival of the original consciousness of the living being—the conscious awareness that one is eternally related to God or Krishna.

By renouncing the material world and leading a life of purification and chanting *Hare Krishna*, the holy names of God, a devotee of Krishna hopes to raise his consciousness and achieve a 'higher taste' of *prema* or love of God and thus ultimately attain a transcendental plane and 'go back to Godhead'.

The transcendence of consciousness offered by the eastern religions is particularly attractive to adolescents. The 'betwixt and between' stage between childhood and adulthood, is a time when individuals are neither one nor the other and have no clear-cut roles or social responsibilities thrust on them. It is a period of doubt, anxiety and tension when the problem of meaning and the need to solve personal problems are particularly acute. In Britain, as well as in America, devotees are intelligent enough to ask 'Why?' or 'Who am I?' and 'What is the purpose of life?' They tend to be acutely frustrated by their situation and feel that 'there must be more to life than this'.

Most importantly adolescence—and, for the most immature, this goes on into the early twenties—is the age when individuals begin to define their adult identities and face up to and evaluate the beliefs and values of the adult world. Having no clear-cut roles and social responsibilities of family and career to constrain them, they are more able to question the belief system. It is the age when if people are going to question the system they will. The questioning by youth of society is thus not a new phenomenon; what differentiated it in the 1960s from previous generations was its intensity and its overtness.

This general questioning of belief leads young people of course to evaluate religious and spiritual beliefs and values as well. We tend to associate young peoples' interest in oriental faiths and religion and the spiritual life in general as new and part of the unique 1960s youth phenomenon. But, in fact, young peoples' interest in the religious and spiritual and their conversion and overt commitment to religion are an integral part of adolescence, as a number of studies have shown (Argyle 1958:59-70). It was not just a product of the social chaos and upheaval in America in the 1960s or a product of the 'Swinging Sixties' in Britain. The whole Billy Graham evangelical movement in Britain in the 1950s was youth orientated for example. The modal age of individuals converted in Britain by Billy Graham in 1954 was 15, about the age at which Billy Graham himself found God.

Adolescence appears to be the age when individuals either develop a religious orientation or give it up altogether or will convert to another religion if they are prone to do so. Understandably so, since it is the age when they are brought face to face with religious and spiritual values and are forced to evaluate and reconcile them as they develop their adult sense of identity and place in society. What broadly differentiates modern youth's religiosity from previous generations is its intensity which is generated by the modern milieu. In addition, the lifting of traditional social constraints has enabled this integral part of adolescence to blossom and flourish.

Obviously if people have had some kind of contact or connection with religion then this is likely to act as a catalyst either way. Clearly, social factors are all important reasons why people join sects like ISKCON. But many people who feel frustrated and fed up with the material world do not join sects like ISKCON. A major factor differentiating ISKCON devotees is that they often appear to have had some prior connection with religion. Either they have a past history of religious commitment, having been brought up in a family where either one or both parents were religious, or they had a latent religious orientation which has been brought to the surface by participation in ISKCON. Many appear to have been interested in religious questions since childhood—one devotee, Seamus, said he had conducted church services for his friends when he was six—or had some connection with religion in the formative years of their lives such as pious parents, attendance at Sunday school or education in a Catholic school. Krishna Consciousness is not thus usually their first religious experience but a continuation of a past contact with religion.

Actually a quite high proportion of devotees are Catholic by birth (according to Judah [1974:147] 18 per cent of the parents of devotees in the San Francisco and Los Angeles temples were Catholics). Catholicism of course, parallels ISKCON's belief and social structure in a number of important ways. It is easy for Catholics to convert to ISKCON for they are very similar, both being iconolatrous, devotional, strong on discipline and highly ritualistic and both pray using rosaries.

In the States too, indicating their prior interest in religion, a great many of the devotees had dabbled in various forms of eastern mysticism and the occult before joining the movement. In Britain however the esoteric subculture is relatively small-scale and to a great degree focused around the cities and big towns and few devotees came into contact with other forms of eastern mysticism prior to joining the movement. Thus, for the majority of British devotees ISKCON was their first experience of eastern mysticism.

Experimentation with forms of eastern mysticism and drug-taking on the part of western youth, particularly hallucinogenic drugs appear to go hand in hand and are directly related. Both eastern religions and hallucinogenic drug-taking focus on mind expansion and aim to transcend the senses. The drug-taking past of ISKCON devotees predisposed them to be interested in an experiment with mystical forms. It also made devotees aware that there was more to the human mind than what our keen senses tell us.

ISKCON, however like the majority of eastern religions, denies that you can induce a mystical experience by artificial means such as drugs. Contact with the Supreme Personality of Godhead, it is held, can only be achieved by *bhakti yoga*, by personal loving devotion to Krishna. Whilst neophyte devotees sometimes say they obtained a mystical experience when they took acid, devotees who have been in the movement long enough to know the philosophy are quick to deny that mystical experiences can be obtained by a 'cheap thrill' like L.S.D. Rather, they interpret their drug-taking past as a symptom of their 'fallen state' and of the low standard of their life prior to joining the movement, and drug-taking is one of the most strictly enforced prohibitions in the movement. Anyone caught taking drugs is immediately expelled and I never came across a case in the three years I visited ISKCON temples in Britain.

The influence of devotees' drug-taking background is reflected in the movement. They have brought with them into the movement the terminology of the drug scene and their hippy days and communicate with the public, particularly in America, in terms of the language of the drug scene. For instance, the Haight Ashbury temple in 1968 had on its walls a four-foot high poster which stated:

STAY HIGH FOREVER. No more coming down. Practice Krishna Consciousness. Expand your consciousness by practicing the Transcendental Sound Vibration. Hare Krishna, Hare Krishna, Krishna Krishna, Hare Hare, Hare Rama, Hare Rama, Rama Rama, Hare Hare. The chanting will cleanse the dust from the mirror of the mind and free you from all material contamination. It is practical, self-evident, and requires no artificial aid. Try it and be blissful all the time. *Turn on* through music, dance, philosophy, science, religion, and prasadam (spiritual food). *Tune in*. Awaken your Transcendental Nature! Rejoice in the Ocean of Bliss! The process of Sankirtan brings about transcendental ecstasy. *Drop out* of movements employing artificially induced states of self-realization and expanded consciousness. Such methods only lead to spiritual laziness and chaos. *End all bring downs*, flip out and stay high for eternity. Bhaktiyoga has been practiced for many centuries and is authorized by India's great acharyas. Swami Bhaktivedanta is in the bonafide line of Krishna's disciplic succession. He has especially come to this country to spiritually guide young Americans. (Johnson 1973:41.)

Not only is the focus on altered states of consciousness of the new eastern religions attractive to westerners, but the beliefs, symbols and rituals in which these new eastern religions are embedded are also highly appealing for they offer a very good explanation of devotees' situation and provide a meaningful frame of reference for them. This is especially true of ISKCON, where there is an amazingly high congruence between the teachings of Gaudiya Matha philosophy and devotees' social situation and the existential and social problems that confront them in their daily lives.

The majority of eastern religions which have attracted modern westerners in the last decade, such as the Divine Light Mission, or Swami Muktananda's Siddha Yoga group or TM, have not taught the intricacies of Hindu philosophy. They have tended rather to concentrate on inner experience, consciousness raising, meditation and mind control and have been essentially practical in nature. Since they involve little change in life-style they have been easy to assimilate and accept by westerners. But joining ISKCON involves the total rejection of a devotees' natal western culture and the substitution of Vaishnava culture as interpreted and taught by Prabhupad, the movement's spiritual master and a member of this culture himself.

Outsiders, particularly antagonistic academics, tend to assume that ISKCON philosophy bears little relationship to 'real' Hinduism and that it must be a lot of superficial misunderstood mumbo-jumbo. But, significantly, Prabhupad adhered closely, with only a few minor deviations, to the teaching of the Gaudiya sect to which he belonged and to the beliefs and practices of his natal Bengali culture.

Prabhupad was, like many of his generation (who matured before Indological scholarship had ascertained the factual history and chronology of Indian religion), a fundamentalist and adhered to a literal extremely orthodox and conservative interpretation of the Gaudiya scriptures.

It is a truism to say that the beliefs and practices, as well as symbols and rituals, of one culture take on new meaning and significance when transposed to another but this is particularly true of ISKCON. Prabhupad did not teach just a hotch-potch of Vaishnava beliefs and practices. He was very sensitive to the needs of his young followers and gradually, in response to their perceived needs and demands, made minor deviations and placed more emphasis on certain aspects of Vaishnava teaching than is generally done, traditionally, in India. In so doing he remodelled and adapted Vaishnava culture to form a coherent whole attractive to western youth. Also, the devotees themselves, particularly in the last few years, have laid greater emphasis on some traditional beliefs and practices than is customary and in one or two instances have reinterpreted them. These minor modifications, reinterpretations and different emphases have resulted in ISKCON's belief system, ritual and social organization appearing superfically very similar to traditional Gaudiya Matha belief and practice and Bengali culture. But in practice it has resulted in the infrastructure of ISKCON's belief system, ritual and social organisation in some spheres developing very differently from the traditional.

Nevertheless, the very fact that ISKCON, adheres so closely to traditional belief and practice is in itself socially significant... Why does ISKCON do so? Transposed out of their traditional setting, Vaishnava Gaudiya Matha beliefs and practices, with their emphasis on Krishna, his consort Radha and their attendant demigods, appear to outsiders, both to the average man in the street and antagonistic academics (educated on a diet of rationality), to be a set of gobbledegook beliefs and practices. 'How can they believe in such rubbish' they say. But it is precisely because Krishna Consciousness philosophy contains such beliefs and practices that they are attractive to the kind of people who join ISKCON. For new devotees, frustrated with their own western society as they often tend to be, the idea of rejecting western society is in itself attractive. But incredible as it may seem, there is a striking compatibility between the content of Gaudiya Matha belief and the devotees' own social situation and mental orientation. The actual beliefs provide them with a meaningful explanation of and the means of coming to terms with and dealing with them.

The religious beliefs and practices of the Gaudiya sect from which ISKCON's beliefs and practices are derived, has its roots in Bengal and has a long history in India stemming from the Middle Ages, a point devotees are quick to make; since they are determined on being taken seriously by the outside world and are keen to be accepted as they put it as 'a genuine bonafide religion'. They have even taken legal action in America to do so. They point to the long history of Krishna worship in India and their own close adherence to traditional Vaishnava beliefs and practices to justify their claims to legitimacy. They are also quick to maintain that they are not 'Hindus' or a 'sect', that Krishna Consciousness philosophy is *Sanatana dharma* (eternal truth) and that, being eternal and true, it is above parochial and social forms and thus applicable to all times and everywhere:

> Krishna Consciousness is not a sectarian religion. It is 'sanatana-dharma', which literally means the eternal activity of the soul to render service to the Supreme Personality of Godhead. Sanatana-dharma is the constitutional nature of each and every living entity regardless of colour, class, creed, nationality, background, even species of life. (HKD 1979:8.)

Like the teachings of the Gaudiya sect, ISKCON's beliefs are centred around the worship of Lord Krishna, whose name etymologically refers to his supposedly dark complexion. Krishna is a god renowned and worshipped throughout India, particularly in Bengal, Gujarat, Uttar Pradesh and parts of the Punjab. Traditional and fundamentalist Hindus, such as Prabhupad, claim that Krishna descended to earth as an *avatara* (earthly incarnation) 'five thousand years ago'. The preindustrial peasant society of the period when Krishna lived on earth, which is referred to in ISKCON as 'Vedic culture', has been used by Prabhupad as the blueprint for ISKCON's own social organisation. This 'Vedic culture', with its rural focus and emphasis on the keeping of cows, is of course the exact opposite of modern industrial technological western society and is clearly an example of the use of inversion as a means of social protest. To people such as devotees, frustrated by urban civilisation, the 'back-to-nature' way of life offered by ISKCON is very attractive.

The setting up of a society 5,000 years ago as a model has provided ISKCON with a very flexible framework for social organisation. Since very little is known historically about the society of Krishna's supposed lifetime, just about anything, therefore, can be said to be a belief and practice of this period without fear of contradiction. 'Vedic' culture, in fact, provides the legitimisation and basis for ISKCON's deviation from modern Gaudiya belief and practice. ISKCON justifies any deviation the movement makes by saying it is 'Vedic', and therefore more valid.

Krishna, as represented in medieval Vaishnava writings, does not appear in the earliest Indian scriptures, the Vedic literature of the Aryan invaders who swarmed over northern India in the third millennium BC. The vedic literature, which orthodox Brahmins consider to be divinely revealed *shruti*, dates from 3000-800 BC. It is essentially pantheistic and is concerned with fire sacrifice, nature and nature Gods such as Rudra, the god of Storms, and Agni, the God of Fire.

The Upanishads, which developed out of the Vedas around 800 BC, although essentially monotheistic in outlook, make only a passing reference to Krishna. Krishna makes his first important appearance in the *Bhagavad Gita* (The Song of the Lord), a part of the *Mahabharata*, the great epic poem which functions as a kind of bible for Hinduism and is an important canonical source for both the Gaudiyas and the Gaudiya Matha and ISKCON Prabhupad claims that his own commentary on the *Gita—The Bhagavad Gita As It Is* (1968)—the basic text of ISKCON—is a literal interpretation of it and harks back to its true original meaning. It is claimed by the movement that he is able to capture the true intrinsic quintessence of the *Gita* because he is a 'pure devotee' of the Lord and his teachings, of which devotees make a great point, are considered to be part of a *parampara*, a tradition of direct disciplic succession from Krishna himself.

It is primarily the Gita that fundamentalists use as a basis for their interpretation of Krishna. According to the *Gita*, before the battle of Kurukshetra, where the Pandava family were about to fight their kinsmen the Kauravas, Krishna expounded to Arjuna his message of liberation to the world. In the *Gita*, a new feature appears in Hinduism, that of man's love for God and God for man. In the *Gita*, too, it is held that the most important way to salvation is that of *bhakti yoga*, namely personal loving devotion to God. The *Bhagavad Gita* is reckoned by scholars to have been composed some time after the third century BC. Orthodox Brahmins view the *Gita* as epic poetry (Smriti), but fundamentalists such as Prabhupad and ISKCON hold the *Gita* and a later work, the *Shrimad Bhagavata*, to be revealed texts and Shruti, too, and that the events depicted in them are historical and that they originate from the period 5000 years ago when they claim Krishna descended to earth.

Krishna, from the scholastic evidence available, appears to have been worshipped in some form from the third or fourth century BC, though the precise form appears to have varied from area to area. Gradually, however, the many different forms of Krishna worship fused syncretically to form, devotional Vaishnava sects (those which worship Vishnu and/or Krishna and Rama incarnations) which followed a path of total adoration and personal devotion to God. These *bhakti yoga* sects appear to have originated in the south in the sixth century.

The decline of Buddhism in the first ten centuries after christ, and reactions to both Brahmin domination and the threat of the Muslim invasion, have been put forward as reasons for the spread and development of the Vaishnava sects. At all events, the first of the five main Vaishnava sects, the Shri Vaishnava sect, was founded by Ramanuja in the south in the twelfth century. It was the sixteenth century, however, that saw the development of both the Vallabhacharya sect in Gujarat, which worships Krishna in his child form, and the Gaudiya sect in Bengal, whose founder Chaitanya Mahaprabhu lived from 1486 to 1533.

Chaitanya was not an originator, but a revivalist of Krishna *bhakti*, for there is evidence of bhakti movements in Bengal from AD 11th-12th centuries. Sri Chaitanya Mahaprabhu was a religious mystic who developed an ecstatic relationship with Krishna and was thought by his followers to be an incarnation (*avatara*) of Krishna in devotee form; also, as being a joint incarnation of Krishna and his *Gopi*, shepherdess, consort Radha. A Brahmin, he was born in Navadwip (Nadia) in Bengal (where ISKCON has established their 'Mayapur' temple and farm) and devoted his adult life to Krishna. According to the ISKCON *Teachings of Lord Chaitanya*, a pilgrimage to Gaya at the age of 16-17 witnessed the real beginning of his religious life. There he took spiritual initiation from Isvara Puri, a renowned sannyasi and from then on dedicated his life to Krishna. Indeed, he entered into ecstatic communion with the Godhead and behaved like a man inspired, so intense were his religious feelings and sentiments. So passionate was his devotion and adoration of Krishna that he continually chanted his names. So powerful was his love, too, that he would cry and go into trances and fall on the ground in ecstasy or swoon at the mention of Krishna or go into a frenzy at the sight of anything that reminded him of Him.

The apparent genuineness of his ecstatic relationship with Krishna rapidly gained him followers. He inaugurated *Sankirtana*, a form of congregational chanting. He and groups of his devotees would parade through the streets dancing and singing the names of Krishna to the accompaniment of drums and cymbals, as an expression of their love for him, a custom which has become a distinctive feature of ISKCON in western cities. So passionate was Chaitanya's devotion to Krishna that he took the renounced order of *sannyasa* and settled in Puri, in Orissa and never saw his wife and family again. Chaitanya disappeared in 1533. ISKCON devotees claim he disappeared into the deities in the Gopinatha temple in Puri. Others maintain that whilst in a trance he rushed into the sea and drowned or that he died from an infected wound in his foot.

Chaitanya engendered so powerful a religious revival of devotional religion that by the time he died, and in the period immediately after his death, his version of Krishna *bhakti* had spread throughout much of eastern India. After his death the movement split into two factions, those who followed Advaita and those who followed Nityananda—his leading disciples. It is to Nityananda's branch that Prabhupad belongs. Later centuries saw some decline in the initial impetus of Chaitanya's *bhakti*. However, in the 19th century there was a revival, one of the leaders of which was Bhaktivinoda Thakura, a Brahmin judge and superintendent of the Gopinatha temple in Puri. His son was Bhakti Siddhanta Sarasvati Thakura. He founded the reformist proselytising Gaudiya Matha (Mission) in 1918. It was he who was the guru of Prabhupad who himself joined the mission as a householder (*grihastha*) in 1932.

Chaitanya himself, although renowned as a scholar in his youth, was not a theologian but emphasised experience rather than rationality. He left a scholarly heritage of eight verses only, known as the *Siksashtaka* and the Hare Krishna *mantra*, which essentially is an invocation of the holy names of God. His philosophy was codified by disciples of his known as the six Gosvamis. Two of whom, Sanatana and Rupa Gosvami, on his orders went and settled in Vrindaban, near Mathura in Uttar Pradesh, Krishna's supposed birthplace on earth. Vrindaban still has a large Bengali population and Prabhupad himself lived there in Radhadamodara temple after he took *sannyasa*, the renounced order, in 1959. It is in Vrindaban that ISKCON built its first temple in India, Krishna Balarama Mandir, and later a comfortable International Guest House and school (*gurukula*) for devotees' children.

The Gaudiyas (taking their name from the Gauda province in Bengal), as Chaitanya's sect later became known, use as a source for their dualistic philosophy and literature not only the *Bhagavad*

Gita but the *Bhagavata Purana* or *Shrimad Bhagavata* as the devotees call it. Although, Prabhupad, fundamentalist Gaudiyas and ISKCON regard the *Shrimad Bhagavata* as divinely revealed and as Vedic, scholars believe the *Shrimad Bhagavata* dates from about the 9th century only.

The *Shrimad Bhagavata* supplements the *Bhagavad Gita* by dealing in detail with the early life of Krishna and it is highly erotic in tone. It is primarily around Krishna's early life and adolescence that Gaudiya and ISKCON philosophy is based. For ISKCON devotees, Krishna is the flute-playing cowherd boy who dallies and plays sensually with his milkmaid consort Radha and the shepherdesses (*gopis*) in transcendental Vrindaban, situated in Vaikuntha, his abode in the heavenly planets.

Both the Gaudiya sect and ISKCON profess a religion of 'love' and this is fundamental to understanding the movement. As is clear from Dimock's (1966) study of the Sahajiyas, as Chaitanya's sect was called in its early days, the imagery of their beliefs and practices is highly erotic and passionate and focuses around Krishna's love for the gopis. One gopi that Krishna favours in particular is his consort Radha. Modern Gaudiyas believe that Radha emanated from Krishna himself and that he created her to experience his own pleasure potency.

Radha's love for Krishna is powerfully and highly idealised. It was love at a distance, and love in separation. The relationship between Radha and Krishna provides a symbol for Gaudiya and ISKCON dualist philosophy, namely that man and God are eternally separate. Radha longs to be united with her lover Krishna and devotees are supposed to put themselves in Radha's place and emulate her relationship with Krishna. They are supposed to try to feel the longing and love she has for him. The pure bliss of her relationship with Krishna is the purity of emotion and joy that they are to receive themselves.

Clearly, the similarity in age of Krishna and Radha and the devotees is a reason for devotees' attraction to Krishna Consciousness philosophy. The traditional, long-bearded old man sitting up in heaven of Christianity has little relevance or symbolic significance for modern youth, particularly as they have rejected the older generation and its values. Being the same age, they are more in tune with and better able to identify with Krishna and Radha and are able in their fantasies to participate in their lives, love-making and frolics in Vaikuntha.

'Love' and particularly 'romantic love' are highly valued in western society. Young people are continuously bombarded with it by the media and often with highly erotic and pornographic forms of it. Thus a religion of love that is highly erotic in tone such as is offered by ISKCON, also fits in neatly with westerners' own emphasis on and preconception of love.

Most importantly, love in western society is so over idealised and people's expectations about it are so high, that the majority of people often find it impossible to attain. In consequence, they feel frustrated at the lack of love in their lives; particularly young people who have been brought up to expect it as a right. It is not uncommon either for devotees themselves to have had unhappy love affairs prior to joining the movement, or to have had difficulty developing satisfying loving relationships. An identification with Krishna in his relationship with, or developing an 'actual' love relationship with him, provides a powerful substitute for the love that they cannot find in their everyday lives. This relationship, moreover, is particularly meaningful, for devotees can obtain a highly idealised form of love which is unobtainable in reality. Since it is a transcendental relationship and not part of actual social life, devotees can manipulate and make of it what they will, unlike their everyday relationships.

Followers of Chaitanya believe that Krishna rather than Brahma, Shiva or Vishnu is the Supreme Personality of Godhead and original form of God, and that all other deities such as Brahma, Rama and Narayana are but expansions of him. Krishna Consciousness philosophy is essentially dualistic in nature. Krishna is viewed as both creator and ultimate controller of the world and all that exists, though he remains separate from all phenomena and is untainted by them. He is characterised as having numerous *shakti* (powers) which, whilst originating in him, are separate and different. Krishna is believed to be able to transform himself into other deity forms and is able to perform different functions through the medium of these forms, such as Jagannatha, Lord of the Universe, a form in which he is also worshipped by ISKCON devotees. Most importantly, in times of crisis and peril on earth, he is believed to descend and take the form of a man in order to help the world, such as the Krishna of the *Bhagavad Gita*, or as Chaitanya. He also enters his image so that he may receive the worship of his devotees.

ISKCON's system of belief is thus not only dualist but significantly monotheistic, which makes it easy for devotees, being brought up in a similar monotheistic tradition themselves, to identify with and accept a monotheistic God such as Krishna. Many see the Christian God and Krishna as one and the same. It has been easy for devotees to accept Krishna Consciousness too, because they have not had to reject their basic traditional Christian and Jewish beliefs either. Jesus, the prophets and Mohammad are seen as 'pure' devotees of God and as such to be respected.

ISKCON stresses the monotheistic features of its belief system more than do the majority of traditional Hindus. Hindus, whilst some sects may acknowledge Krishna as the supreme God, customarily worship other deities too. It was not even unknown for Prabhupad himself if he was in India and passed a Kali shrine, to pay his respects to this goddess, the most popular deity in his native Bengal. But in ISKCON Krishna is supreme, whilst the 'demigods', as the other deities are referred to, are acknowledged and respected, they are not worshipped and their status is underplayed. Nor is Chaitanya himself given the status attributed to him by traditional Gaudiyas.

Gaudiya philosophy also stresses that God is a person with human attributes. Great emphasis is attached to this point by devotees. 'God', they frequently say to outsiders, is a person. As Mukunda, one of the original devotees who brought ISKCON to Britain remarked:

> You can love what you think is God may be, but we know from practical experience that you can't love even air, sky or music. You have to love a person. This is what love is all about. It requires reciprocation. It requires two entities, one on each side. (Judah 1974: 173)

The greatest sin in ISKCON is 'impersonalism'—to believe that God is not a person but formless. They describe all 'karmis' and anyone who disagrees with their philosophy, as 'impersonalists', whether they believe in God or not. Prabhupad himself frequently referred to Shankaracharya and the monistic Vedanta school which views *atma* (soul) and Brahman as ultimately merging in the Absolute as 'Impersonalists'.

In fact, whenever anyone criticises their beliefs they immediately reply scornfully, 'Oh you are an impersonalist like Shankaracharya. You believe you are God.' Devotees continually attack what they refer to as the 'impersonalism' of the outside world. One of their most important and frequently repeated *mantras*, quoted at the beginning of this chapter, thanks Prabhupad for delivering western countries not only from 'voidism' but 'impersonalism'.

The degree of emphasis placed on impersonalism in ISKCON indicates that it is of great significance to devotees. Actually it is loaded with symbolic content. The development and stress on impersonalism in ISKCON and its corollary, an emphasis on and development of a personal and idealised relationship with a God with human attributes, is a clear parallel and expression of the impersonalism and alienation of western urban life and is an attempt to deal with it. Devotees themselves appear to be people who feel the impersonalism and alienation of urban life particularly acutely, partly perhaps because they themselves frequently have difficulty making and developing personal relationships. Emphasising Krishna as a person with human attributes and by developing a personal human-like relationship with him, devotees have created a substitute for their own alienation and lack of close personal relations.

The material world, according to Krishna Consciousness philosophy is created from Krishna's lower energy (*mayashakti*). Living entities, it is held, have a warped view of the mundane world and all phenomena because they perceive them through the veil of *maya* which ISKCON equates with 'sense gratification', or 'illusion'. Mankind's cognition is thus conditioned by *maya* which causes him to view the mundane world in which really all phenomena are only temporary, as real and permanent. As a result of *maya*, man fails to perceive the true eternal reality which is Krishna and the spiritual and transcendental world. Human consciousness became warped and clouded through material conditioning, leading man to identify himself with his physical body and to believe that people are the controllers and enjoyers of the world, when it is really Krishna who is. ISKCON maintains that humans suffer because of this false identification with their bodies and their physical desire for sense gratification.

All living entities, including man have, according to Gaudiya and ISKCON philosophy, a soul (*atma* or *jiva*) which whilst being part of Krishna is separate from him. According to devotees, Krishna as supersoul (*paramatma*) resides in the heart of man where he is of the size of an 'atom'. It is in his role of supersoul that Krishna acts as the inner controller of man's actions, allowing him some degree of freedom, even though his soul is trapped in material existence. However, at the same time, Krishna subjects all living entities, including human beings, to the laws of *karma* (action) and *samsara* (reincarnation). The supersoul directs man's actions, but because of *maya*, his desire for sense gratification and misidentification with bodily needs, man is unaware of the role of the supersoul. If a living entity wants to indulge in *maya*, in sense gratification, Krishna will allow him to do so but he will subsequently be punished in present and future lives. It is held that if a man performs good acts he will attain a place in heaven and higher status in this life and in the next. Whilst if he performs bad acts he will accordingly be given lower status in future lives, such as being reborn as an ant.

Vaishnava philosophy thus emphasises the impermanence of all material phenomena, suffering, unhappiness and illusion. They all have obvious parallels in western thought too and, as such, readily invoked a positive response in devotees' hearts. Also, these beliefs have been given special emphasis in ISKCON for they provide devotees with a very meaningful frame of reference and orientation for action.

An obsession with impermanence and change appears as a major theme that pervades all spheres of ISKCON and references to both continually crop up in devotees conversations. The emphasis in ISKCON on the impermanence of material phenomenon is an indicator and reflection of the rapid social upheaval that has taken place in western society and indicates devotees' awareness of it and concern. Their emphasis on it provides them with the means of airing and articulating the problem, of expressing their own unease at the rapidity of social change in modern society, and, by so doing, coming to terms with it.

Moreover, the nuclear family's focus around expressive relationships also lays great stress not only on love, but on feelings such as happiness, and suffering, which have encouraged young people to strive after happiness and inculcated in them a strong desire to avoid suffering. In their everyday speech, devotees frequently refer to happiness and suffering as well as to impermanence.

The Science of Self Realisation

'Everybody wants to be happy', they say. Yet western society frustrates these desires, and devotees are people who feel particularly acutely the gap between the ideal and the practical realities of life very acutely. ISKCON's belief structure, by stressing similar beliefs provides an ideal framework for articulating these feelings and reconciling them. Even if you think you are happy, say devotees, all happiness is impermanent and illusory. It is short-lived and will lead to unhappiness and grief. It is better to renounce all and follow the path of *bhakti*. Only through *prema*, love of God, can true happiness and relief from the misery of material existence be achieved. Devotees say that people who think they are happy are too caught up in *maya* (sense gratification) to be interested in spiritual life, and that only those who know suffering are able to tread the spiritual path. Devotees always tend to mention and introduce their ideas about suffering to visitors in order to test out whether the newcomer thinks along the same lines as themselves, and is therefore a potential devotee. Typical of this approach are the lines used by Hare Krishna Dasa, a former temple president of Soho Street, when chatting up a girl visitor one day: 'Are you interested in spiritual life?' he asked. 'Do you follow spiritual life? Do you know what it is? To follow spiritual life you have to know that you suffer. Some people say they are happy; Prabhupad says they are fools and it is false ego. Everybody is suffering, everybody wants to be happy.'

For those who feel they have suffered, the devotees' attitude to suffering strikes a responsive cord in their heart. To feel that others think along the same lines as themselves and have the same problems is an appealing rationale. As one male devotee said, 'Some come for "prasad" (free meals) others from distress. I came from distress, I was out of work, I used to think it was just me. I came here and realised that others felt like me. This dull world. Life in the world is suffering.'

ISKCON also places emphasis on continuity and one way it is stressed is through the legitimacy of the belief structure, which justifies Prabhupad's teaching in terms of disciplic succession, by holding that Prabhupad's teachings have been passed on in direct line from Krishna himself and are therefore true. Reference to *parampara* (disciplic succession) is made so frequently by devotees that it is obviously loaded with symbolic significance. By stressing the continuity and eternal nature of Krishna consciousness philosophy devotees provide themselves with a coherent permanent framework within which to combat the problems of rapid social change.

According to Gaudiya and ISKCON philosophy, man has forgotten that God consciousness is his true and original nature because he is trapped in material existence and desires sense gratification. The aim of Krishna Consciousness is through 'self-realisation', 'to go back to Godhead'—to liberate oneself from the trap of material existence and the chains of *maya* and realise one's original state of God consciousness and obtain love of Godhead. This is to be achieved through *bhakti yoga*, by chanting the holy names of the Lord and through the help of a guru or spiritual guide. Some pure devotees such as Chaitanya, are able to obtain spontaneous love of God and are able to cast off the chains of *maya* and immediately return to their original state of God consciousness, having become aware that they are eternally related to Krishna. But, for the ordinary devotee, to reach Krishna and to love, know and associate with him, it is necessary to cultivate the right relationship with the Godhead and follow the path of *bhakti*.

Bhakti is a total way of life, based on complete adoration, selfless devotion and loving service to God and devotees are expected to completely engage themselves in his transcendental loving service. As the Bombay devotees said in an eulogy to Prabhupad in honour of his birthday in 1976, known as his 'Appearance Day' in the movement:

> Sense gratification can never satisfy the soul. The tongue is dictating, the belly is dictating, the genitals are dictating, all of the senses are dictating: "I want to enjoy." But instead of enjoying we are suffering. We are not the enjoyers. We are meant to serve Krishna. Thus the mind is constantly agitated, falsely trying, to enjoy, accepting and rejecting, never caring to remember the lotus feet of Krishna or His representative. Therefore the Lord advises us to give up all of our materialistic plan-making and just surrender to his plan. The basic desire for sense gratification expands into so many "isms," such as communism, socialism, humanitarianism, altruism and philanthropism, but still the basic principle is sense gratification limited or extended. Therefore the Lord advises us to give up all these 'isms' and just

take to Vaishnavism—service to Vishnu or his representative. (SVPB 1976:67.)

The true devotee longs for God, and, in order to overcome false identification with his body sees himself as Krishna's servant and in recognition of this position most devotees attach the terms *dasa* (male) *dasi* (female), meaning servant, to their names. Man must dedicate himself and live in permanent loving service to God. If he does, he will be liberated from the bonds of *maya*. Through the raising of his consciousness to the transcendental plane, he will become aware of his true relationship to the Godhead, and will achieve his original untainted God consciousness and attain transcendental bliss and knowledge.

A true devotee who follows the path of *bhakti* should glorify Krishna at all times, should think, feel and speak only of Krishna and should use all his talents and resources for the service of Krishna. All actions should also be performed with Krishna in mind and for Krishna alone. Everything is at the disposal of Krishna and all services performed for Krishna should be performed without thought of reward, though Krishna, because of his affection for his devotees, will reward them many times over. Ritual or good works and knowledge—the other forms of yoga expounded in the *Gita*—are not considered effective unless infused with bhakti. By giving pleasure to Krishna, devotees experience pleasure without desire for personal gratification. Towards Krishna a devotee has multiplex relationships. He feels not only the love of a servant for a master, but the love that a human being feels for his children and siblings. Most importantly, the exquisite pure untainted love that a lover feels for his loved one, though this point is underemphasised by male devotees, who find it embarrassing because of its homosexual implications.

For a devotee, everything is Krishna's mercy, everything is in Krishna's control. ISKCON devotees frequently remark that 'karmis' think they are in control, but they are etupid fools. For it is Krishna who is in control. For the alienated, insecure and confused, as are devotees in varying degrees, to surrender to Krishna, to the security which *bhakti* offers, to the belief that their lives are ordered and controlled by Krishna, is highly appealing. Performing all actions as service for Krishna also gives meaning and purpose to life which devotees, prior to joining the movement, often did not have, particularly those who lived the transient life of Haight Asbhury hippies and, in England, those who had lived on the dole. As one American devotee said—when discussing a book written by an American journalist about the movement, which made a sensationalist interpretation of devotees' sexual customs—all she was interested in was the 'weird sexual rites of the Hare Krishnas', she didn't realise the *bliss* of surrender to Krishna, she said, dismissing the book with scorn.

Chanting the holy names of the Lord is also considered an ideal means of consciousness raising, attaining bliss and obtaining the right relationship with the Godhead. The present epoch is regarded as *Kaliyuga*, the Age of Strife and Quarrel. For early devotees in America, brought up amidst the Vietnam war and the social chaos of the late 1960s, it was a very fitting and apt description of their own civilisation and attractive for this reason. Chaitanya himself maintained that in the Kali Age chanting the holy names of the Lord, what has come to be known as the Hare Krishna mantra, rather than words or actions, was a better and more direct means of raising consciousness and thus going back to Godhead.

The Hare Krishna mantra—Hare Krishna, Hare Krishna, Krishna, Krishna, Hare Hare, Hare Rama, Hare Rama, Rama Rama, Hare Hare—is perhaps the feature of ISKCON best known to outsiders, partly because George Harrison made a record of it which was played on television pop shows in the early 1970s. The Hare Krishna mantra is an invocation of the holy names of God. Krishna refers to his blackish appearance, 'Hare' is a name of Vishnu (who according to the Gaudiyas is an expansion of Krishna), and Rama is another of his incarnations. Though ISKCON itself defines the Hare Krishna mantra as:

> The word Hare is the form of addressing the energy of the Lord, and the words Krishna and Rama are forms of addressing the Lord Himself. Both Krishna and Rama mean 'the supreme pleasure', and Hare is the supreme pleasure energy of the Lord, changed to Hare in the vocative. The supreme pleasure energy of the Lord helps us to reach the Lord. These three words, namely Hare, Krishna and Rama are the transcendental seeds of the maha-mantra. The chanting is a spiritual call for the Lord and His energy, to give protection to the conditioned soul. This chanting is exactly like the genuine cry of a child for its mother's

presence. Mother Hara helps the devotee achieve the Lord Father's grace, and the Lord reveals Himself to the devotee who chants this mantra sincerely. (H.K. Diary 1979:26-27.)

Traditional Vaishnava philosophy holds that the names of God invoked in the mantra are indeed God himself in the form of sound vibrations. Devotees, by saying the mantra and invoking his name are able to associate and make a connection with the Godhead, and thus are able to obtain bliss, peace and inner tranquillity and, ultimately, to regain their original God consciousness.

In ISKCON, the Hare Krishna mantra has become a major focus of attention and forms part of devotees' daily routine being changed both individually and communally. Individually, devotees chant using a rosary of 108 beads to count the number of times the mantra is repeated. Chanting on the full 108 beads is known as a round. The *sannyasins* of the Gaudiya mission chant 64 rounds a day, but when Prabhupad ordered his devotees to chant similarly they said that they were 'fallen souls' and could not manage 64 rounds a day and so 18 rounds a day was agreed upon instead. To say 18 rounds consecutively takes a devotee about two hours. Some devotees do their rounds before *mangala arati*, the first ceremony held in Britain at about 4.15 a.m. at which the deities are worshipped. Most devotees, however, do not manage all their rounds first thing in the morning and have to say them whenever they have a spare moment during the day.

The mantra is also recited communally to the accompaniment of drums and cymbals at the morning *mangala arati* ceremony and in the evening *arati* ceremony in the main temple room where the deities are worshipped. This is referred to as 'kirtan' (*kirtana*) in the movement. The mantra is also recited by the congregational chanting parties which parade through the streets and which have become a familiar sight in most major cities in the west.

The saying of the Hare Krishna mantra provides a 'here and now' emotional experience, said Jnana Dasa, the Oxford graduate, at hourly lectures he gave on Krishna Consciousness philosophy at the 1978 Mind and Body Festival where ISKCON had a stall. At these lectures he would invite the audience to recite the Hare Krishna mantra and would say:

Focus your mind on the sound of the mantra, the mantra automatically works to make your mind peaceful and it purifies the heart, we become free from anxieties and happy. The reason is that the Hare Krishna mantra is not an ordinary sound, it is a spiritual sound vibration. It's full of special energies by which we can understand that we are not this material body—I'm eternal spirit-soul. The problems of life come from our mistaken idea that I'm this material body. There're so many problems concerned with the body but actually we have nothing to do with this material body, our real self is eternal. Just feel how peaceful and relaxed the mind is when we chant Hare Krishna. The reason for this is that the Hare Krishna mantra is not an ordinary sound, it is the spiritual sound vibration and when we chant the Hare Krishna mantra we actually experience genuine spiritual happiness. So there are three important energies within the Hare Krishna mantra. The first is called the 'sat' energy by which we realise that we are not these material bodies we are eternal spirit-souls. The material body is like a covering but our real self is eternal and spiritual. By the *chit* energy we understand all sorts of transcendental knowledge which is revealed within the heart about ourselves, about the world we live in and about how to live and find real happiness and finally by the 'ananda' energy we awaken our original-blissful happy consciousness. So when we chant Hare Krishna we get a higher taste and the mind no longer has to go restlessly from one place to another looking for enjoyment.

Whilst some devotees get very little out of saying it and either do not say all their sixteen rounds a day or else they get satisfaction out of just managing to perform the required number of rounds, some devotees derive a great deal of emotional satisfaction and inner tranquillity from doing so.

This emotional feedback too reflects a feature of ISKCON and of the other new eastern religious groups, that is little dealt with in the literature, namely the degree of emotional satisfaction derived from membership of these religious groups. Krishna Consciousness, 'the Religion of Love', has contained within it a set of beliefs and practices which provide an ideal channel for the development and expression of highly charged emotions and for the achieving of a high level of emotional experience. ISKCON has focused on, and in a number of cases developed further, the traditional emotional content of these practices so that the movement provides an 'emotional trip' par excellence, and it is a major reason why 'advanced' devotees remain in the movement for so long. ISKCON is more geared to the emotional level than any other of the new eastern religious groups, having the most highly charged and emotional feedback of all the new cults which derives from the nature of *bhakti yoga*.

A great deal of emotional and mystical feeling and energy is often generated in a devotee's relationship with Krishna. Lord Chaitanya himself was, of course, an archetypal mystic and his life and behaviour both legitimises and sanctions the mystical 'trip' in the movement. A small proportion of devotees with particularly strong emotional and experiential inclinations have taken him as their ideal and attempt to emulate him and attain similar states of ecstasy.

What ISKCON has to offer is instant ecstasy. 'Kirtan', as devotees refer to dancing and chanting the holy names of the Lord in ecstatic love of Godhead, has been developed into a more important role in ISKCON that it has in modern India, where public *sankirtana* has largely died out and where 'kirtan' at *arati* ceremonies rarely involves dancing. In ISKCON 'kirtan' has become the central focus of the movement's ritual system, being performed not only publicly in the streets but also forming part of devotees' daily routine as it is performed at the morning and evening *arati* ceremonies when devotees come together to worship the deities communally. As will be discussed in detail later, devotees often achieve highly charged emotional and ecstatic states during 'kirtan' and these states, as well as the music and dance are themselves appealing to young people.

So ecstatic do some devotees get during *arati* that they even see the deities move'. Ecstasy has become institutionalised and routinised in the movement. In a sense devotees can plug into their emotions and derive emotional satisfaction as part of their daily routine. It is, as such, one of ISKCON's major attractions —quick emotional thrill.

The high level of emotional intensity generated by ISKCON is reflected in the kind of people attracted to the movement. People with an artistic and musical bent tend often to be emotional personality types. ISKCON has a high incidence of people with artistic and musical talents, many of them long-term or 'advanced' devotees as ISKCON refers to them. Drug-takers, particularly 'acid-heads' who are into the psychedelic experience, are people seeking such an experience too. That so many artists and acid-heads have joined ISKCON tends to suggest that it is able to provide them with a highly charged and satisfying emotional experience.

Art and aesthetics, reflecting the artistic bent of many devotees, play an important role in ISKCON, more so than in other new eastern religious groups. Many temples have their own art departments. Artistic talent is highly valued and respected and creative people receive preferential treatment in ISKCON. Pictures painted by devotee artists are hung in prominent positions in temple deity rooms and are included in, and have pride of place, in literature published by the movement.

ISKCON art, publications and temple decoration are essentially 1960s psychedelic in style. Art in the movement usually depicts scenes from the *Shrimad Bhagavata*. Devotees have, within a psychedelic framework, copied the realistic style of the 19th century Malayali painter Raja Ravi Varma who, himself, was influenced by contemporary western Christian painting. As devotee artists have developed and matured however, they have modified their psychedelic style. Whilst still using Raja Ravi Varma as a basic model, they have been influenced by and have started to copy and paint in the sensual and vibrant style of Reubens and Raphael.

ISKCON art and temple decoration is fascinating and reveals a great deal about ISKCON devotees and the movement as a whole. On one level ISKCON visual art is a 'psychedelic trip' and pure 'kitsch'. It is, too, an example of ISKCON's use of inversion as a form of social protest. They are deliberately 'cocking a snook' at the values of bourgeois art, and, in painting in a realistic manner not only the fashion in modern art for abstract painting but the 'impersonalism' of the 'karmi' world. But, most importantly, the vibrant colours and sensual figures (so at odds with ISKCON's ascetic ideal) reflect, and indicate, not only devotees' previous experience of hallucinogenic drugs, but are also expressive of the heightened intensity of the emotional level in ISKCON.

The devotees themselves are aware of the highly charged emotional experience that ISKCON offers. They often say, as did Jnana Dasa in his description of the mantra, that ISKCON offers a 'here and now experience' which, incidentally, is also an important factor in the appeal of the great majority of the new sects. Devotees would often criticise my intellectual analytical social-science approach to understanding the movement. 'You can't understand it', they would say, 'unless you join in and participate. It is an experience. It is like honey. You cannot determine the taste of honey no matter how much you examine and analyse its consistency. You can only do so by actually tasting it'.

But, most importantly it is clear that the 'real world' in ISKCON is the transcendental and spiritual world of Krishna and the gopis in Vaikuntha. True reality is one of transcendental experience, a world that in one's expanded consciousness is indescribable in terms of material experience. The unreal world is the world of devotees' everyday lives, the material world of *maya* in which they experience frustration, lack of meaning and have problems with which they are unable to cope. By projecting reality onto the spiritual level, devotees have provided themselves with a framework for protest on the belief and symbolic levels and with a basis for 'resistance through ritual'. It has enabled ISKCON to develop on the symbolic level a model of the world, society and social relations which enables them to deal with the existential and social problems which confront them personally in their daily lives. The acceptance in ISKCON of the spiritual world as being the 'real' world sanctions and validates the projection of their problems onto the level of belief and provides devotees with a framework for overcoming them. Being able to see the spiritual level as the real world enables devotees, for instance, to see the problems which confront them in their daily lives as being unimportant and irrelevant and therefore more easy for them to bear.

CHAPTER FOUR

'All Glories to Srilaprabhupad':
The Role of the Guru in ISKCON

Oh, Srilaprabhupada, because of your Divine Grace only, there is still joy in the world, there is still hope in the world, there is still some future worth living for, some work worth doing, some words worth saying. Because of Your Divine Grace, man's search still has a chance of reaching a worthwhile conclusion. I think, therefore, that because of your continued presence on earth, the sun and moon still rise at their appointed hours, the cows still give milk and the Deities in the temple shine forth in all Their Splendor.

The whole world is deluded by impersonalism out of frustration because in our experience all persons have exploited us and cheated us and know that I am also a cheater. But in you we have found a true friend and well-wisher, and we can see by your example what a person is really meant to be. So we worship your lotus feet and pray for your benediction.

—His Divine Grace Jayatirtha Maharaj, Guru of the
United Kingdom and Mid West. SVPB. 1977: 75

The term 'guru' became a household word in the 'Swinging Sixties'. Gurus by the score descended on the West from the East, all offering different paths to salvation. Young people in their thousands, including pop stars, made their pilgrimage to Asia in search of a guru. It became not uncommon for even the man in the street to admit to having one.

Gurus have a long tradition in India, being essentially repositories and teachers of traditional knowledge. They may teach any subject including such things as music or dance. In the religious sphere, a guru is a spiritual guide, initiator and teacher of a specific set of religious beliefs and practices. These teachings may be his own or, if he is a member of a particular sect as was the case with Prabhupad, the teachings of his sect. Successful gurus may attract large followings. If they do so, as happened with Chaitanya and Prabhupad, their followings may develop into sects.

Devotees frequently point to sloka 34 in *The Bhagavad Gita As It Is* (p. 87) in which it states:

> Just try to learn the truth by approaching a spiritual master. Inquire from him submissively and render service upto him. The self-realized soul can impart knowledge upto you because he has seen the truth.

'That's how you have to act towards a spiritual master', they say. 'You have to surrender to him and obey him always. You are his servant.'

In *Vaishnava* sects such as the Gaudiyas, the guru is exalted and worshipped almost like a God. Similarly in ISKCON, Prabhupad is highly revered, hero-worshipped and greatly loved by devotees. Prayers are said to him at every ritual and chanting generally includes the prayer:

Nama om visnupadaya krsna presthaya bhutale
Srimati bhaktivedanta svamin iti namine

(I offer my respectful obediences upto his Divine Grace Bhaktivedanta Swami, who is very dear to Lord Krishna having taken shelter at his lotus feet).

Prabhupad led a very ascetic and renounced life, a fact which gave him credibility and legitimacy in the eyes of devotees. They frequently compare him favourably with the other gurus that came to the west, such as Guru Maharaj Ji, the 'Boy God' of the Divine Light Mission who lives surrounded by luxury, and whom they denounce and refer to derogatorily as 'bogey yogis'. Prabhupad, because of his saintliness was considered to be a 'pure devotee' of the Lord who, because of his purity, was able to see the truth and articulate the teachings of the Supreme Personality of Godhead.

Prabhupad was exalted by devotees to an even greater degree than gurus traditionally are in India. So great was the power attributed him by devotees that they claimed, when he finally died at the age of 82 after a long bout of illness, that he did not die because of old age and illness, but that he died when he did because he chose to.

Essentially, he 'sold himself' to the devotees as a scholar and religious authority. Prabhupad's status, rationale and means of attaining legitimacy from very early on in the movement, were attained not just by demonstrating his purity of life-style. His 'book learning', intellectualism, knowledge of the scriptures and scholarship were major factors in his retention of devotees' long-term support and his success as a guru. To legitimise his own position he himself emphasised the importance of belief and the scriptures at all times which consequently developed as a major focus, and framework of the movement.

Most of the American devotees having some college education, had been through an educational system that attached great value to the written word, books and intellectualism in general. Devotees brought up to respect intellectualism found Prabhupad's theologising and scholastic ability impressive and attractive, particularly as it was only superficially intellectual. Although Prabhupad's teachings were couched in intellectual terms and appeared to convey the impression of great learning (he used a great deal of Sanskrit terminology for instance), nevertheless he used a very simple and basic vocabulary. His books were simple, unacademic and polemical in style. As such they were readily understood by all, and for this reason, were attractive to devotees. Intellectuals are few and far between in the movement, as is clear from the fact that most devotees who went to college found academic life unsatisfactory and dropped out. Nonetheless, devotees are not without intellectual pretensions. Prabhupad's easily understood, yet seemingly intellectual style, is very attractive to them, not only because they could understand it, but because it made them feel intellectual. This is particularly true of the less well educated British devotees who were easily able to understand Prabhupad's teachings. Having been brought up to consider themselves totally unacademic, they gain great satisfaction from being able to easily understand Prabhupad's philosophy and from being able to feel intellectual. This is no doubt a contributory factor of the appeal of ISKCON in Britain to the lower status groups.

Prabhupad's life time's work in the movement became the translation and writing of commentaries on the Krishna Consciousness scriptures of the Gaudiya *sampradaya*. The devotees saw their role as printing and publishing his works and preaching Krishna Consciousness to the world through their distribution to the public. Over forty pieces of his work were published in all by the movement, though many were reprints in various forms of the same works. These include a translation and commentary of the *Chaitanya Charitamrita* and the *Shrimad Bhagavata* in eleven volumes.

The devotees are very proud of Prabhupad's scholastic ability and sustained literary output. His continued flow of books justified their respect and belief in him and demonstrated his genuineness to them. It legitimised his position as far as they were concerned, and provided a major basis for their respect for him. It made him a cut above the other gurus and differentiated him from other 'bogey yogis'. Devotees try to emulate him. One or two, including Swami Satsavarupa, a leading devotee, have written books on Krishna Consciousness literature and great status and respect is given to anyone in the movement who has similar literary ability.

Devotees continually make reference to the amount of time Prabhupad spent translating and the number of books he has written. Devotees frequently remark with awe that Prabhupad used to work late into the night at his translations, and that he only took three hours' sleep. Many even maintained, though he was ill for a year before his death and patently unable to work, that he was translating right up until his death. Devotees consider his books so revered and sacred that, despite the fact that they are only English translations and commentaries, they are considered to be *shruti* (divinely revealed texts). They are never put on the floor or allowed to fall on the ground. Many hold that his translations and commentaries supersede the original Sanskrit texts and make them unnecessary. Devotees claim that where his editing and interpretations differ from the original texts, it is the original texts that are incorrect! For the majority of devotees his texts, commentaries and translations being divinely inspired, contain total truth and make any other scripture irrelevant and unnecessary reading.

Because Prabhupad's teachings are considered divinely revealed, no criticism of them is allowed in the movement. Like most gurus, Prabhupad had a great deal of power and control over his devotees, but the divine authority of his teachings put him in an exceptionally powerful position. I never once in the three years I visited ISKCON temples ever heard any criticism of him or his teachings by devotees. His commands were obeyed without question and devotees would do anything he wanted them to do.

The devotees' adulation and love for Prabhupad and the type and content of the relationship they developed with him is reflected in the *Sri Vyasa Puja* books. They contain eulogies contributed and written by leading devotees and temples throughout the world.

A few excerpts from these eulogies will now be quoted, so that devotees can speak for themselves about their feelings for Prabhupad. Letting devotees speak for themselves is highly illuminating. It reveals a great deal about the devotees themselves, as well as the way they view the universe, and it will give the reader far better than any analytic description could, the feel, colour and tone of ISKCON.

(i) Oh, Venerable Vaishnava, dearly beloved spiritual master, you are the life and sustenance of our existence. Just as the sun activates lifeless trees at winter's end and ushers in the flower-bearing spring, you have, by your presence, given life to a lifeless world. Please give us the shade of your lotus feet.

Oh, ocean of auspicious qualities, please wash away our faults and passions, and as the cloud pours water on the forest fire, extinguish this blazing fire of material existence in which we have been burning since time immemorial. Please give us the shelter of your lotus feet.

Oh, lionhearted and fearless father, out of your ceaseless kindness you have informed us of our eternal blissful nature as servants of Krishna. Now please bestow upon us the faith to carry on this sankirtan movement, which is benefiting all humanity. Please give us the shelter of your lotus feet. Oh, Srilaprabhupada, protector of fallen souls, please accept our humble offerings of homage and make our lives successful. If you do not accept our tiny offerings, then our lives are ruined and we will surely be lost again in the whirlpool of material suffering. Please Srilaprabhupada, give us the mercy of your lotus feet.

(ii) The spiritual master is the mercy incarnation of the Supreme Personality of Godhead. His message is the message of God, and his pleasure is the pleasure of God. There is no other way to approach Krishna than through the medium of His beloved servant, the spiritual master. Therefore, we must fall at his feet in all humility, without personal prestige or motivation, and beg his merciful glance upon us. Without becoming his unalloyed and thoroughly devoted servants, there is absolutely no escape from the miserable conditions of material existence. We must therefore be ever vigilant not to mistake him to be an ordinary man of whom we might become envious. Rather, we should be always proud of our spiritual master—proud of his courage, proud of his wisdom, and proud of his purity. He is actually Krishna manifested before our crippled vision because he is delivering the message of Krishna. He speaks what Krishna speaks, and he lives it for all to see.

(*iii*) Please accept our most fallen and worthless obeisances at your sacred lotus feet. We are certainly incapable of saying anything poetic, and any attempt to praise you will be marred by our filthy consciousness, and our words remain the mumbling of fools. We are facing the burning of samsara. Maya is dancing before our senses and you and Krishna are calling us to come home. We are running toward your shelter father, but we are crippled, and we are always falling down and getting lost on the path you tell us to follow. Dark clouds of illusion are surrounding us and death like a fierce dog is closing in on our so-called youth. O Father! We are terrified of this material world. It is the worst nightmare; we are crying. Lost in the forest of illusion we fall again and again, but there is no time to count our bruises and lament. We are running toward you begging for shelter; we are running with you in defeating the atheism of the world, spreading the brilliance of Krishna Consciousness, and we are running for you in the performance of our prescribed dharmas trying to please you—our most wonderful and divine guru-maharaajah. O Srilaprabhupada! We are your servants, souls surrendered to you, now and forever. Kindly tell us what to do.

(*iv*) Srilaprabhupad, we feel you are our real father because you have given us birth against the hellish existence of material life. By your ideal example and your patient and kind instruction, you are teaching us everything. You are teaching us how to eat, how to clean ourselves, how to sleep, how to pass stool, how to dress, and most of all, you are teaching us how to live. Srilaprabhupada, we are your children, and it is by your mercy that we exist. You are taking us gently by the hand as helpless babies in the lap of maya and teaching us to walk naturally in Krishna Consciousness. It is painful and frustrating for us, and we fall down, but you help us up with encouraging words, Prabhupada, we are afraid that if you take away your helping hand now we will simply fall on our faces and not be able to get up. Please do not leave us like that.

The prose style of these eulogies is fulsome and flowery. It is the exact opposite to the restrained prose style acceptable in scholastic and intellectual circles in the West. Thus in the way devotees have conceptualised their relationship with Prabhupad. they have followed their general orientation to life, namely social protest through inversion. These eulogies also indicate the powerful idealised quality and emotionally charged nature of devotees' relationships to Prabhupad. Their relationship with him is as much of a personal emotional 'trip' as their relationship with Krishna, and satisfies similar emotional needs.

It is often argued that the gurus of the 1960s functioned as 'father figures' for disorientated and alienated youth. Although this is something of a cliché, there is an element of truth in it as far as Prabhupad was concerned. The devotees view him as a surrogate father and themselves as his children and they play-act out a father/child role with him. Prabhupad, though, did not play the role one generally assumes gurus to play, namely that of a gentle ascetic renunciate. Rather, he acted out the 'traditional', archetypical, autocratic, dominant father figure role, the exact opposite role to devotees' own liberal permissive parents, a point of crucial significance for understanding the nature of devotees' relationship with him. He had a dynamic, rather arrogant and 'bossy' personality. He was very autocratic and expected his orders to be obeyed immediately. He never shillyshallied but gave direct, clear-cut, practical advice and answers to questions.

That devotees themselves saw Prabhupad as a traditional father-figure and played a filial role themselves is clear from the eulogies. He is often depicted as such, too, in pictures of him painted by ISKCON's artists and in photographs which appear frequently in the literature. Generally, he is portrayed as regal, confident and dignified.

It is precisely because Prabhupad played the dominant autocratic father-figure role that he attracted and retained devotees' allegiance. Devotees, being people who appear to find the multiple norms of modern society difficult to cope with and who need clear-cut guidelines for behaviour, found Prabhupad's 'no nonsense' approach and clear-cut answers to their questions understandably attractive and ideal for them. He offered them security by providing them with a spelt out frame of reference for action

Prabhupad, like devotees' relationship with Krishna, provided a substitute for the emotional relationships they could not achieve in the outside world. As one American middle-class Jewish mother said, when trying to explain why her son had remained in the movement for 10 years, 'he really loved Prabhupad'.

Again, although young people appear to grow up earlier than in the past and are given much more responsibility at an earlier age, they are often not as emotionally, mature as they appear. Indeed, the emotionally charged relationships developed within the nuclear family, foster a need in devotees for dependence right up into late adolescence. Yet modern parents, assuming them to be young adults, do not provide this need and so modern youth, understandably, look elsewhere. Gurus such as Prabhupad provide them with an ideal and function as dependence substitutes. Reference to their need to depend on him comes up again and again in the *Sri Vyasa Puja* homages.

But the content of devotees' relationship with Prabhupad were often not developed through actual contact with him. Most devotees, since he spent much of his time travelling from temple to temple, had little contact with him. An actual conversation with Prabhupad was something to be treasured. Also, to give himself charisma, he deliberately kept himself at a distance, only appearing for what the devotees refer to as 'darshan' (audience). Many devotees never saw him at all. Yet, significantly, all developed the same kind of relationship with Prabhupad, as is reflected in the previously quoted excerpts from the *Vyasa Puja* books. It is a powerfully idealised relationship of love at a distance, one highly charged emotionally. As is indicated by an experience that Saruabhavana a middle-class Jewish devotee and ex-engineering student from the Mid West, states he had when he went to the airport to see off a devotee friend. Whilst waiting to see off his friend he said he 'all of a sudden' had an all powerful emotional experience, a total overwhelming sense of the nearness and sacredness of Prabhupad. He said he felt the tears run down his face as he felt Prabhupad's love for him. He maintained, prior to this experience, that he had not been sure of his belief and had not been fully committed to ISKCON. He in fact had never even met Prabhupad. But this experience had so overwhelmed him that it had convinced him of the truth of Krishna Consciousness philosophy and committed him totally to Prabhuped and ISKCON. Further it had been a major reason for his remaining in the movement some seven years.

The fact that most devotees had little actual contact with Prabhupad and that their relationship with him was one of idealised love rooted in the mind, was to have significant consequences for the institutional structure of the movement and the changes that took place on Prabhupad's death. It made the transition easy.

Prabhupad's age and obviously imminent death was a constant worry in the late 1970s making devotees fear for the future of ISKCON, particularly in the two years prior to his death when he was ill and obviously nearing the end. Many devotees felt that he was the force that kept the movement together, that on h's death factionalism would develop and the movement would fall apart. Reflecting their fears, in the two years prior to his death and in the period immediately after, ISKCON's generally cataclysmic view of the world intensified and the movement became apocalyptic. It became a generally accepted view in the movement that a third world war was imminent, and that after the world had been devastated by war, a saint would come out of the Himalayas and, with the help of the devotees who would be amongst the survivors of the holocaust, would spread Krishna Consciousness throughout the world. Such a belief gave the movement at a time of great uncertainty and worry both a framework for organisation and a goal. Devotees believed they had to strive and prepare themselves for the imminent holocaust. It thus gave proselytizing further justification and legitimacy, and street preaching increased. But, in fact devotees' fears proved groundless. Although Prabhupad's death led to some fragmentation within the movement, the continuity of the movement was unaffected and the change took place remarkably smoothly.

No one devotee was appointed overall head of the movement. Rather from amongst the leading devotees eleven new gurus were appointed to be acharyas and initiators, each with his own regional sphere of influence. All of the new gurus are *sannyasins* except His Divine Grace Jayatirtha Maharaj, who was appointed the guru for the British Movement and also has the Chicago, Detroit and South African temples in his jurisdiction. Jayatirtha Maharaj was born in 1948 in Saipan where his father was a career Air Force Officer. He travelled around frequently as a child as his father was posted from base to base. Brought up a catholic, he dropped out of the University of California and joined ISKCON in 1967. He and his wife Manjvali came to England in 1976 and have since had one son.

When Prabhupad 'passed over', as devotees refer to his death, the new gurus literally 'stepped into his shoes'. His death revealed that it was his symbolic, dominant, autocratic father-figure role and the idealised love-at-a-distance relationship which devotees had with him that were important rather than their actual personal relationship with him, for the new gurus have taken on exactly the same role and function that Prabhupad had. They have been structurally, functionally and symbolically slotted into Prabhupad's position and are treated now as if they were Prabhupad himself, as figures of authority, and the older ones as father figures. Devotees have projected an idealised love relationship on them too, and hero worship and revere them in exactly the same way as they did Prabhupad. They too are considered as representatives of the *parampara* and their orders are obeyed without question. Like Prabhupad, they are believed to be present in their pictures, to which offerings are made in the daily *arati* ceremony. Similarly, their shoes are kept on the *vyasasana* (throne) and *puja* (rituals) performed in front of them. *Sri Vyasa Puja* books are published in honour of them on their birthdays as well, and share a similar content.

In sum, they are treated no differently. Clearly, a major reason for ISKCON's avoidance of destructive factionalism and successful and smooth transition in the months after Prabhupad died lies in the fact that ISKCON retained the same role structure, merely changing the personnel.

The continuity of role structure after Prabhupad's 'passing over', as the devotees refer to his death, was the result of a symbiotic relationship between the gurus and rank and file devotees. On the one hand the gurus wanted to be gurus like Prabhupad and tried very hard to copy him, and act like 'pure devotees' and real ascetics too. The new gurus, who range in age from 26 to the early forties, developed their new roles amazingly quickly within a few months of Prabhupad's death. They were able to do so because of the connivance of the other devotees who aided and abetted them. The rank and file devotees, fearing that without a strong leader the movement would disintegrate and needing a strong authority figure to depend on and love, were only too willing to play up to the 'spiritual master' and saintly roles that the gurus were developing.

The majority of new gurus are in their twenties and early thirties. One of the most powerful Ramesvara Swami is, in fact, only 26. For such youthful people as are the new gurus, to head an organisation as large and wealthy as ISKCON is no mean achievement, and is of interest for this reason. What the future holds for these young gurus is as yet unclear. But the smoothness of the transfer of control and power in the movement since Prabhupad's death has been almost miraculous, which suggests they have organising ability and are competent to perform their roles.

CHAPTER FIVE

Bhakti Yoga and the 'Personal Trip':
The Individual Versus the Group in ISKCON

> The completeness of human life can be realized only when the human form of life is engaged in the service of the complete whole... Krishna is the complete whole, and everything else is his part and parcel. The relation is one of the servant and the served, and it is transcendental and is completely distinguished from our experience in material existence. This relation of servant and the served is the most congenial form of intimacy. One can realize it as devotional service progresses. Everyone should engage himself in that transcendental loving service of the Lord, even in the present conditional state of material existence. That will gradually give one the clue to actual life and please him to complete satisfaction.
> —BTG Vol. 12, No. 3/4, p. 6

The ideology of *Bhakti yoga* is primarily individualistic in ethic and single stranded in the way it focuses on the individual and his highly personal relationship with God. This emphasis provides the channel and basic framework for ISKCON's belief system and social, economic and political organisation which is predominantly individualistic in orientation. In this way ISKCON contrasts with accepted opinion which views the eastern religious sects and communes which arose during the 1960s as essentially communally-oriented and group-focused.

Scholars have tended to emphasise the communal aspects of the new groups which mushroomed during the 1960s. They have, pointed to their highly developed sense of community and strongly developed group ties as major reasons for their development and attraction for youth. Slater (1970) in the *Pursuit of Loneliness*, for instance, maintains that modern western society frustrates man's innate need for dependence and community and that countercultural groups such as communes and new eastern religious sects provide for such a need. Judah (1974: 102) in *Hare Krishna and the Counterculture* quotes him favourably and sees his theory as applicable to ISKCON. Also Glock (1976) sees the communal focus of the new eastern religious groups as an attempt by youth to counteract and come to terms with, amongst other things, the extreme individualism of modern western society.

Some of the new religious groups which arose in the 1960s, such as the 'Moonies', with their emphasis on the 'family', have a strongly developed sense of community and group organisation. Superficially ISKCON appears similar. It has a well-developed sense of group identity and devotees identify strongly with the movement. This is reflected in an emphasis on boundaries and a highly developed 'them/us' attitude with relationship to 'karmi' society which is expressed in condemnation and rejection of all outsiders. Their strong sense of group is manifested in their emphasis on group harmony, which is considered all-important. No conflict is allowed within the temple and anybody who persistently makes a nuisance of himself or causes trouble and threatens the unity of the group is expelled from the temple.

From the outside, it would appear that ISKCON was extremely communally focused, living together in temples in close proximity and sharing a collective alternative life-style as do devotees; a life moreover in which devotees surrender their personal liberty to the authority of the group. Devotees, too, when they join the movement are supposed to renounce all their possessions and donate them to the movement (though in practice, most devotees have little to renounce) in favour of a life-style in which all resources are pooled and shared. ISKCON, in return, supplies each devotee with his basic needs, a feature, of course, which further fosters the development of a communal focus in ISKCON.

Group identity and communal life is also developed by the physical boundaries and internal structures of ISKCON's temples, which are not, as is often supposed by outsiders, organised on the lines of a loosely structured and amorphous hippie commune with little role differentiation. Rather, all temples have clearly bounded, complexly intertwined and highly organised inward-looking internal structures, which further generate a communal orientation.

ISKCON is divided for administrative purposes into regional zones. The British temples comprise the 'Northwest European Zone', whilst America is divided into five zones. The German,

Bhakti Yoga and the Personal Trip

French, South American (ISKCON seems to do well in Catholic countries) and Indian temples all form separate zones too. Whilst Prabhupad was alive, he was the final arbiter of decisions. But for everyday affairs and management, ISKCON was governed by a 'Governing Body Commission' made up of some 20 leading devotees, each of whom was assigned a regional zone to control and organise or given some specific organisational duty. On Prabhupad's death, whilst control of devotees' spiritual welfare was put in the hands of eleven gurus, the administrative control of ISKCON throughout the world was placed in the hands of the Governing Body Commission (GBC). Northwest Europe and the Central American Zone (Detroit and Chicago temples) are governed by his Divine Grace Jayatirtha Maharaj, the devotee who was made the guru for this zone after Prabhupad 'passed over'.

Each temple within a zone is autonomous and is governed by a President appointed by the regional Governing Body Commissioner (GBC) and a board of 'managers' made up of leading devotees. Each manager is assigned a specific function, e.g. treasurer, publicity officer, temple commander (who is in charge of domestic day to day chores) and so on.

Wide areas of behaviour in ISKCON are also governed and regulated by what often appear to be a multitude of restrictive and pettifogging rules and rituals which further fosters commitment and binds the individual to the group. For instance, devotees must always remember to take off their shoes when entering the temple, keep their heads shaved at all times; they must dress in a certain way; they are expected to interact with other devotees in a particular manner, even the way devotees defecate is governed by specific rules.

A number of ISKCON rituals are in fact communal and provide the social framework for the devotees' daily routine. The most important are the *arati* ceremonies held four times daily (the first—*mangalarati*—in England is at 4.15 a.m., then at 12 a.m., 4 p.m. and 7 p.m.). At *arati*, the deities are treated as though they were living people and are bathed, washed, clothed, fed and, at the evening *arati*, put to bed. At *mangalarati* and the evening *arati* ceremony at 7 p.m., devotees join together in congregational chanting. They dance ecstatically in front of the deities expressing their love of Godhead to the accompaniment of cymbals and drums, and sing the Hare Krishna and a number of other mantras. Devotees also, of course, perform 'kirtan', as they refer to congregational chanting, in the street. *Bhagavad Gita* classes are held twice daily in the morning and evening too.

In a way, ISKCON is somewhat like a youth club, where people can meet other people, enjoy themselves and have fun. It not only provides the companionship of similar, like-minded people but also offers a varied social life. Bhaktivedanta Manor especially has a very cheerful and happy atmosphere which is often remarked on by visitors. The brightly coloured rooms are inviting and attractive to young people. In summer, visitors and devotees sit out on the lawns, whilst the children scamper about. Often, Asian devotees dance and sing *bhajans* on the lawn. New devotees, impressed by the atmosphere and environment, often remark that ISKCON is like a 'family', though significantly I never once heard a long-term 'advanced' devotee make such a remark. For them their frame of reference is always Krishna.

Both Diner (1976) in her study of the Boston temple, and Johnson (1973) in his doctoral thesis study of the San Francisco temple, emphasise the communal focus of ISKCON as being an important reason for attracting devotees to the movement and retaining their commitment. The San Francisco temple, set up in 1967, was originally situated in the notorious Haight Ashbury district, where the hippie community was entrenched during the 1960s. Young Americans in their thousands migrated to this 'ghetto' during this decade. Johnson (1973: 24-29) points to the instability and intransient nature of the relationships in the Haight Ashbury during this time, to the rootlessness of the Haight Ashbury life-style and absence of purpose and ties between people and to the lack of community life and focus there. He characterised typical Haight Ashbury hippies as being motivated by unrestrained egotism and geared to the pursuance of personal pleasure. He says that 'seeker' devotees joined the Haight Ashbury temple to obtain an alternative communal life-style which they thought, when they migrated to Haight Ashbury, that they would find there, but which hadn't materialised, or were ex-hippies disillusioned with their previous life-style and desirous of communal life and stable relationships. He sees them as renouncing and rejecting their unfettered, ego-focused individualism in favour of ISKCON's communally focused group life. He sees devotees' personal lives as becoming suffused with the objectives of the movement and stresses the importance of 'kirtan' (singing and chanting) both as fostering communalism and as a major reason for attracting devotees to the movement.

ISKCON's group focus and communal life is, no doubt, a reason why devotees both join the movement and sustain their commitment to it. To some degree devotees do appear to be group-focused and communally oriented. Identification with a group such as ISKCON and participation in group rituals such as 'kirtan' and community life provides great satisfaction particularly for the lonely and frustrated and for those who, prior to joining the movement, suffered from psychological problems or were involved in some form of crisis. The fact that the majority of devotees first come to the temple alone, particularly the men, tends to indicate their loneliness to be an important factor. ISKCON provides them not only with companionship, but with the security and confidence derived from belonging to a group. For those who have led a chaotic and transient life prior to joining the movement and have suffered stress because of it, the routine of a highly regulated temple life provides a satisfying and attractive alternative.

But, to over-emphasise and regard ISKCON's group focus and communal life as the major orientation of the movement, and to emphasise ISKCON's group structure as the all important reason for joining the movement and for retaining devotees' commitment, would also be to give a misleading picture of ISKCON's belief system and social organisation and the relationship of the individual devotee to the movement as a group. In ISKCON, the stress is as much on the individual as on the group and community life, if not more so. ISKCON legitimises, reinforces, as well as fosters, and channels individualism. It sanctions a 'personal trip' and allows devotees to pursue their own ends.

What is noticeable in ISKCON temples, apart from the *arati* ceremonies, 'kirtan' and the *Bhagavad Gita* classes is the absence of enduring groups. Some temples, including the British ones, have restaurants, candle and incense factories and travel agencies attached, but they are small concerns and only employ a few devotees. The only other major grouping in ISKCON temples is the 'sankirtan' groups, *Sankirtana* is a word which, in India, refers to group singing or chanting, particularly through the streets and is used in the movement to refer to small groups of devotees who work together as a group selling ISKCON literature and records. British

ISKCON has bought a fleet of buses and vans in which groups of devotees travel around the country selling literature and preaching. But the composition of these groups is always changing for most devotees tend to move from group to group, job to job and temple to temple with amazing rapidity, particularly in the States. Kirtan is very group-focused too—participation in it, and being part of a group, helps foster ecstasy and heightened emotional experiences. The devotees themselves say that the more people who take part in 'kirtan', the larger the group, the greater the ecstatic and mystical feelings they obtain. But whilst the communal and group nature of 'kirtan' may provide the means of inducing mystical experiences and may be functionally important, nevertheless in the dance, the overt relationship is not with other members of the group but with Krishna.

It is thus an ego-focused dyadic single-stranded relationship and the mystical experiences obtained, whilst generated primarily by participation in the group, are personal. As such, the structure and function of the dance is as much individualistic as group-focused. Devotees' individualism is also seen in the structure of the dance itself. Although the movement has devised one or two of its own dance steps, including the 'Swami Shuffle', nevertheless the dance steps in 'kirtan' are fairly free-form and the dancer can improvise as he goes along and develop his own individual variation of the dance. Devotees in 'kirtan' appear to be a collection of individuals all 'doing their own thing' and going their own way. This is particularly true of routine daily 'kirtan' at the evening *arati* ceremony. Generally, only a small number of devotees take part in them. Dancing tends to be routinised and to have little emotional content. In them, the absence of heightened emotional content, the smallness of numbers and big spaces between the dancers, make devotees' isolation from each other very apparent. Watching devotees dance by themselves, the outsider is reminded not of a group but of the isolated, alienated individual typical of urban society.

Most relationships in ISKCON are, in fact, ego-focused and dyadic. When a devotee joins the movement he develops a personal network of relationships rather than just joins a group as such. Although devotees generally know large numbers of other devotees by name and sight and have superficial ties with them, their personal social network and close ties are frequently limited. Often, because they are people who find it difficult to develop close ties, but also because their relationships tend to be contractual and transient as devotees change jobs and move from temple to temple. The composition of the 'sankirtan' parties which travel all over the country, for instance, is based on a small network of friends and the turnover of personnel in them, as has been mentioned, tends to be rapid.

The group focus and minutiae of rules and regulations which govern wide areas of devotees' behaviour, would lead one to conclude that devotees have little choice of action available to them—that they are unable to pursue their own ends and that individualism would be nigh-on impossible. On one level it is highly constrained in that it regulates behaviour in a detailed way, e.g. having to remove shoes on entering the temple, etc.

In practice, however, the movement allows devotees a wide leeway of behaviour. ISKCON has not as yet really developed a clearly defined ethical and generalised value system. The movement places more emphasis on rules than ethics or general values. Although the movement has a highly developed system of detailed rules which cover wide areas of thought and behaviour, with a few exceptions they refer to specific actions rather than general orientations. This is reflected in the 'Four Regulative Principles' which form the core of ISKCON's system of rules, namely (1) no illicit sex, (2) no eating of meat, fish, eggs or even garlic and onions, (3) no intoxication, and (4) no gambling, speculative enterprises or wastefil activities such as watching television or going to the cinema. Providing devotees abide by the 'Four Regulative Principles' and the minutiae of pettifogging rules, as far as values are concerned, devotees can believe very much as they choose. In important areas such as where devotees live, what job they do, how hard they work, what income they may obtain, whether they marry or not or even whether they may leave the movement, the system is very flexible and is open to individual manipulation, allowing devotees to pursue their own ends to a great degree.

This is reflected in devotees' attitudes to possessions. In practice, devotees are much more individualistic with regard to possessions than the movement's sharing ethic might suggest. In the early days devotees did tend to donate their possessions to ISKCON on joining the movement, though even then a not inconsiderable number did not. Nowadays the majority do not. Amburisha the grandson of Henry Ford for instance, who joined the movement in the early 1970s, retained control over his own fortune. Those devotees too who, prior to joining the movement owned expensive items such as cars and motorbikes, whilst they usually donated them to the movement when they joined, nevertheless retained control over their use and continued to use them in the movement. Also, the majority of devotees retain at least part, if not all, of their money when they join the ISKCON.

Rank and file devotees are only provided with the bare essentials by the movement; food, clothes, a place to sleep and washing requirements such as a toothbrush. Thus, there is a big gap between what the temple supplies to a devotee and his actual needs. If devotees want any extras such as tape recorders, cassettes of Prabhupad's speeches and cameras (and the authorities, deviating from the communal ethos, allow them such personal possessions), they are expected to provide them. Also, in most cases they are expected to finance themselves if they want to visit other temples. In practice, rank and file devotees lead a very hand-to-mouth existence and the average devotee is permanently and chronically short of money. The majority of potential devotees soon become aware of this fact after visiting the temple once or twice and, generally, rather than donate their money to the temple on joining ISKCON, they prefer to keep it for future expenses. As Radha once remarked, 'most devotees have a little something salted away for a rainy day'.

It is true that the devotees do appear, on the surface, to share with each other a great deal, more so perhaps than 'karmis', particularly items of clothing—especially the girls, who frequently swap saris. But when it comes to more expensive possessions, devotees are generally none too willing to share, and only lend to those whom they like and respect. Usually they keep their belongings in lockers or cases with padlocks, a necessary precaution since anything left about in ISKCON has a tendency to 'walk' and theft is not uncommon. Understandably so in a community where devotees lead such a hand-to-mouth existence.

Leading such a frugal existence fosters devotees' individualism and makes them very manipulative. They have to become so in order to make ends meet and to obtain the things they need which are not provided by the movement. Some devotees, too, as the next chapter will show, own a great many possessions—a far cry from the renunciation of individualistic materialism and the ethic of communal sharing which lies at the heart of the ISKCON belief system. In fact, the internal structure and group organisation of

ISKCON provides a stage and backcloth to act out an 'individualistic trip'.

To explain this emphasis on individualism and the sanctioning of a 'personal individualistic trip' in ISKCON, it is necessary to examine devotees' lives prior to their joining the movement, particularly the former lives of the earliest devotees and especially those in the Haight Ashbury temple, for it was they who influenced and determined the form that ISKCON was to take. The Haight Ashbury temple functions, of course, as ISKCON's 'nursery', for it was there in the late 1960s that the basic framework and belief structure of the movement developed. Significantly, it was devotees from this temple who spread ISKCON throughout the world, including to Britain. But it would be naive to assume that Haight Ashbury hippies, on joining the movement, totally renounced all vestiges of unfettered egotism and a desire to pursue their own ends. It seems more reasonable to assume that devotees would take their former experiences and predispositions with them into the movement, albeit latently, and that their behaviour in ISKCON and concomitantly the institutional development of the movement, would be influenced by their previous life-styles.

Zablocki (1971), in his study of several hundred collective living units in the U.S., most of which failed in the first year, concluded that the majority failed because of the absence of constraints on individuality. Certainly there are many constraints on individuality in ISKCON, such as the emphasis on the all-importance of harmony and the forbidding of criticism which are no doubt major reasons for the movement's continued survival. But it is precisely because the movement has developed a flexibility that can cater for devotees' latent individualism and has provided clear-cut channels for its expression that the movement has survived. Otherwise devotees would rapidly have become as frustrated and disillusioned with constraint as their former loosely structured hippie past. Devotees in temples other than Haight Ashbury, in recent years too, often appear to come from similarly fluctuating, transient and single stranded relationships as the early Haight Ashbury devotees, and show symptoms of being loners who are motivated to pursue their own ends. Thus, the early flexibility built into the movement has stood ISKCON in good stead for accommodating itself to later devotees' predispositions and needs.

The sanctioning of an 'individualistic trip' in ISKCON is also directly related to the ideology of *bhakti yoga*. *Bhakti yoga*, with its stress on the purification of the individual soul and attainment of one's original God consciousness and its emphasis on the individual's highly personal relationship with God and lonely and individualistic path back to Godhead, both sanctions, encourages and channels devotees' individualism as does its focus on personal mystical experience. The frame of reference for long-term 'advanced' devotees, well socialized into the philosophy, is always their relationship with Krishna. Relationships within the movement are not directed to undifferentiated fellowship with the entire community but are always centred on God rather than on other people or the group. Both the movement as a whole and other devotees provide the backcloth for acting out the individual's relationship with God. All relationships other than that with Krishna are unimportant and irrelevant. Since the only 'real' love is *prema* (love of God), love between people is considered an illusion and impermanent.

Bhakti thus underplays all other attachments, including social relationships with other devotees and people in general. As such, it encourages individualism and provides devotees with a blueprint for pursuing their own ends and personal 'individualistic trip'. Actually the individualistic ideology of *bhakti* parallels ISKCON's social structure which tends to be single stranded too. It channels ISKCON's social, economic and political organisation and system of belief into an individualistic framework. Even ISKCON's symbolic model of social protest, as will become clear, is focused around the individual and expressed in individualistic terms.

ISKCON individualism is, reflected in the detachment evident in devotees' relationships with each other. Collective fellowship within the movement is essentially on the level of ritual rather than evident in personal relationships which tend to be single stranded. Although some of the more long-term devotees have developed close friendships, and it is not uncommon for siblings to join together, relationships between devotees are not generally very close. Nor do they go out of their way to help each other. If a devotees needs help or has a personal problem such as illness, they do not expect and, generally, do not get help from other devotees. Also it is not uncommon for devotees to 'rip each other off'.

Nor are the temple authorities paternalistic in their attitudes to rank and file devotees. They do not interest themselves in devotees unless they are a source of trouble and bring the movement into disrepute. Devotees are expected to deal with their own problems and look after themselves. As a very prominent British devotee remarked when discussing the devotees' lack of concern for each other, 'You can be lying up there dying', referring to the sleeping quarters above Bury Place, 'and no one will lift a hand to help you'. Certainly people who are ill do appear to be left to fend for themselves.

Neither do ISKCON authorities have a paternalistic attitude towards devotees' children. Parents themselves are expected to provide for their needs and deal with their problems. For single parent mothers, this lack of concern and interest in others can present problems. If their child becomes sick they find it almost impossible to get help or find anyone to take them to the doctor or hospital.

In fact, single mothers and their children are not encouraged to join as full-time resident members of temples.

Relationships between husbands and wives are also influenced by the under-emphasis placed in *bhakti* on relationships with others and the lack of stress placed on love between people. Although celibacy is the ideal, devotees are free to marry if it will further their service to Krishna. Marriages, however, are arranged by temple authorities. Until recently, devotees often did not meet their spouses until just before the marriage. Understandably, initial pairbonding tends to be underdeveloped in ISKCON and relationships between couples tend not to be intimate. Because their main concern is their personal relationship to Krishna, little emphasis is placed in practice on the marriage bond. Spouses frequently appear to go their own way rather than work together and develop their relationship.

Though it is too early to say whether this will happen with English devotees, as most of their children are still toddlers, American devotees tend to show a lack of close attachment to their children, which is reflected in their attitude to their children's schooling. Despising 'karmi' schools, which they view as atheistic and subversive, ISKCON has set up its own schools for the movement's male children. American devotees send their children, often at the age of 6 to 7, to these schools, many to the *gurukula* in India, they frequently do not see them for long periods. Parents could, if they so chose, reside at the temples where their children are at school, but very often they do not. It is not uncommon either for older adolescent children to reside in different temples from their parents, particularly girls, who are not sent to school. Such separation naturally fosters further detachment on the part of not only the parents, but the children too.

Pursuing their service for Krishna also sanctions devotees moving from temple to temple and job to job. This rapid moving around further hinders the development of close bonds in the movement, causing devotees to be inward looking and preoccupied with their own selves. In general, the longer devotees stay in the movement, particularly Americans who tend to move around more than other nationalities, the more detached from relationships they become; a consequence of the philosophy of *bhakti yoga* which seeks to break personal material attachments in favour of the relationship with the Godhead.

But whilst *bhakti* fosters detachment, individualism and, in some cases, selfishness, it also fosters self-reliance. Membership of ISKCON might well be characterised as 'survival of the fittest'. The provision of only minimal basic needs by the temple and the lack of help given to devotees by the temple authorities and other devotees, teaches them to stand on their own feet and to fend for themselves. They soon learn to manipulate the system to their own advantage in order to survive in it. Moreover late adolescent (17-21) devotees are often far more self-reliant, manipulative and better able to fend for themselves than their 'karmi' counterparts. Many often by themselves, use the world-wide temple structure as a means of travelling, to Europe, America and India--some all over the world. Not infrequently, the devotees' well-scrubbed fresh-faced look, which they interpret as a reflection of the 'pure' lives they lead, belies a manipulative interior. This emphasis on self-reliance, manipulation and general individualism is reflected in ISKCON's economic and political structure.

CHAPTER SIX

Preaching Krishna Consciousness and the Economics of Bhakti Yoga

'Nature has already given us everything. There is no need to become rich by starting some huge factory to produce auto bodies. By such industrial enterprises we have simply created troubles . . . "We simply have to depend on Krishna. Krishna does not say, 'Yes, depend on Me, and also depend on your slaughterhouses and factories.' No. He says 'Depend only on Me.'"
—BTG Vol. 13, No. 12, p. 4-5

Rejection of the material world and renunciation of all possessions for the austerity of an ascetic temple life in which all resources are pooled and each member owns only the minimum possessions necessary for existence is the ideal in ISKCON. But, like other features of ISKCON, this, too, is an inversion of the values and norms of western society; as is their rejection in favour of a mystic contemplative and ascetic community life of the competitive rat-race for material success which forms the basic framework of the western capitalist economic structure. Indeed, ISKCON's anti-materialism is a direct attack on western affluence and is a rejection of the materialism and capitalist economic basis of western society.

But ISKCON's anti-materialism is more symbolic than actual. It is an ethical statement of intent and a value rather than a practical reality. The economic structure of ISKCON and the individual devotee's own economic behaviour are, actually, a mirror image of traditional western economic forms. In practice, devotees are very materialistic in their attitudes. The movement is a parody of capitalism and the individualistic and competitive ethic which forms its base. ISKCON has developed its own internal capitalist 'rat-race'. It operates within a framework of economic competitiveness, albeit under the sacred canopy of Krishna. Moreover, far from renouncing the capitalist economic structure of the outside 'karmi' world, the movement's economic structure is intricately tied in with it. It is totally dependent on 'karmi' society for its income and the technology it uses to gain such an income.

For instance, devotees' rampant individualism, which is a product of their former 'karmi' lives, is evident in ISKCON's economic organisation. Whilst the basic economic framework of ISKCON is group-focused, its economic relations nevertheless tend to be predominantly ego-focused and individualistically oriented, just like the concept of *bhakti yoga*. ISKCON's system of belief and economic organisation developed hand in hand and are closely intertwined. The individualism which underlies both *bhakti yoga* and the economic structure of the movement developed together and are symbiotically related, for each justifies, reinforces and encourages the other. *Bhakti yoga*'s focus on the individual and its emphasis on detachment from personal ties has promoted individualism in the economic field. At the same time its individualistic orientation provides both legitimation and a channel for devotees' personal egotism and desire to pursue their own ends economically. A number of other social, economic and political factors have also fostered the individualistic focus of ISKCON's economic organisation for which *bhakti yoga* also provides a rationale and an outlet.

In essence, ISKCON's economic system might well be characterised as 'order within chaos'. ISKCON has developed economically so as to allow each individual to pursue his own economic ends within a basically communal framework. The movement derives its income primarily from individualistic enterprise and small-scale, but highly successful, capitalistic petit entrepreneurship. This provides a basic framework within which individual devotees are able to pursue their own personal 'trip'.

ISKCON has temples in some hundred countries dotted about the world. Although ISKCON has not expanded rapidly in terms of numbers, it has grown very fast financially, so that in terms of wealth and real estate it is becoming quite a rich movement. It has substantial properties and income in many of the major countries where it has established temples, as is clear from the properties they own in Britain. Its property in Soho Street, for instance, cost £ 120,000 and a further £ 200,000 was spent renovating it. As an indication of ISKCON's financial stability in Britain, devotees were able to get a large mortgage to help pay for Soho Street from a major bank. As a result of their solvency and credit-worthiness, they find it very easy in general to get credit in most countries where they have properties.

Like most of the new eastern religious groups that sprung up during the 1960s, ISKCON was quick to take advantage of the tax benefits of being a registered charity. According to the accounts they filed with the British Charity Commission, their annual income rose from £ 6,000 in 1968 to £ 800,000 in 1977. ISKCON's financial solvency is no doubt surprising to critics who see them merely as workshy hippie dropouts. Considering the youth of the average devotee and the kind of people who join ISKCON, particularly in America—dropouts, hippies, etc.—it would seem surprising that the movement should have become so wealthy and financially sound.

ISKCON is not alone in its economic success. Some of the other new eastern religious groups which mushroomed in the 1960s, such as Transcendental Meditation and the 'Moonies', have also been very financially successful and accumulated a great deal of wealth. Those groups which survived the 1960s at Haight Ashbury tended to be those that became wealthy rapidly. ISKCON, along with these other groups, accumulated wealth so quickly that it rapidly developed a sound financial base. At the same time, the movement also developed an internal institutional structure geared ideologically, socially and economically to the making of money and the generation of wealth. This enabled the movement to transcend the economic 'take-off' stage and develop a social organisation that has been able to promote further economic expansion.

Although Prabhupad was in control of ISKCON and was the final arbiter of decisions, the movement did not develop a highly centralised bureaucratic system of economic organisation. Rather the few attempts at centralisation that there have been soon proved to be unsuccessful. ISKCON has instead developed economically into a loosely federated group of financially autonomous and self-sufficient temples which have become even more loosely federated since Prabhupad's death.

Each temple has a well defined internal economic organisation and its economic affairs are governed by a hierarchial chain of command, reflecting the complex development of ISKCON's institutional structure. The finances of each temple in a GBC zone are controlled and exploited by the GBC, temple President and the Board of appointed 'Managers' who meet usually once a week to discuss temple affairs and make decisions. Each temple's income is used to cover its overheads, as well as to feed and clothe devotees, and provide both transport and finance for expanding the movement.

But in Britain, although ISKCON's annual income is very large, its overheads are enormous and, the leaders have difficulty making ends meet on a day-to-day basis and there is always a shortage of ready cash. Devotees themselves are no conservers of energy and the Bhaktivedanta Manor electricity bills alone are nearly £ 1,000 a month.

Initially, the first ISKCON temple in New York (founded in 1966) and later the temple in San Francisco where Prabhupad moved with some of the early devotees, were financially supported by some of the devotees, e.g. Swami Satsvarupa, holding outside jobs and contributing their salaries to help maintain the temple. But by 1971, the selling of books and Krishna Consciousness literature on the streets had become the basis of ISKCON's economic structure. Most of the new eastern religions publish, if at all, only a few books and magazines. Prabhupad's scholastic ability and literary output, however, was harnessed to the economic structure and laid the foundations for a form of economic structure, namely the selling of Krishna Consciousness literature which facilitated money-making and which had great influence on the resulting success of the movement's economic organisation.

Prabhupad claimed, though this was disputed by some of his God-brothers in the Gaudiya Mission, that he had specifically been sent by his spiritual master and guru, Bhaktisiddhanta Saraswati Goswami, to preach Krishna Consciousness to the West. Preaching was incorporated into ISKCON from its conception and rapidly became the movement's basic rationale and justification for book distribution on the streets. Prabhupad's 'mission to the West' was interpreted in the movement as meaning that Krishna Consciousness was to be spread through the medium of Prabhupad's books and the primary aim of the movement came to be to distribute as many books as possible. The interrelationship of preaching and book distribution, of ideology and economics, was to prove to be a potent economic force and was to have a very beneficial effect on the development of the finances of the movement. It proved a very lucrative and successful way of attaining a large and regular income and it soon became the movement's major source of income, and a very profitable source of income at that.

Development of preaching and book selling on the streets as the basis of the movement's economic structure was to have a critical effect on ISKCON's institutional organisation, as it had to remain primarily an urban sect since it is in the towns and major airports (Chicago airport, along with London's West End, are considered amongst the most lucrative centres) that they are able to distribute their literature most profitably. Thus ISKCON's book focused economic structure has prevented the development of ISKCON's ideal, namely the development of a 'back to nature' contemplative community farm life.

A factor crucial to the success of ISKCON's book distribution and without which it might never have got off the ground, is the movement's attraction from the earliest days of artistic and creative types. A number of the earliest devotees had journalistic, artistic, photographic and printing skills which provided ISKCON with the necessary skills and capabilities to get book publishing off the ground and make it a success.

In 1972, devotees set up their own publishing company, the Bhaktivedanta Book Trust, which is now situated in Los Angeles, and is run by devotees. It publishes its own books using highly sophisticated modern equipment and techniques, including computer typewriters, though the actual printing itself is farmed out to a 'karmi' printers in Tennessee. Using devotee labour, BBT is able to keep the overheads low and print Krishna Consciousness books cheaply; hard backs costing about two dollars a copy and *Back to Godhead*, the movement's magazine, a few pence. Being able to draw on a lot of artistic, journalistic, and photographic skills, the standard of BBT publications is very high and they are very attractively presented, albeit in a somewhat 'kitsch' style. Also ISKCON has won a number of eminent printing prizes in America for its books. BBT claims to have published some 66,000,000 pieces of literature since its inception, including some three million *Bhagavad Gita As It Is*! They claim that 'someone buys a BBT book every 2.4 seconds'! Though this is a somewhat wild exaggeration, the movement's literary output is enormous.

BBT sells the books it publishes at a small profit to temples throughout the world. Any profit it makes it ploughs back into BBT. Any surplus is lent on interest to temples throughout the world who want to undertake projects which they cannot afford, such as buying more property or erecting buildings, as well as setting up projects in India; including contributing towards the building of the Vrindaban and Mayapur temples.

Devotees in each temple are then given the books to distribute to the public and sell on the streets and in American airports. Books are also sold by BBT and the temples to colleges and university libraries and over the telephone to individuals through using magazine subscriber lists. The devotees are expected to give the money they make, which is referred to in the movement as *Lakshmi* (the name of the Goddess of Wealth) to the authorities of the temple where they reside and/or obtained the books. The proceeds from book distribution are used communally and go towards temple maintenance and overheads, and feeding and clothing devotees.

Because devotees see book distribution as the primary means of spreading and preaching Krishna Consciousness, it is referred to in the movement (deriving the term from Chaitanya's ecstatic street chanting processions) as 'sankirtan' or street-preaching. 'Sankirtan' is never referred to as 'selling', but 'book distribution' or 'preaching', and the money received in return for the literature is viewed as 'a donation'. The overt aim is not primarily to make money (though devotees are very aware of the need to do so in order to cover the ever-increasing temple overheads), but to make the public aware of Krishna Consciousness and to 'plant Krishna in their hearts'. Even if people who buy Krishna Consciousness literature do not read it, devotees maintain that merely by association with Prabhupad's books and their Krishna content, they will be purified.

Female devotees, particularly pretty girls, are generally more financially successful than men at 'sankirtan', since they make a point of 'chatting-up' male passers-by. In America, on an average, a girl devotee who works a full day can make between 200 and 250 dollars, though some make much more. Rukhmini, one of the most famous 'sankirtan' devotees, who lives at a Californian temple and who is considered to be very religious-minded and 'into Krishna', sold over 800 large books in a week at Christmas 1978, making over 2000 dollars. Whilst in England, the champion 'sankirtan' devotee, Anandalila, a very pretty girl in her midtwenties, once made 1200 pounds in six days. However, the majority of the other 'sankirtan' girls in London, some ten in number, make much less. In England, about 56 people do 'sankirtan' each week, though the amount of hours they do varies. Some do eight hours a day six days a week, whilst others only go out for a few hours a week. About 13000 pounds was collected in one week in June 1978. If this reflects an average weekly 'sankirtan' taking, since half the money collected is profit, it becomes understandable how ISKCON has become economically successful so rapidly in Britain.

In Britain, records, including 'Goddess of Fortune', a record made for ISKCON by George Harrison, are being increasingly substituted for books, which are proving to be uneconomical to import from the States and too costly to print in Britain. Also, these records sell very well to the public, not only because of George Harrison, but because they sell for a pound; a quarter the price paid in shops for records, and as such they are viewed as bargains. Records are a very profitable and quick means of making money for the movement, as each record only costs 30p to cut. To the purists in the movement, however, the substitution of records for books is condemned and frowned upon, for it is not considered to constitute preaching. For the more money-minded authorities, however, it is a very successful and therefore acceptable and necessary means of making money.

Devotees are often accused by critics of being a 'nuisance' and of lying to people as to who they are and what they are selling when they do 'sankirtan', 'begging', 'hustling', 'hassling', 'ripping off passers-by', using 'a hard sell', are other criticisms made against them. Devotees, of course, viewing it as preaching do not see it as such. Nevertheless, some selling techniques used by devotees do mislead and some devotees do lie. In many cases, the charge of unethicalness is well warranted. Some devotees use white lies and say they are students, or collecting for children or people in underdeveloped countries. They defend themselves by arguing that as *brahmacharins* they are students and that they are collecting for children, the gurukula in India and for people in under-developed countries—and they sometimes do donate money for famine relief in Bengal. Others lie outright. One devotee in Hawaii, for example, who has become something of a legend, used to tell rich tourists on Waikiki beach, much to the amusement of other devotees, that he was collecting for 'The Volcano Relief Fund'. Encyclopedia salesmen methods are also used.

In America, devotees stop passers-by and, as a means of opening up a conversation, pin a flower or candy on their lapel, or, if they are tourists, ask them where they come from and whether they are enjoying their holiday.

But some subterfuge is necessary. If they did not, 'sankirtan' would be financially unsuccessful and ISKCON's economic organisation would collapse for the majority of the public are antagonistic towards ISKCON and uninterested in eastern philosophy and Krishna Consciousness in particular. If devotees were to say who they were and to start explaining about Krishna Consciousness immediately, the public would just walk away without making a donation. Devotees do not have the time to discuss philosophy with every member of the public whom they engage in conversation. If they are to make a profit, they have to go for a 'quick sell'. They have to use some kind of subterfuge, or a gimmick which makes a quick sale possible. But ISKCON shrugs off criticism of lack of ethics in 'sankirtan' by claiming that any publicity is good publicity; it does not matter how bad the criticism is. It is making people aware of Krishna and planting Krishna in their hearts that is important.

This element of unethicalness which underpins 'sankirtan' pervades the whole of ISKCON thinking to some degree and is related to the ideology of *bhakti yoga*. As has been mentioned, *bhakti yoga*'s emphasis on detachment from relationships with others does not foster sensitivity towards others. Much the opposite. For devotees, other people are not their frame of reference and how they act towards them is not of great importance. Such an attitude, of course, fosters unethicalness. But some devotees, generally the more religious and sincere, unable to accept the lack of ethics in 'sankirtan' and the hassle involved in doing it, will not do 'sankirtan' as a full-time job. They prefer to perform some other service for Krishna, such as cleaning the temple, cooking, temple odd jobs, administration, deity worship, including making clothes and garlands for the deities. The latter is generally considered women's work.

Although ISKCON rejects the 'rat-race', competition which both reflects and harnesses devotees' individualism underlies book distribution. A competition is held each week in each temple to see who distributes the most books and collects the most money. The winner's name is read out at the Sunday morning *Bhagavad Gita* class and as a reward, the winner is given a leaf of the sacred *tulasi* plant (which is venerated by all Vaishnavas and regarded by Gaudiyas as a sacred goddess) to eat. Competition also takes place internationally between temples on a monthly basis. A Newsletter, the 'Sankirtan Newsletter', is published monthly and sent to all temples throughout the world stating, by means of a points system, the number of books distributed and the amount of money made by each temple and the top scoring devotees. Every Christmas, too, a 'sankirtan' marathon is held, when temples compete with each other internationally to see who can distribute the most books. At this time of the year all devotees are expected to go out all day to distribute books and collect as much money as possible. In New York, at Christmas, devotees wear, improbably, Santa Claus suits and carry a bucket for donations and distribute sweets to the public.

Looked at from the outside, it might appear that the leaders are manipulating devotees and using competition to get them to make as much money as possible for the movement. Indeed, leaders often give 'pep' talks on the subject of competition and try to get the devotees 'fired up' with enthusiasm for 'sankirtan' and for beating other temples. But the introduction of competition in ISKCON was a reaction to a real need and a necessity, for devotees are not the most motivated of individuals and it is often difficult to get some of them to do anything at all. If the movement is to attain the necessary finance to support itself, devotees have to be motivated with a meaning and purpose to their work, and the introduction of competition and related incentives has provided a very successful answer to this problem. But in doing so, far from renouncing the 'rat race', ISKCON has introduced its own variety into the movement one that is a parody in microcosm of the outside world. Indeed, ISKCON's incorporation of competition is another example of its close integration in practice with the wider society and further demonstrates that its rejection of western society is essentially symbolic rather than actual.

Devotees are in fact not forced to go out on 'sankirtan' except at Christmas, when everybody is expected to do so. ISKCON devotees are not exploited by their leaders and forced to go out on the streets selling books for long hours and at all times of the day. To a large extent, devotees choose the kind of 'service' they perform for Krishna. Only about a third of the devotees in the London temple do 'sankirtan' regularly. To be successful at 'sankirtan' and to enjoy doing it, a devotee needs to be an outward-going personality, adept at handling people and verbally articulate. Many devotees detest 'sankirtan' and will not do it, particularly the inarticulate and those with psychological problems. Not just because of the lack of ethics in it, but because they cannot deal with the public and cope with the frequent abuse and insults which they receive. In fact, a devotee needs a tough personality to cope with 'sankirtan'. On the whole, though, those that do 'sankirtan' do it voluntarily because they like it, or, at least, do not detest it, and the hours they work are up to them.

It is certainly more attractive than the other jobs in the movement which are open to the majority of devotees. Such as making flower garlands for the deities, deity worship (*pujari* work), cooking or cleaning—and this is especially true of female devotees without any particular talent. For pretty girls, too, there is the added bonus that the responses of male passers-by are often ego-boosting.

There are also, as would tend to be assumed if people are willing to spend such long hours at it, a number of perks involved and benefits derived from doing 'sankirtan'. On one level devotees are highly materialistic. Money in the movement is highly revered—'Lakshmi'—and how much individuals make, is a frequent topic of conversation. The big 'sankirtan' moneymakers are highly respected and enjoy great prestige. Prior to joining the movement few devotees were in positions of prestige and status; much the opposite. For people who lacked self-confidence in a wider society, being a big fish in a small pond is ego-boosting and satisfying and the prestige derived from big 'sankirtan' takings appears to be a major incentive for doing it.

The more money a devotee makes for the movement, the better the movement looks after them. Generally, as soon as a temple has got off the ground economically, it invests in pleasant living accommodation for the 'sankirtan mothers', as female 'sankirtan' devotees are called. 'Sankirtan mothers' are generally controlled and organised by a male householder and in Britain Bhaja Hari, the British 'sankirtan' leader and the 'sankirtan mothers' moved into their own house in Clapham in 1978. Bhaja Hari keeps the 'sankirtan mothers' well supplied with pleasing saris, including silk ones and pretty 'karmi' clothing for 'sankirtan'.

ISKCON holds festivals at Mayapur and Vrindaban annually in March which are attended by devotees from all over the world. Devotees who make a great deal of money are taken to this festival, as well as on a tour of other sacred Krishna places in India.

'Sankirtan' also provides devotees with a varied life with minimum routine. It is, too, less boring than most other jobs open to them in the movement. The 'travelling sankirtan parties' in Britain, most of which consist of groups of *brahmacharins* travel all over the country, particularly in the Midlands where there is a large Asian community. They are provided with a particularly varied life which is often a lot of fun.

Also, 'sankirtan' is a service that can be performed by anybody in any temple and 'sankirtan' devotees can move easily from temple to temple; which many in fact do, particularly in America. Also, because they are money makers they are very welcome in any temple. Some devotees travel from temple to temple and 'see the world' on 'sankirtan'.

Moreover, for devotees who are very devout and 'into Krishna'—as the devotees refer to each other's piety—the religious element itself is an important incentive and they get great satisfaction from performing this service for Krishna and are willing to put in as many hours as possible. Often, it is the most religious, the most 'fired up', who spend the longest hours at 'sankirtan' and are the most successful book distributors.

Some critics of ISKCON also maintain that its leaders exploit the devotees because they take their earnings. But such a view is misleading and misrepresents the actual situation in ISKCON. It is true that some devotees make thousands of pounds a year for their temple. But devotees can only make this kind of money because they are in such a movement as ISKCON, which goes in for this method of selling. Bearing in mind the work pattern of the average devotee prior to joining the movement, they could not make this kind of money themselves if they were to work outside the movement.

Balanced against their earnings, too, is the kind of lifestyle they lead in the movement. While devotees' physical accommodation may be minimal, uncomfortable, crowded and lacking in privacy (a circumstance that generally does not appear to worry young people or put them off anyway), it is a much more interesting life and more fun—a bit like a social club—than the life they would probably lead outside. This is particularly true of English devotees who come typically from 'man in the street' backgrounds. Although their parental homes may have a high living standard, American devotees' own accommodation, prior to joining the movement, often tended to be little more than a 'hippie pad' and their previous social lives equally boring and routine. Few ordinary people do the job they choose, lead a varied life or travel all round the country and go to India every year, as do many ISKCON devotees.

Prabhupad's age and personality are also important factors that have to be taken into account when discussing exploitation. Given the total respect, worship and obedience gurus receive from their followers, they are easily able to exploit them. ISKCON was lucky in the kind of guru it got. Prabhupad was already seventy when he came to the West and past the age when he was likely to be highly motivated by a desire for material wealth or great luxury, as some of the gurus appear to be, such as the boy-god Guru Maharaj Ji of Divine Light. Prabhupad, although it was discovered that he had very large sums of money in his personal bank account when he died, lived a relatively austere and ascetic life. This earned him the respect of devotees and in their eyes gave him legitimacy and made him a bona fide guru. It made him, for them, a cut above the other gurus, whose luxurious lives devotees were quick to criticise and compare with Prabhupad's asceticism.

Relatively speaking, little money was spent in ISKCON on supplying Prabhupad with a luxurious life. Rather, the money was ploughed back into the movement. So too, has been the money Prabhupad left in his private bank account (excluding a monthly allowance of 4,000 rupees which he willed to his family). It has been used to buy transport, technical equipment and property, including temple buildings and farms for devotees to act out their 'back to nature' ethic. There is far more economic waste in ISKCON than the average commercial company. Devotees, like most young people, tend to be slipshod in the way they look after things. Nevertheless, money made by ISKCON devotees has not been frittered away. In fact, ISKCON, particularly in America, has a lot to show for the hard work put in by devotees and its income has been used in such a way as to benefit the ordinary devotees. For instance, money is spent on such items as cars, expensive photographic, art and theatre equipment, which are of interest to the devotees and which they can use themselves; particularly talented devotees who have censiderable influence in the movement.

It is still too early to tell, especially as far as exploitation is concerned, the way the movement is likely to develop in the future. However most of the eleven new gurus who took over when Prabhupad died appear to be trying to emulate him. They have much better food, clothes, accommodation and travelling facilities—they fly all over the world than the average devotee. They nevertheless seem to be trying to follow a relatively ascetic life too. They appear, also to be ploughing ISKCON money back into the movement in a way beneficial to all devotees. Only one has so far shown any sign of a desire for a very luxurious life. Internal constraints on the American gurus as will be discussed later, are developing which should limit and prevent their abuse of power and exploitation of devotees.

One control devotees have over the misuse and misallocation of funds is that the size of the income derived from 'sankirtan' is, to some extent, common knowledge for devotees discuss their 'sankirtan' takings frequently. In fact, at Bhaktivedanta Manor, lists are put up on a notice board each week of takings, and each temple's takings are published in the monthly Sankirtan Newsletter. Devotees also know roughly how much the business enterprises, such as Spiritual Sky and the restaurants, are making. In England, only money donated by individual donors is not common knowledge. Thus, any devotee using large amounts for his own personal use would soon be spotted and this acts as a control over misuse. It is not unknown, however, for devotees, particularly temple treasurers, to run off with temple money. One devotee in Laguna Beach, is alleged to have appropriated 4,000 dollars.

Exploitation is not just one way—the leaders exploit the rank and file, the ordinary rank and file devotees exploit the movement too. Some devotees, albeit a relatively small minority, manipulate 'sankirtan' to their own advantage and the ability to do so is a major incentive for them to do 'sankirtan'. Devotees, wishing to keep up a good appearance, adamantly maintain to outsiders, that all the money collected goes to the temple for communal use. But in practice many devotees take a personal cut from the money they collect. Because the average devotee is permanently and chronically short of money, he may bridge the gap between the basic necessities that the temple supplies him with and his actual needs by taking a cut from his 'sankirtan' takings, or any other project that he might become involved in. To do so is informally considered a legitimate perk. Although some ask the temple's permission before doing so, others, albeit a minority and often the least sincere and least religious devotees, take a cut without permission.

ISKCON also formally allows devotees to finance personal projects through their 'sankirtan' takings, provided they first ask permission. Devotees have to pay to send their children to the ISKCON schools (the main gurukula in Vrindaban charges 60 dollars a month) and they are allowed to make the necessary money through 'sankirtan'. Similarly, if they want to go to a temple in another country or make the pilgrimage to India. Devotees who have financed trips round the world through 'sankirtan', and maintain that they can make enough money to finance a trip to India in a week.

Whilst book distribution is still the backbone of the movement, ISKCON has also embarked on other commercial enterprises. Jayatirtha Maharaj began a candle, incense and perfume-making factory in the Los Angeles temple in the early days of the movement which proved to be financially successful. Many other temples including Bhaktivedanta Manor have followed suit and set up their own 'Spiritual Skies', as these enterprises are called in the movement.

The movement has also entered into the restaurant business. 'Govinda's', in the basement of the New York temple, provides the basis of the temple's financial support and serves Indian vegetarian ('Krishnatarian') and health food to a large outside clientele who are attracted by the quality of the food and the competitive prices. The English movement opened its 'Healthy, Wealthy and Wise' restaurant in 1979, which has been decorated in a tasteful style reminiscent of 'Cranks', the famous Soho health food restaurant and within a short time after opening was getting 300 customers a day. ISKCON also has its own travel agency—'Three Worlds

Travel'—which mostly caters for devotees who want to go to India or the States, but which is also trying to expand into the outside 'karmi' market.

In sum, ISKCON, far from being a hippy movement with a poorly organised and minimally developed economic structure, has evolved a highly developed economic organisation. As the movement has expanded in numbers, role differentiation and complexity have concomitantly increased. In order to cope with the expansion, it has become progressively bureaucratic, particularly in the large American temples such as Los Angeles, where 250-300 devotees reside. In Britain, the management committee which, in the early days of the movement numbered five, has now expanded to 14 to deal with the ever increasing role differentiation. Nowadays, British ISKCON even has its own Public Relations Officer. In fact, to cope with ISKCON's rapidly increasing institutional complexity and bureaucratic needs, Vijitravirya, the assistant Governing Board Commissioner in Britain, bought himself some books on 'management' and has become the movement's 'guru' on management problems! He studied on the subject so that the movement could learn how to organise itself rationally and how to set up committees, etc.

The internal finances of ISKCON are bureaucratically organised too, 'Chitties' are given out and signed for everything, especially in the big temples such as Los Angeles. There, the role of treasurer is a time-consuming one. In Los Angeles, reflecting ISKCON's individualistic ethic, everything is accounted for on an individual basis. Individuals or the departments for which they work, e.g. BBT., Art Department, or FATE, are expected to pay for their accommodation and food if they live within the temple complex. At the *gurukulas*, everything is accounted for individually and parents are expected to pay their own children's school fees. In Britain, bureaucratisation has not developed so far that everything is accounted for on an individual basis, but nevertheless 'chitties' are also the norm and the role of treasurer is full-time.

The Life Membership Scheme introduced in 1969 is perhaps the best and most extreme example of rational bureaucratic norms at work in ISKCON. The Life Membership Scheme enables Krishna worshippers who do not want to become full-time devotees to join the movement. For a once-and-for-all fee which, in 1977, was £150, an individual may join ISKCON as a lay 'Life Member'. ISKCON allows the life membership fee to be paid in instalments. It has bureaucratically had membership forms printed in the form of bank standing orders.

ISKCON too always seeks the best legal advice money can buy—a reason, no doubt, why ISKCON always does well in its legal battles. Its bureaucratic and rational allocation of resources is also indicated by its creditworthiness and the ease with which it gets loans. One or two of the devotees, including His Divine Grace Jayatirtha Maharaj, are very shrewd real estate dealers, and allocate resources wisely. For example Soho Street appears likely to be a very successful investment.

On another level, however, due to devotees' individualism and desire to pursue their own ends, ISKCON appears to be immensely chaotic and always on the brink of disaster. This is reflected in the movement's lack of ready cash and over-spending in its day-to-day expenditure. Projects get started enthusiastically, but soon fizzle out. Some never get off the ground, or take a great deal of time to get done. The Soho restaurant premises, for instance, were bought in 1976. ISKCON originally intended opening the restaurant in 1978, but so dilatory were the devotees at converting the premises, that it was not opened until the summer of 1979. Devotees themselves are well aware of the slowness with which things get done in ISKCON. They refer to it jokingly, with tongue-in-cheek, as 'devotee time'.

This is partly due to devotees' own individualism but also to the nature of the chain of command, which while overtly clear-cut, is diffuse in practice. Orders tend to get lost, or never quite carried out, or carried out incorrectly. It is, of course, often difficult to get devotees to do anything, particularly the more unmotivated ones. The job of temple commander, who is in charge of running the day-to-day domestic life of the temple and of handing out domestic jobs to devotees, is a particularly frustrating and unrewarding one. The turnover of temple commanders, due to job frustration is rapid. The presidency of Bury Place, which was more an administrative role than a position of power, also had a high turnover and partly for the same reason. Even the President had difficulty in getting the devotees to work. For instance, it is not obligatory to go to the evening *mangala arati* and many devotees do not go. It is not an unfamiliar sight to see the temple president or an assistant ineffectively trying to drum up custom for the evening *arati* ceremony, telling devotees that they must go. In fact, reflecting the individualistic orientation that runs throughout ISKCON, everybody in the temple appears to be going his own way and doing his own thing.

ISKCON has become wealthy precisely because it operates within its highly formalised institutional framework, an essentially loosely structured and ramshackle organisation. This apparent disorganisation masks a rational and realistic use of ISKCON's work force. The chaos itself is an expression and necessary part of the rational allocation of resources and labour force in ISKCON, ISKCON's economic organization is based on a realistic appraisal of the type of people that devotees are and it has been adapted to their needs, motivation and personality type. It is ideally suited to channel and cater for devotees' individualism and their desire to pursue their own ends. Through its very chaos, ISKCON has been able to harness devotees' individual abilities and economic potential so as to get the maximum out of them.

Devotees, as is clear from the number who were on the dole prior to joining the movement, recoil from the whole idea of a nine-to-five routine or having to do the same job for any length of time. They joined the movement precisely to get away from the rat-race and the eight hour day. Thus any attempt to get all devotees to do a routinised permanent nine-to-five job, given devotees' 'flightiness', would be doomed to failure from the out set. The movement has implicitly faced up to devotees' attitudes to the nine-to-five routine and realistically worked within the limitations imposed by the type of people who join the movement. Instead of developing a large-scale monolithic centralised economic organisation based on an eight hour working day, ISKCON has set up economic projects which are not dependent on a nine-to-five routine for success or a skilled or stable permanent workforce.

For instance, although, in theory, the temple president allocates the service a devotee performs for Krishna, in practice, the system is flexible. A devotee's own wishes are always overtly underplayed. It is always maintained when a devotee takes up a new job that it was 'Krishna's mercy' or the temple authorities that decided it. Devotees, in general, however, are allowed to do much as they choose. Since there is an acute manpower shortage in most temples, once devotees have become initiated and are seen to be worthwhile acquisitions, temple authorities attempt to accommodate their desires. They try to provide them with satisfying and rewarding jobs, for they are well aware that devotees with good reputations are welcomed at any temple and if they force devotees to do work they do not like, they may leave.

Symptomatic of their dislike for routine, devotees rarely stay in the same job in the movement for long, unless they have some speciality such as an artistic skill or they are hardened 'sankirtan' devotees who enjoy the associated life-style and the perks that go with it, or they are in positions of power. Even leading devotees tend to change their jobs and/or the projects they are involved in quite frequently. Bored by routine, most devotees, particularly the male celibate *barhmacharins*, especially in the United States, soon lose interest in any job they do and flit from job to job, and even temple to temple. Devotees are well aware of their own attitudes to work and refer to their work orientation as 'flighty' or 'unstable'. Realistically accepting the situation in order to make sure that Healthy, Wealthy and Wise was financially successful and had a reliable labour force, paid 'karmi' help was employed behind the counter.

Also, the economic projects that ISKCON has set up need few skills. An important and realistic point as far as devotees are concerned for few of them, particularly the college dropouts, have any useful skill. Allowing petit entrepreneurship has also proved a shrewd move, for it has provided an incentive to the motivated, ISKCON has thus developed an economic structure which caters for both the slackers and the highly motivated hardworkers and in so doing, has managed to maximise the output of both groups!

Although working within devotees' limitations has enabled ISKCON to make the most out of devotees economically, it does have its economic drawbacks. In particular, it has, in some areas, hindered and prevented economic expansion. A case in point is Spiritual Sky in Britain. Puranjana, the thirty year old American who runs Spiritual Sky in the U.K. frequently complained that there was a big market in the 'karmi' world for ISKCON's high quality candles. They could sell far more than the two thousand a week they produced. But he moaned devotees were 'unreliable'. They were here one minute and gone the next. Some days no devotees turned up for work at all. Since he did not have a permanent workforce he could rely on, he said he could not expand as he could never be sure he would be able to fulfil his orders. In consequence when he opened a shop in 1979, he employed 'karmi' labour.

Book distribution ('Sankirtan') has proved an ideal economic venture for ISKCON to embark on, for it is not dependent on a permanent or skilled workforce. It can be done by anybody at any time. Devotees can do it where and when they choose and when they get bored they can move on without jeopardising the economic set-up of the temple. Restaurants and candle-making factories are excellent economic ventures for ISKCON for similar reasons. The turnover rate in ISKCON restaurants and candle-making factories is incredibly high.

The movement also harnesses devotees' personal interests and latent talents and abilities that have gone unrecognised. This not only provides motivation but also contributes towards maximising devotees' potential and output. Devotees are encouraged to develop any talent they have, from handyman and do-it-yourself skills to music and artistic talents for the service of Krishna. They are allowed to perform them in the movement as their job. One devotee, Atma Atma, a pixie-faced young man of 22, had been in and out of work before joining the movement, though immediately prior to joining the movement he had a job switching on the fountains in Trafalgar Square. He was a keen and able handyman and derived great job satisfaction from doing any carpentry or plumbing that the temple needed. As he remarked, 'It's only in ISKCON that your job's your hobby too'. Anandadasa, a New York Jewish householder now in charge of Prabhupad's Museum in the New York temple, had an unsettled history of psychiatric disease prior to joining the movement some seven years ago. He remarked that he had found motivation and fulfilment in the movement. As an adolescent he said he had not known what he had really wanted to do and had dropped out of college. He had subsequently developed an interest in music which his family frowned upon and discouraged. The devotees, Anandadasa said, were the first people to encourage him and really understand him. They had said to him that he could utilise his interest in music as his service for Krishna and he felt immediately drawn to the movement; it was one of the major reasons why he joined the movement. The movement has provided a number of unemployed musicians, writers and artists with an outlet for their talents.

ISKCON is far more involved in films, music and drama than

any of the other eastern religious groups. Most temples for instance have not only art departments but drama groups too. The movement also makes its own films which are used for preaching purposes. This emphasis is clearly a reflection of the high proportion of creative and artistic types in ISKCON. But it also demonstrates how the movement adapts to and harnesses these talents and interests.

Most of the creative people in ISKCON, particularly the artists, are technically quite skilled. But most do not, in general, show any real original creative talent. They could not hope to become successful professional artists or compete with established 'karmi' artists. Since creativity and artistic skills are very highly respected in the movement, it enables such people to bloom and become 'stars', for any demonstration of creativity attains prestige and status. This is an important factor in keeping such creative and talented people in the movement. Would-be photographers and film-makers are given the chance to develop their interests in a manner which they would be unlikely to be able to do outside. For example Yadubara and Visakha his wife, who make most of the ISKCON films have attained a high standard of competence over the years. They, too, are amongst the most highly respected of devotees.

Most devotees who survive the first six months tend to stay in the movement if not permanently, then at least for several years. Creative and talented devotees, in particular, tend frequently to be long-term devotees. Yadubara and Visakha, for instance, have been in the movement over ten years, whilst Yadurani, the head of the art department in Los Angeles was the first female devotee. Providing devotees, particularly the more intelligent ones with jobs in the movement that are stimulating and interesting is clearly a major reason for their remaining in the movement. They stay because they have created for themselves a satisfying occupation and rewarding niche in the movement. Those who do not, leave. Indeed, much of the movement's success, and financial success in particular, is in its building its framework around and adapting to devotees' interests and talents, and providing them with the kinds of jobs that they can do and enjoy doing; and a satisfying life. In so doing, ISKCON has been able to maximise devotees' economic output.

Preaching Krishna Consciousness

Indicating how ISKCON's rejection of western society is symbolic rather than actual, devotees hold that anything, including western technological products, can be used in the service of Krishna. It is no accident that the movement has bought in a great deal of modern technology and highly sophisticated gadgetry, such as computer typewriters for book printing, complex electronic equipment for sound effects in their FATE waxwork museum, sophisticated equipment for their art and film-making departments as well as, on a mundane level, a fleet of buses and cars and even modern stainless steel kitchens. In essence, ISKCON has invested in gadgetry that young people would find interesting, stimulating and fascinating. This supplies them with further motivation and stimulation for hard work and high output.

FATE (First American Theistic Exhibition) Studios is perhaps the prime example in ISKCON of the movement's abundant usage of sophisticated modern technological gadgetry. FATE Studios, situated in the Los Angeles temple complex, is an autonomous department of ISKCON. FATE is *the* hot-house of ISKCON talent and some of the most gifted and talented devotees work there. FATE Studios makes waxworks. It opened its own waxwork museum costing about a hundred thousand dollars in Los Angeles in 1977—'The First American Theistic Exhibition'. As an indication of the high degree of skill and talent the movement can call upon, the standard of the waxwork exhibits and dioramas is as high, if not higher than that of Madame Tussaud's the famous waxworks museum in London. The dioramas in the museum, somewhat reminiscent of Disneyland, as are the accompanying high quality, realistic, sound effects. They depict scenes from the *Shrimad Bhagavata*, the *Bhagavad Gita* and, of course, there is a waxwork of Prabhupad at work translating, which both moves and speaks. Not to be outdone, an even grander museum which, it is estimated, will cost several hundred thousands of dollars has been conmissioned by Jayatirtha Maharaj for the Detroit temple which is in his zone. It is reported that it will be paid for by Henry Ford's grandson who resides in the Detroit temple.

FATE Studios in Los Angeles have taken over a large new warehouse and have invested in every type of modern gadgetry necessary for the project. This new project has provided the most talented section of ISKCON with stimulating and interesting work for the next few years. Understandably, there is great competition to get asked to join FATE Studios and much prestige attached to working there. At FATE, an enormous amount of ISKCON money is being used to provide not the gurus, but the rank and file devotees themselves with interesting and stimulating work. FATE demonstrates that the 'spoils' of the movement are broadly distributed through the movement as a whole, but it bears witness to the sizable influence the devotees themselves have on the shaping and development of the movement.

Devotees also go, on the pretext of doing 'sankirtan' or 'harinam' (as devotees sometimes also refer to the street-chanting parties) to places of interest to young people such as Pop Festivals, The Mind and Body Festival and even the Earls Court Boat Show. All such outings supply devotees with stimulation, an extra source of interest and a varied and fascinating life; one which minimizes boredom and routine.

Thus ISKCON, by allowing devotees to be independent and go their own way, by allowing them to choose the job they do and even the temple they reside in, and by allowing them to pursue their own interests, has provided them with stimulation and motivation. As such it has been able to get work out of them which they would probably have not undertaken otherwise. Most importantly, this form of loose organisation has been a major reason for devotees staying in the movement for such long periods. A more coercive and organised form of economic organisation would very likely have caused them to leave rapidly. By playing up to devotees' egotism and rampant individualism and by allowing them to act it out, ISKCON has become financially successful.

Individualism, self-interest and emphasis on the 'personal trip' in ISKCON also lie at the heart of the petit entrepreneurship which pervades economic activity in the movement. Individual devotees in the movement are allowed to pursue their own economic self-interest and to go in for personal economic aggrandizement and by allowing them to do so, ISKCON has harnessed a potent money-making force for the movement.

The 'poor man made good', the highly respected symbol of success in capitalist American society, is personified in Prabhupad himself, a circumstance which evokes admiration and respect in devotees also brought up to respect the 'rags to riches' ideal. Prabhupad came to

America by boat, having been given a free ticket by Mrs. Sumati Morarji, the owner of a shipping company. According to ISKCON myth, he arrived in New York with 'only forty rupees' in his pocket, a fact which devotees are quick to point out to outsiders. Often they go on to say with pride—'and look what he has achieved in ten years'.

Prabhupad's own behaviour provides a shining example of and justification for devotees' own economic ventures. Many devotees, especially the Americans, have started their own money-making projects and have become small-scale entrepreneurs, setting up projects on their own which significantly use the terminology of the 'karmi' world and are referred to in the movement as 'doing business'. Given devotees' general lack of education, skills and personal finance, small-scale entrepreneurism which needs little skill or capital investment is thus a rational answer and a realistic approach to devotees' personal situations.

Entrepreneurism which was started by devotees very early in the movement has become an accepted and legitimate part of the ISKCON economic structure. In fact, it underpins and articulates the formal 'sankirtan' economic system and is a prime reason for sankirtan's rapid financial success. Entrepreneurism is rationalised in ISKCON in terms of Krishna. It is all viewed as being done for the glory of Krishna and in Krishna's service. Following what ISKCON maintains was the custom in 'Vedic' times, devotees are expected to donate fifty per cent of what they make to the temple to be used communally, though owing to devotees' individualism and self-interest, few actually pay the full fifty per cent.

Devotees have utilised their Indian connections. Most import and export Indian goods. Some devotees living in India have set themselves up as middlemen and export to temples in the West the religious paraphernalia they need—clothes for the devotees and the deities, altar clothes and ritual objects. The most famous of such middlemen in the movement is Dhananjaya, who is British. He is thirty years old, a very thoughtful and sincere devotee, and an example of the best kind of ISKCON devotee.

Dhananjaya liked India, and Vrindaban, where he lived in particular. He learnt Hindi and developed close relations with the local Indian community, unlike most other western devotees who do not bother to learn Hindi when they come to India. He was able to put this knowledge of Hindi and his local contacts to good use. He cornered the market and became the principal ISKCON middleman in India. Some devotees have estimated that during the March Festival in 1978, some £ 200,000 was spent in Vrindaban in a fortnight. A great deal of this money passed through his hands and he, of course, took his percentage.

Individual devotees in the West have also entered the business of import and export of Indian goods, often using Dhananjaya as the go-between. They, too, import Krishna Consciousness paraphernalia, including such things as small personal deities and deity clothes, cheap jewellery, cheap western style clothes and sari silk which is sold as dress material. They sell these goods to other devotees and to outsiders including outside commercial interests. They also supply these, in some cases, to the temple for resale within the temple; particularly if the temple runs its own shop or stall.

In fact, most devotees because of the gap between temple provision and their actual everyday needs, do some business, in order to provide themselves with a small income; unless they have psychological problems that prevent them from organising themselves and communicating with others. Indeed, there is quite a lot of buying and selling between devotees themselves.

Some devotees, as has been mentioned, also manipulate 'sankirtan' to their own advantage. In fact, a major reason for 'sankirtan's' rapid success as a money-making venture was due to individual effort. Most of the ideas and projects that got 'sankirtan' off the ground were initiated by individual devotees themselves rather than Prabhupad. The idea of 'sankirtan parties', of buying fleets of buses and sending devotees round the country to distribute literature, which has made a lot of money for the movement, was thought up by Bhaktivedanta Swami, one of the most prominent of all devotees.

Also, those devotees who control 'sankirtan' money and either have their own party or, because they are Governing Board Commissioners and/or gurus and/or temple presidents and as such have access to and/or control of temple 'sankirtan' funds, as will become clear, can use it to their own advantage politically if they so choose and many do, they thus have the incentive to make as much money as possible.

One former *sannyasin* in the movement, Swami Govinda and

one of the most famous, or rather most notorious devotees, operated a group of 'sankirtan' boys, some fifteen to twenty in number. They operated in both Europe and the Far East. Swami Govinda and his boys were so successful and made so much money that he was reputed to be the wealthiest devotee in the movement. Certainly his quarters in Vrindaban were luxurious and his personal deities expensive.

ISKCON's other enterprises: Spiritual Sky, the restaurants and Three Worlds Travel, are essentially one-man shows and reflect the energy and dynamism of one individual. In England, Spiritual Sky run by Purangana, who began the factory in England. The Three Worlds Travel is directed by Emanuel, the middle-aged eccentric. He buys cheap tickets direct from airlines and sells them to devotees at a profit, and has a reputation in the movement for being rich. In 1979, he set himself up in the restaurant business and rented a sandwich bar in Soho.

Great emphasis is placed on money in the movement. Indeed, whilst ISKCON's symbolic model of social protest is expressed in transcendental beliefs and a non-materialist ethic, the devotees in practice are materialistic in outlook. They are quick to take as much money off outsiders as possible, often using very unsubtle techniques. Of course, too, although it should not be exaggerated, is it not unknown for one devotee to 'rip off' another. In fact, 'transcendental gossip' abounds with tales of these 'rip offs'.

Devotees' materialism is partly due to the way the economic system has developed, particularly the influence of 'sankirtan' and the techniques involved in it. Since obtaining enough money for their needs is always a constant problem and worry they have to continually manipulate which understandably has fostered a materialist attitude. Few, for instance, have the money to pay their train fare from Central London to Bhaktivedanta Manor. Many, particularly the men, use devious means to circumvent paying.

Prabhupad himself encouraged their materialism. Hinduism is, in theory, perhaps one of the most transcendental of all religions. Yet at the same time it is perhaps the most materialist in practice. Popular Hinduism focuses around gift giving to the gods. Though Vaishnavism officially teaches that gifts are to be made to please Krishna without expectation of reward, in practice, gifts are always given on the assumption that they will be returned, hopefully threefold. Like all Hindus, Prabhupad had an element of materialism in him and this appears to have influenced the way he shaped the movement. He encouraged devotees' money-making activities and rewarded the economically successful with high status in the movement.

Great value is placed on being able to make money in the movement. Money and money-making abilities are, as well as the degree of asceticism, the criteria by which devotees judge each other. The movement's emphasis on hierarchy is reflected here too. Devotees rank each other according to the amount of money they make and contribute to the movement. Devotees who are successful at 'doing business' and are wealthy, are attributed high status and prestige. Often they become legends as Dhananjaya and Swami Govinda, and his friend Swami Vrindavan who between them raised a great deal of money for the building of the Krishna Balaram temple in Vrindaban (some £ 5,0000). The latter two were known as the 'Mean Swamis' because of their alleged nefarious activities and their general lack of ethics in 'doing business'. They were looked down on by the more ethical devotees. But, nevertheless, they were highly respected and even hero worshipped by some of the young boys, who were impressed by the swashbuckling life they appeared to lead.

The way devotees rank each other in terms of their money-making abilities clearly indicates, as do all the features of ISKCON's economic structure, how far removed ISKCON is in reality from its ideal of renunciation and its anti-materialist ethic. Far from renouncing western society totally, ISKCON's economic organisation is the capitalist economic structure of western society in microcosm.

CHAPTER SEVEN

Power and the Politics of Asceticism

The International Society for Krishna Consciousness intends to re-establish the true Vedic System of varnashrama, the four classes and four orders of life, whereby each and every person in society works cooperatively according to his own natural position in life so that society may progress on the path of spiritual enlightenment.

—H. K. Diary, 1979: 11

'It's all politics' moaned an erstwhile ISKCON leader who gave up his own leadership position because he could no longer put up with the internal bickering and factionalism that goes on in ISKCON. The Indian manager of the Vrindaban International Guest House complained that 'They all want to be boss' and said that he could not stand being ordered about all the time and having his orders continuously countermanded by other devotees. He found his position so intolerable that after a month as manager he resigned.

Paradoxically, for a movement which condemns the politics of 'karmi' society and which has renounced materialism for a spiritual life, a substantial proportion of devotees appear to spend a great deal of their time playing politics and competing with each other for leadership positions, and for power, influence and control over the decision making processes in ISKCON. Since ISKCON is becoming quite a large and complex organisation and a wealthy movement with substantial resources at its disposal, the leaders have a great deal of power. The rights and privileges that go with leadership roles including the right to control the decision making process, are, of course, attractive and heavily competed for.

The movement is extremely hierarchical. Symptomatic of ISKCON's general pattern of social protest through inversion in contrast to the egalitarian ideals of the Permissive Society, it has introduced as the basis of its internal organisation both the Indian caste system and the four orders of Hindu religious life namely *brahmacharin* (student), *grihastha* (householder), *vanaprastha* (renounced householder) and *sannyasin* (totally renounced celibate). A male devotee is expected to progress gradually during his life through these four stages from being first of all a student of religion, to marriage and a family, afterwards in middleage whilst still a householder to begin a renounced life. Finally, in old age he is expected to renounce the world all together and become a *sannyasin*.

ISKCON has fitted its members' religious and administrative roles into a caste framework. At the top of the traditional four grade caste system is the *Brahmin* or priestly caste. Below it is the *kshatriya* caste to which traditionally warriors and administrators belonged and below them is the *vaishya* or merchant caste. At the bottom of the caste hierarchy is the *shudra* or labouring caste. The administrative roles in ISKCON are considered to belong to the *kshatriya* caste, whilst 'doing business' is categorized as a *vaishya* occupation and work around the temple that of the *shudra* labouring caste.

But there is a crucial difference between ISKCON's interpretation of the caste system and the practical realities of caste in modern India. In India, an individual inherits and is born into a caste. But ISKCON condemns the inheritance of caste affiliation and harks back, as it always does when it wants to reinterpret modern Indian society to fit in with its needs, to Vedic times, when it maintains caste was not inherited but achieved. Thus, whilst ISKCON has a caste system, Brahmin status is not inherited as in modern India, but achieved by demonstration of commitment to spiritual life. In fact, Brahmin status is conferred on all devotees after they have shown that they intend staying in the movement and are willing to obey the rules. Usually after some six to eighteen months.

Indeed in ISKCON this re-interpretation of caste, particularly as it relates to Brahmin status, is a necessity for only Brahmins can traditionally perform rituals (*pujas*) and cook pure food for the deities. Without its own Brahmins the movement would be unable to function for deity worship and *puja* are at the heart of the movement and a central focus.

ISKCON's Vedic interpretation of the caste system is reminiscent of the basic fundamental capitalist idea that a person's position in society is determined by their capabilities; that people are what they are because of their abilities and it is up to individuals what they make of their lives. This belief of course, is at the heart of and justifies the rabid individualism and self interest that provides the basic framework of capitalism. It also, of course, legitimises a devotee's own individualism and competitiveness within the movement.

Nowhere is devotees' individualism more blatantly expressed than in ISKCON's internal politics. It provides the framework within which ISKCON's internal political structure is articulated.

Devotees of course rank each other not only according to their money making abilities but also by their degree of asceticism. Moreover there is a direct correlation between money making abilities in ISKCON and the actual power structure. These abilities are, as in the capitalist 'karmi' world, directly related to leadership including, amazing as it may seem, religious leadership roles.

Power and responsibility accrue to those devotees who make a lot of money for the movement and/or have organising abilities which will contribute towards this end. Those devotees who show a flair for business and organisational ability, are, as in the outside 'karmi' world given positions of responsibility and power e.g. GBC, President, Sankirtan Leaders and so on. Parodying the terminology of the outside world they are referred to as 'managers'. Conversely, if a devotee wants to attain a position of power and prestige in the movement, he must demonstrate a flair for organisation or business or preferably a combination of both, for those who combine both organisational ability with a flair for business attain the most power.

Nearly all those devotees who hold high-ranking positions in ISKCON, including, in particular, the spiritual guides or gurus have at one time or another, demonstrated such talents and abilities. Jayatirtha Maharaj the British guru and GBC is highly respected in the movement as a businessman and is considered particularly expert at real-estate deals. His business expertise is frequently called upon by temples throughout the movement. Prabhupad thought highly of his keen business mind. According to ISKCON mythology, Prabhupad is supposed to have said that he was the 'smartest' devotee in the movement. Because of his business abilities Prabhupad made him an executor of his will, along with Atreya Rishi, a Persian Jewish ex-Harvard Business School Graduate who runs a very successful accountancy business in Teheran. Because of Atreya Rishi's flair for business he became a leading devotee soon after he joined the movement and he has a great deal of influence and say in how the movement uses its finances.

The other leading devotees too have demonstrated their business abilities and organisational talents similarly: Bhaktivedanta Swami who was Prabhupad's private secretary, was not only the initiator of the lucrative 'Radha Damodara Travelling Sankirtan Party' but was involved in numerous other money making projects. Ramesvara Swami, a baby faced twenty six year old who is GBC of the South West Coast of the USA, including the Los Angles temple complex, made his name through organising the finances of BBT very successfully. Hamsaduta Swami, of German American extraction, whose GBC zone is the northern part of the American West Coast and includes the Berkeley and Seattle temples in his region, successfully developed ISKCON in Germany. Kirtanananda Swami on the other hand made his name through the New Vrindaban farming project in West Virginia, which he started and developed.

In Britain, however, because fewer devotees 'do business' on a large scale, the emphasis is on demonstrating organisational abilities as the means of attaining power. But, even in Britain, those devotees who show money-making abilities such as Dhananjaya and Bhaja Hari, have carved out for themselves positions of great power and influence.

ISKCON, particularly in Britain, does not in general attract, by its very nature, the most motivated and competitive people or people with well developed organisational ability, and so does not have a large pool of managerial talent on which to draw. Consequently, anybody who joins ISKCON and shows any sign of drive and managerial and business talent can, and often does, rise to the top of the movement very quickly. In fact in Britain with a few exceptions ISKCON is dominated and controlled by the better-educated who tend to be amongst the most motivated.

Those who are good at doing business and are therefore a potential source of income for the temple, as well as people with organisational talents, can move very easily from one temple to another and are welcomed anywhere. Often, if a manager wants to move to another temple and it is acceptable to his temple authorities, they will arrange a trade with the temple where he wants to go who will send a replacement of equal status.

Power and the Politics of Asceticism

ISKCON is governed by a clearly defined hierarchy of GBC, temple president, temple commander and so on, and its religious life is dominated by the gurus and, as will be seen, by the *sannyasins* too. Because of the nature of ISKCON's economic structure and its emphasis on economic individualism, however, it is an individual devotee's economic pull that really determines his power in the movement—both administrative and religious. In general, real power, both administrative and religious, in the movement is determined by the amount of money and resources an individual actually makes by 'doing business' and/or is able to control through a position such as GBC, temple president, guru or *sannyasin*.

Those GBCs, Presidents, *sannyasins* and gurus who have control over large amounts of money either by 'doing business or because they directly control large temples with large numbers of devotees and concomitantly have big incomes or have access, to temple finances, resources and manpower, which they can utilise as they choose, have real power and influence in the movement for they can use them to control the decision-making process and thus attain power and control in the movement. Those leaders that do not, whilst they have status, prestige and some influence, have no real power or influence on decision making in ISKCON. Thus the GBC's of western temples who have within their zones large temples with many devotees doing 'sankirtan' and concomitantly a large income, such as Jayatirtha Maharaj Bhagavan Goswami (France), Harikesa Swami (Germany), Ramesvara Swami (Los Angeles), Hamsaduta Swami (Berkeley and Seattle), Adikeshvara Swami (New York, Gita Nagari and Boston) and Bhaktivedanta Swami (Houston and Dallas) are all very powerful and influential in the movement. Those leaders who hold vital administrative roles and control the biggest temples with the largest numbers of devotees doing 'sankirtan' as well as being good at 'doing business', themselves as is the case with Jayatirtha Maharaj and Ramesvara Swami are the most powerful of all, because they have the largest resources to draw upon.

Those GBCs and Temple presidents who have status and prestige but no real power tend primarily to be either non-Caucasians or hold positions in the Third world where temples and incomes are small or where they have no real control over the temples finances and man-power resources. The best example is Padma Dasa the GBC of India prior to Prabhupad's death. He is a Bengali in his late thirties who started the movement in Canada.

He is one of the movement's frontmen in India and acts as a buffer between the movement and the wider Indian society. Whilst he is highly respected and has some influence, he has little real control over decision making, for he has no real economic pull because the Indian temples are poor and dependent on the western temples for financial support. Moreover, in practice, the Indian temples are under the control of some of the most powerful western devotees so that he has no direct access to temple funds or resources. Nor does he have his own personal income as he does not control a 'sankirtan' party or 'do business'. As such, he is dependent on handouts from other western devotees for his material needs. As one devotee remarked of him 'He even has to ask for the hundred rupees for his train fare'.

The same factors which determine real power in the administrative structure in ISKCON also underly the religious leadership in the movement namely the *sannyasins* and gurus who are the movement's spiritual guides and represent ISKCON's ascetic ideal. Indeed, in ISKCON, there is a direct relationship between economics and asceticism.

The *sannyasin's* role and its development is an interesting phenomenon in itself. It symbolizes and is the epitome of the 'personal trip' side of ISKCON. It reflects also ISKCON's symbolic rather than actual renunciation of the material world. The *sannyasin's* role is not only the ideal in ISKCON, but, until Prabhupad died, it was the highest pinnacle that a devotee could attain. Ordinary devotees treat the *sannyasins*, who number some twenty, with immense outward respect and adulation, prostrating themselves before them when they pass.

Traditionally, theoretically, in India when an individual takes *sannyasa* he renounces the world and all social ties and encumbrances totally. He literally becomes 'dead to the world'. Though in practice *sannyasins* in actual Hindu sects often tend to be heavily involved in 'this-worldly' affairs. Although ISKCON maintains that they uphold and act out traditional 'vedic' ideals in the movement, ISKCON *sannyasins* do not follow the ideal of renunciation. Ironically, they are often the most materially involved devotees of all in the movement. Generally, they are the most actively involved in 'doing business' and in ISKCON politics. As is the case with the former Swami Govinda of Vrindaban, Swami

Hamsaduta of Berkeley and Seattle and Bhaktivedanta Swami of Dallas and Houston and Swami Ramesvara of Los Angeles. Indeed, the *sannyasins*' role is directly related to the power structure, for they also function as political leaders. The amount of political influence and the control over the decision-making process they have in the movement is, as in the administration of ISKCON, directly related to their economic power and the degree to which they control temple finances and manpower.

Their lack of real asceticism and material involvement is reflected in the way of life they lead. They have much better accommodation, food and clothing than the average devotee and far more money at their disposal. Often they have large incomes. They belong to the jet setting fraternity too, and travel widely on the pretext of preaching or 'doing business' from country to country usually by plane. Indeed, the majority of them are also GBCs and heads of the administrative structure.

To understand why asceticism in ISKCON is so closely linked to the economic structure, it is necessary to examine the way the movement developed and the nature of the young male devotee's commitment to ISKCON in the early years. In the early days of ISKCON the movement was at the height of its function as a vehicle for social protest. The *sannyasin* emphasis on total renunciation and rejection of society was, of course, an ideal symbol for expressing devotees' dislike for and rejection of society and attractive for that reason. Also, so strong was their attachment to Prabhupad that they wanted to be like him as much as possible and so be a *sannyasin* like him. It was the leading devotees, those who had carved out leadership positions by demonstrating money-making and organisational talents, many of whom were presidents and GBCs, who initiated *sannyasin* status. Although traditionally in India individuals are not supposed to take *sannyasa* until they are sixty, after they had had a family life, Prabhupad initiated many who were in their twenties into *sannyasa*. Thus, from the very earliest days, asceticism and power in ISKCON have been closely entwined.

Traditionally, in India, anybody with a spiritual inclination for total renunciation can become a *sannyasin*. In ISKCON, the early link between the *sannyasin* role and leadership has continued. In order to protect their own *sannyasin* status, the leaders of ISKCON only allow other devotees who have also become leaders to become *sannyasins*. Since Prabhupad's death, *sannyasins* have been appointed by the GBCs and the conferring of *sannyasin* status on a devotee is de facto recognition of his leadership status and power in the movement, i. e. of his total involvement in this 'worldly materialism'.

This link between power and asceticism in ISKCON is, of course, clearly demonstrated by the fact that so many of the GBCs and temple presidents are also *sannyasins*. *Sannyasin* roles have such a high status and are only conferred on devotees who are recognised internationally as leaders. Many devotees, motivated by a desire to become powerful leaders, try to get themselves made *sannyasins* as a means to this end.

Within the *sannyasin* group, some of them have more power and influence than others, such as Swami Ramesvara, Swami Govinda, Swami Hamsaduta, Bhaktivedanta Swami and Swami Kirtanananda. A *sannyasin's* degree of power is related to his amount of economic pull, his ability to do business and the degree of control he has over temple finances and manpower resources. Such *sannyasins*, including those just mentioned, have large personal incomes derived from doing business or from their position as GBCs and Presidents of large and rich temples with big financial incomes and large manpower resources. This enables them to control directly the decision-making process in ISKCON and have the most power. Those *sannyasins* who do not 'do business' or do not have direct control over a large temple or access to temple finances and have very little money of their own, whilst they have status and great prestige, have very little real power or say in the movement's affairs, either spiritual or administrative. This is true of the *sannyasins* in the poor Indian temples, such as Swami Jagannatha, the former President of the Vrindaban temple, and Swami Acyutananda, an alleged draft dodger with a very fine singing voice and colourful past, who was at one time President of the Calcutta temple. Although they were temple Presidents, neither had a large income and power base which they could use to influence the decision-making process. Nor did they do business and have a personal income. Jagannatha's lack of real power was clearly indicated after Prabhupad died and Swami Govinda was put in charge of Vrindaban temple. Vrindaban was always chronically short of funds and it was hoped that Swami Govinda would use his own personal wealth to shore up the temple's finances. His first act was to push out Jagannatha from his post as

President and install one of his own men. Jagannatha, having no economic clout of his own and no stable population of devotees to back him up, was unable to withstand him and had to leave.

The appointment of the new gurus as spiritual guides in ISKCON also fits in with this general pattern. They are also directly related to the power and economic structure. Prabhupad was supposed to have made a list and appointed them just before he died, ostensibly because they were considered to be the most spiritual of the devotees and best suited to be in charge of the movement's spiritual welfare. Though some leading devotees dispute this point and state that these appointments were concocted by some of the leading devotees, Prabhupad being too ill at the time to have made any list. In practice, it was the most powerful devotees of all in the movement who were made gurus. Significantly, they were all Americans. Most control or had controlled, the big western temples and, with one exception, Satsavarupa Goswami, they were all GBCs. Indeed, one of the new gurus, Bhaktivedanta Swami, had been Prabhupad's personal secretary until his death and because of his direct access to Prabhupad, had been the most powerful devotee of all. Thus, the appointment of gurus was de facto recognition of the actual power structure in ISKCON.

In fact, the appointment of gurus paralleled that of the existing GBC zones in the West. Thus Jayatirtha Maharaj the GBC of the U.K., was made the guru for Britain; and Bhagavan Goswami the GBC of France, its guru. Indeed GBCs and zones were juggled about and realigned so that GBCs and gurus were coterminus. A guru's area of spiritual authority was thus identical with his GBC regional zone. This realignment resulted in each GBC region of the world having its own guru.

In essence the most powerful devotees shared the temples throughout the world amongst themselves and the most powerful of all were given power bases and control of large rich temples with big resources in the West. Both Bhaktivedanta Swami and Hamsaduta Swami had given up their power bases in the West, sometime prior to Prabhupad's death and had been living a great deal of the time in South Asia. In compensation Bhaktivedanta Swami was given Dallas and Houston and Hamsaduta Swami, Berkeley and Seattle as well as smaller temples in other parts of the world.

Swami Satsvarupa, the only devotee made a guru who was not a GBC, is nonetheless a very powerful and influential devotee.

He had demonstrated organisational and leadership abilities by editing *Back of Godhead* for several years. He is also considered one of the movement's leading intellectuals having written a book on Krishna Consciousness entitled *Readings in Vedic Literature.* Indeed he is in the process of taking over Prabhupad's scholarly role in the movement and at the moment is writing a biography of Prabhupad himself. He is also one of the earliest of Prabhupad's devotees and is highly respected in the movement for having supported it in the early days by taking an outside job. He is also admired for the ascetic life he leads. All these factors contributed to his being made a guru. He followed the zonal pattern of the other gurus when he was appointed and became the guru for the zone of Adikeshvara Swami, the GBC of the New York and Boston temples and Eastern Seaboard.

Adikeshvara Swami was not made a guru even though he was amongst the most powerful devotees controlling as he did the New York temple because he was considered too young, being in his early twenties. Also he was thought of as somewhat flighty besides being involved in a court case at about the time of Prabhupad's death. The other leading devotee who was not made a guru, was Swami Govinda. Prabhupad is supposed to have insisted that he was too unethical and had been involved in too many shady deals to be acceptable as a guru.

Demonstrating that it was the most powerful rather than the most spiritual devotees who became gurus, those *sannyasins* such as Jagannatha, Acyutananda and Brahmananda and those GBSs such as Padma Dasa who were without strong power bases and large personal incomes were not made gurus; much to the chagrin of some of them.

Because politics, like economics and *bhakti* is an 'individualistic trip' in ISKCON it would be misleading to examine each temple and its internal relationships and the relationships it has with other temples alone. It is more revealing to focus on its individual members and to look at its politics internationally.

The ISKCON political system has developed, what can perhaps best be described as a 'big man' system based on 'fiefs' and articulated in terms of patron-client relations. Until Prabhupad's death leading devotees competed with each other on an international basis for the control of temples, financial resources, manpower and the right to make decisions. The degree to which they got control of positions such as GBC and Temple President and gained control of large and rich temples with considerable numbers of devotees, (e.g. Los Angeles, London, New York and Paris) the bigger their power bases and the stronger their control over the decision-making process and the greater their influence over the day to day affairs in the movement. Those leading devotees who were able to combine a leading administrative role with that of a *sannyasin* were further able to consolidate and increase their power and influence because of the high status and respect attributed to the latter in the movement. The same is true of those who were also able to earn a large income by 'doing business'.

By the time of Prabhupad's death some of the leading devotees had begun to develop followings and having a substantial income became a necessity to attract devotees and gain their allegiance. The more devotees whose allegiance they could obtain and attract to their temples the greater their manpower resources and concomitantly the greater their potential incomes. Also the greater the number of devotees owing allegiance to them and living in their temples, the more support they could call upon to back them up in a dispute. Thus they were able to exert more pressure on the movement as a whole. 'Big men' obtained devotees' allegiance for example by providing them with money to set up projects. Also rank and file devotees were always chronically short of money and leading devotees who wanted to attract followings would provide devotees with money, often paying for their travel expenses.

Most 'big men''s followings were centred around the temples they controlled. Generally a devotee owed allegiance to the GBC in whose zone he lived, but this was not always the case. Bhakivedanta Swami had devotees who supported him throughout the movement as did Kirtanananda Swami and Swami Satsvarupa. Economics frequently determined where a devotee lived and since facilities for householders were better in Los Angeles, families tended to congregate there. Nevertheless very frequently devotees who lived there respected and preferred of all the big men Kirtanananda Swami who resides on the eastern seaboard and is widely respected throughout the movement.

The most developed faction in the movement prior to Prabhupad's death was that of Swami Govinda and his followers who operated out of Hong Kong and Japan mostly. They made a great deal of money. Swami Govinda had control of all the money they made and in return for working for him he provided them with a jet set lifestyle and a comfortable, varied and interesting existence.

Swami Govinda is a good example of economic individualism in ISKCON and how in the movement economic power can be translated and converted into political power. He was made GBC and put in charge of the Vrindaban temple when Prabhupad 'passed over' precisely because he was so wealthy and so successful at making money and could afford to maintain Vrindaban.

He used his economic pull in Vrindaban which has no income of its own but also, to squeeze out Dhananjaya who was living at Vrindaban at the time of Prabhupad's death. Dhananjaya was too powerful and influential and far too much of a threat to his own authority to allow him to continue 'doing business' in Vrindaban.

Excluding Dhananjaya and Atreya Rishi, who derived their power from their business abilities, the most powerful devotees in the movement prior to Prabhupad's death were American. The continued dominance of Americans in the movement since Prabhupad's death is due to a number of factors. Firstly, the most powerful leaders in ISKCON have been in the movement from the beginning, since 1967. Some, such as Swami Satsavarupa and Kirtanananda Swami are founding devotees, who attained leadership positions early on and have been able to develop and consolidate their positions over the years as a result of their long-term membership. It was also Americans who spread the movement around the world and developed the movement in foreign countries as did Swami Hamsaduta in Germany. The present American leaders in foreign countries are often the people who built up the movement in these countries. Also, Prabhupad himself favoured Americans —'his American boys' as he referred to them—and he preferred to appoint Americans to the most powerful leadership positions.

Also, the American devotees see the movement as an essentially American one and want to keep it that way, too, and they manipulate the movement to this end. In general, too, the Americans are often more capable leaders and are more motivated to be leaders than devotees of other countries. ISKCON provides them with a means of expressing and using their capabilities. American devotees are a product of American society, a culture that is very 'boss' conscious, and they like, as do many of their country men, to be boss, and enjoy ordering everyone around. ISKCON provides them with the opportunity to do so and some of them become authoritarian.

The appointment of gurus on Prabhupad's death froze the individualistic competition that was going on between leading devotees and institutionalised the status quo and power structure at the time of his death. It gave outright control over the movement to the most powerful American devotees in the movement at the time. Prabhupad stipulated in his will that ISKCON was to remain centralised after his death and was to continue to be governed internationally by the Governing Body Commission comprised of 24 leading devotees. In practice, however, by combining the roles of GBC and Guru, both administrative and spiritual control and outright power fell into the hands of the eleven guru/GBCs who consequently were able to exercise total control over the devotees in their zones. As such they became their own bosses and virtually autonomous. In consequence the Governing Body Commission is little more than a figurehead.

De Facto recognition of the power structure and the appointment of all the most powerful devotees as gurus rather than just one of them, prevented discontent and possible factionalism on the part of those very powerful devotees who were not made gurus. Nevertheless the appointment of eleven new gurus has eventually led to increasing factionalism and fragmentation in the movement. Because in practice a guru's spiritual authority generally coincides with his GBC zone ISKCON's politics to a great extent, have become zonal. It has led to the development of eleven autonomous fiefs. Each guru has his own fief which is coextensive with his GBC zone. Swami Satsavarupa too by joining up with Adikesvara Swami has developed his own fief, on the Eastern Seaboard.

A number of other factors have also helped establish clearly defined boundaries between fiefs and fostered increasing fragmentation in the ISKCON. Whilst Prabhupad was alive new devotees were initiated by him. After his death one of the major reasons for appointing gurus, and one of their main functions, is to initiate new devotees. In theory a new devotee can ask to be initiated by any guru in the movement anywhere in the world. But in practice they take initiation from the guru in whose zone they reside which of course further emphasises, delineates and consolidates a guru's fief.

Long-term devotees are unwilling to accept erstwhile peers as their gurus and have got round this problem by stating that their guru is still Prabhupad and their spiritual allegiance is to him but they nonetheless accept the authority of the guru in whose zone they live. Those devotees who did not like the 'big man' who was appointed to be the guru and GBC of their zone moved out when he took over. The allegiance of all the devotees in a zone to the zone guru has further emphasised and demonstrated boundaries between the fiefs. Factionalism has begun between the gurus too for they are all competing to attract devotees into their fiefs which is leading to further fragmentation of the movement.

In the past the focus of all devotees throughout the world on Prabhupad provided a major unifying factor in the movement. Since his death, however, a devotee's focus and frame of reference has become his guru. In the past devotees chatted incessantly about Prabhupad and sang his praises all day long. Now, they sing the praises of, and identify with, their zone's guru. Indeed a strong sense of solidarity and in-group identification is developing around the new gurus and their fiefs. Devotees spend so much time singing the praises of their own gurus that many devotees find living in fiefs other than their own guru's uncomfortable, so strong is the emphasis on the zone's guru. In fact it is assumed that a devotee will want to live in their guru's zone so that he can share in singing his praises and worshipping him. Each fief has begun to produce *Sri Vyasa Puja books* in honour of the Appearance Day (birthday) of the guru and the eulogies are just as fulsome as those to Prabhupad; all of which of course has led to the fiefs becoming both inward-looking and self-sustaining.

The new gurus vary in personality type. The more sincere and serious minded devotees tend to admire and respect the ascetic and saintly Swamis Kirtanananda and Satsvarupa Swami whose way of life they feel is closer to the movement's ideal. Whilst they tend to consider Bhaktivedanta Swami, notorious for his politicking, to be too 'political' to be acceptable as a spiritual guide. Hamsaduta Swami, known as the 'King of Kirtan' in the movement, is a fine singer and musician, accomplishments which are highly admired in the movement. He also has a reputation for leading a very exciting life and the young *brahmacharins* hero worship him. When he moved to Berkeley after Prabhupad's death a number of them moved to be with him and he paid for some of their travel.

Jayatirtha Maharaj is of course one of the most highly respected of all devotees and has one of the most powerful and important fiefs in the whole of ISKCON. Not only does he control the British movement, but also the Chicago and Detroit temples, as well as

ISKCON in South Africa.

The Detroit temple is of particular significance, for it is in this temple that the grandson of Henry Ford resides. He, in fact, bought the Detroit temple, a palatial mansion, for the movement. Jayatirtha Maharaj has been able to use his friendship with Amburisha to further consolidate his sphere of influence. It is Amburisha who has agreed to fund the Waxwork Museum to be built in Detroit. In so doing he has increased Jayatirtha Maharaj's sphere of influence, since all the FATE devotees have given over their allegiance to Jayatirtha Maharaj and he has become their guru.

Jayatirtha Maharaj was sent by Prabhupad to take over and organise the British movement in 1975. The fact that someone as powerful as Jayatirtha Maharaj controls the British ISKCON has had significant consequences for its development and the role it plays in the movement as a whole. Jayatirtha Maharaj provides a clear example of the continued international domination of Americans in ISKCON, even in countries such as Britain where there are large numbers of native born devotees.

Prabhupad in his will made many of the GBCs, GBC for life, including Jayatirtha Maharaj. Prior to Prabhupad's death, ISKCON leaders tended to move around and change jobs a great deal, but inheriting control permanently over their zones, had a decisive effect on GBCs mobility. GBCs including Jayatirtha Maharaj were no longer able to move around as much as before. Thus, Jayatirtha Maharaj's future, to a great extent, is in Britain, particularly as the British movement is by far the largest and richest part of his fief.

Having an American as guru and GBC in Britain has its advantages for British devotees. Like devotees everywhere, British devotees compete a great deal for leadership positions. By excluding the chief position from such competition it has prevented rivalry amongst British devotees—an important factor in itself for competition over this role might have led to factionalism and the breakup of the movement in Britain.

Jayatirtha Maharaj not only reigns in Britain, but he rules too. He has carved himself out a very strong position in the British movement and is highly respected. To prevent his isolation, to consolidate his position and to prevent British devotees from getting too much control and taking over the movement informally, he has brought in a few Americans to act as a buffer between him and the British devotees. He put one of them in charge of the Healthy, Wealthy and Wise restaurant.

As yet in 1977 none of the British devotees is a real threat to his position anyway. None of them could do his job properly, or have the capabilities to do so. In ISKCON politics it is the fittest who survive, which means that it is the most able and capable devotees who get to the top, as is the case with Jayatirtha Maharaj. He has done an excellent job as GBC and guru in Britain and it is due to his capabilities and organisational power that the movement has developed and expanded so successfully. Indeed it was the acquisition of Bhaktivedanta Manor in 1974 which provided the turning point, the real 'take off' point, in the movement in Britain, for it provided ISKCON with a very attractive setting and housing for a large number of devotees which it had not had previously. It was Jayatirtha Maharaj who organised the redecoration and furnishing of the manor. He reorganised it on more efficient lines and made it the success it has become. He is shrewd too and has used his good business sense to start projects which have provided the basis of British ISKCON's economic success. He also has style and good taste. He chose the decor for Healthy, Wealthy and Wise. Both it and the Manor present a good image of ISKCON to the outside world. Most importantly he is an excellent role player and carries off the role of guru with élan and style—no mean feat for a thirty year old college drop-out.

For their part the British devotees are only too willing to accept Jayatirtha Maharaj as their guru. Like ISKCON devotees everywhere British devotees were very worried about what would happen after Prabhupad died and are only too pleased to have someone like Jayatirtha Maharaj as their guru who performs the role so well. They know that there is no one in Britain as yet who could take up this position. Indeed, not only did they play up to his guru role for all they are worth, but in Britain, as in other countries, they actively connived and helped him develop his saintly guru role. Devotees go out of their way to act towards him as they did towards Prabhupad. Bhaja Hari, one of the leading British devotees at Jayatirtha Maharaj's first Appearance Day ritual for instance acted as Master of Ceremonies. He read the eulogies himself and organised the devotees so that they played their roles properly. He reminded one of a vicar's wife organising everyone at a summer fete!

However, because Jayatirtha Maharaj is dependent on the British movement for much of his power and income, he will have to take into account British devotees' needs and aspirations for fear of alienating them when he makes decisions and embarks on projects. His influential position in the movement as a whole means that the British movement will be able to exert a great deal of influence over the whole decision-making process and the way the movement develops in the future. Any future increase or decrease in his power in the movement will have a backlash on the British movement and effect the course it will take.

Jayatirtha Maharaj, and the gurus in general in ISKCON, represent the epitome of the individualistic trip theme that runs throughout ISKCON. They have reached the pinnacle that individualism can obtain in ISKCON, the control of the other devotees and the decision-making process.

At this stage it is difficult to predict the future course of ISKCON politics. Most thinking devotees hope that a new spiritual master will 'emerge' as they put it, from the ranks of the new gurus and take over informal control of and unite the ISKCON movement once more. Both Satsavarupa Swami and Swami Kirtanananda, whose ascetic way of life commands the respect of most devotees, are frequently pointed to by thinking devotees as the gurus they would most like to see with overall control of the movement. However since the gurus are competing with each other it is possible, as the gurus get further and further entrenched in their fiefs, that factionalism will become so strong that the movement will fragment: the gurus will no longer bother to pay lip service to the Governing Body Commission and will become totally autonomous. Some perhaps will even hive off completely and start separate movements. On the other hand, one of the gurus with the strongest power base and the strongest economic pull such as Jayatirtha Maharaj or Ramesvara Swami, may 'emerge' as the overall spiritual master of ISKCON. The next few years may tell. So far, however, the gurus have managed to control their factionalism and do not appear to be abusing their power to any great extent. In terms of power they appear to balance each other out, preventing any one guru from increasing his power to such an extent that he has been able to take over informal control of the movement or exploit the devotees to any degree. In fact the new gurus seem to be cleaning up and reforming ISKCON. Within a year or so of Prabhupad's death for instance they appear to have forced out Swami Govinda, whose shady deals they felt would bring the movement into disrepute. They appear, particularly in Britain, to be beginning to reintegrate the movement into the wider 'karmi' society.

Clearly ISKCON has come a long way politically from its hippy days in the Haight Ashbury. Within its framework of rampant individualism it has developed a highly complex and sophisticated political structure. But by combining political leadership with asceticism and spirituality from its earliest days, ISKCON has prevented the movement's renunciatory ascetic and anti-materialist ideal from being anything more than a purely symbolic statement of intent. Politically it has just made ISKCON a parody of the outside 'karmi' society.

CHAPTER EIGHT

'I Am Not My Body, I Am Spirit-Soul'

> We're not these skin-and-boney bags,
> But are the souls within;
> Yet, brandishing false fleshy flags,
> We flap with squalid sin
>
> —Citraketu VPB, 1977: 188, Bhaktivedanta Manor

ISKCON's emphasis on individualism, its capitalism, its competitive structure—which imitate traditional western culture—and the close involvement of its social, economic and political institutions with 'karmi' society, demonstrate that the movement's rejection of western culture is symbolic rather than actual. It is a personal rejection in the minds of devotees. ISKCON's replacement of western culture with that of 'Vedic' culture is a symbolic interpretation of reality and provides a 'sacred canopy', albeit an imported one.

Symbolic thought is, of course, a process common to mankind. As Lewis (1977: 1) states:

> The pervasive use of symbols is one of the most distinctive of all human attributes. By "symbols" we mean, of course, something more than signs. Unlike the latter which may be so, symbols are in principle never fully self-explanatory, self-sufficient or fully autonomous...symbols act characteristically as agents, deferentially 'standing', as the phrase has it, 'for something else'. They both reveal and conceal, pointing towards, if not fully disclosing, a different order of reality and experience. Symbols thus are by definition, mysterious. As with that epitome of the essence of the symbolic, perfume, ...they are at once evocative and suggestive, redolent with significance. Symbolism consequently becomes a kind of sign language or semaphore, a code which is only intelligible once you have discovered the key.

Symbols, which may be expressed verbally and/or in ritual and action, are used by people to express their desires, hopes, motivations and experience as well as knowledge and truth. They use symbols to express and interpret reality and to say something about themselves and their positions in it. Symbols thus supply individuals with the means of understanding, imagining and expressing the world and coming to terms with it, and endowing it with significance and order. Symbols, as a means of interpreting reality and society, provide individuals with a means of controlling their own destiny. Symbols stand for something else, generally for something of greater significance than the object or action itself—they express truths that cannot be expressed directly. They offer the means of expressing truths indirectly, or on a level of reality other than that directly open to the senses, i.e. concrete fact. Symbolism is thus, as Lewis says, like a language or code, which it is necessary to decode if it is to be understood.

An examination of the symbolism embedded in ISKCON's world renouncing philosophy and belief system is highly illuminating. Indeed, to understand ISKCON's philosophy, ritual and social organisation, it is important to study the symbols it uses—especially the symbols which devotees use, both to describe and order reality and make statements about themselves and their relationships to society. The way devotees interpret what they do and think in symbolic terms, the way they use and manipulate symbols and the concomitant ritual in their daily lives tell us a great deal about them and the existential and social problems that confront them to as well as their attitudes to the wider society in general.

Judah (1974: 78) maintains that the lives devotees lead is perhaps a more important attraction than the movement's world-renouncing Krishna Consciousness philosophy itself. Johnson (1973: 43-44) in his study of the Haight Ashbury temple, comparing full-time devotees with regular visitors states: 'For both groups, the mantra seemed to be the primary force compelling their participation. The ideology, on the other hand, seemed to be a backdrop, a fortification of the primary purpose of the movement: the performance of the mantra (by which he means 'kirtan'). Certainly, Judah and Johnson's view that the philosophy is less important than the social life that ISKCON offers does not appear to hold nowadays, for by 1979, the philosophy had become a very significant frame of reference for devotees. Indeed, it has become the basic framework of the movement and the importance attached to it and its role and structure is crucial to understanding the nature of the movement as a whole and its symbolic form.

Unlike most of the other new eastern religious sects, most of which have developed relatively simple philosophies, the philosophy is spelt out in great detail in ISKCON's belief system and devotees are continuously made aware of it in their daily lives. In fact, it has great influence on the devotees and structures their thought, behaviour and ritual system, and plays an all important and pervasive role in the movement. ISKCON and the devotees themselves attach great importance to Krishna Consciousness, and the scriptures. Its form, content, nature and development also tend to suggest that this was so from the earliest days of the movement.

Prabhupad's selling of himself to the devotees as a scholar and authority on the scriptures and his own stress on the importance of philosophy, as well as the devotees' own aspirations and desire to emulate him are, of course, important and decisive reasons for the great weight attached to dogma in ISKCON. But the importance of belief and philosophy in ISKCON is also due to Prabhupad's books and his literary output and the part they play in the movement. Since most devotees had little contact with Prabhupad himself, they acquainted themselves with his teachings through his books. As such, it is his books rather than Prabhupad himself which provided the basic framework of the movement's belief system and this was to have crucial significance on the development and role of belief in ISKCON.

Prabhupad's books, of course, underpin ISKCON's economic structure. It is no accident that the development in importance and complexity of ISKCON's belief structure went hand in hand with the development of book publishing as the focus of the movement's economy. The setting up and rapid expansion of the Bhaktivedanta Book Trust, and the establishment of book sales as the movement's major source of income had widespread repercussions within the movement, not only on ISKCON's social organisation but on the form, function and degree of importance of ISKCON's world view. As books became the movement's major source of income and means of proselytizing Krishna Consciousness, an understandably great emphasis was placed on the scriptures and Prabhupad's books in particular as a means of justifying the marketing of books.

The publication of vast quantities of books and devotees' degree of contact with them have helped to deepen the belief in ISKCON. One of the most noticeable things about ISKCON temples is the all-pervasiveness of books. ISKCON devotees come into contact a great deal with doctrinal literature in their everyday lives. Devotees are very proud of Prabhupad's literary output and in most temples they are put in cabinets on prominent display. Large quantities are stacked everywhere, ready for distribution in the streets. This constant contact with books alone impresses devotees with their importance—with the importance of their content, i.e. Krishna Consciousness. Selling books on the street also brings devotees into contact with the philosophy, since it seems reasonable to assume that natural curiosity would make them at least thumb through them at some point.

Knowledge of the philosophy and its importance is brought home to devotees at the Bhagavad Gita classes held every morning and evening in all temples, at which Prabhupad's books are read and sermons given on Krishna Consciousness philosophy. Devotees also come constantly into contact with the philosophy through ritual enactment of it at the *arati* ceremonies. Preaching to visitors and to members of the public during 'sankirtan', as well as chanting 'japa' which devotees do at odd moments throughout the day, also help keep Krishna and the philosophy in their minds constantly.

In fact, of course, *bhakti yoga* demands that all thought and action should be performed in the service of Krishna. Devotees are expected to talk and glorify Krishna at all times. Idle gossip is frowned upon. It is indeed remarkable the extent to which even small talk revolves around Krishna or some aspect of the philosophy in ISKCON temples. In such an environment where devotees are bombarded with the philosophy all day, it is not surprising that it should continually impinge on devotees' consciousness and become their primary frame of reference and orientation and that they should consider the philosophy all important and that it should develop a central role and function in the movement.

The amount devotees actually know about Krishna Consciousness, however, varies considerably. All devotees can quote, in Sanskrit, long passages of the *Bhagavad Gita* by heart. However, only one or two have actually attempted to learn Sanskrit or Bengali, the other language of the Gaudiya scriptures. Many, particularly some of the less educated English devotees, find the philosophical intricacies of the *Bhagavad Gita* and the *Shrimad Bhagavata* difficult to comprehend. They rely instead on *Back to Godhead*, which is in simpler prose and much easier to understand, for obtaining knowledge of the philosophy. But a surprisingly large number of devotees, particularly long-term 'advanced' devotees, are extremely knowledgeable about Vaishnava culture.

In fact, the standard of knowledge attained by the intellectual elite in ISKCON would not put a student of Hinduism to shame. It is no accident that ISKCON devotees are far more knowledgeable in general about Hinduism than followers of any of the other eastern religions.

Reflecting the importance and emphasis attached to philosophy in ISKCON and its basis as a continual frame of reference, devotees, regardless of their degree of knowledge, are only too willing to discuss philosophy whenever the opportunity arises. They will immediately start a philosophical discussion with any stranger who comes to the temple or anybody they meet in the street who appears interested. Indeed, Krishna Consciousness philosophy provides the basis for this interaction with the outside world.

Although social organisation varies to some degree from temple to temple, Krishna Consciousness philosophy is uniform in temples throughout the world and variation is minimal from country to country. This has had significant consequences for the role the philosophy plays in ISKCON. Uniformity of belief in ISKCON is fostered by a number of factors. Prabhupad's teachings, being considered divinely revealed—*shruti*—are held to be true, infallible and to supersede all other beliefs. Other points of view, including the teachings of the other Vaishnava sects, are considered irrelevant and devotees are actually discouraged from reading any other literature than Prabhupad's. Although some devotees are also knowledgeable about Vaishnava religion and culture, as seen through Prabhupad's eyes, they are ignorant about any other Indian philosophy.

Prabhupad's books also foster uniformity of belief and help retain the integrity of his teachings. Although most devotees had little contact with him, all his books were available to them. This discouraged the development of personal interpretations of his teachings and any diversity of belief, for whenever a point of controversy arose or any idiosyncratic interpretation was suggested, devotees referred to his books to solve it. Even after Prabhupad's death, the integrity of his teachings has been maintained because of everybody's direct access to his books.

Bhaktivedanta Book Trust, too, only publishes Prabhupad's works and those of leading devotees such as Swami Satsavarupa's *Readings in Vedic Literature,* and scientific studies of the Bhaktivedanta Institute, which endorse Prabhupad's teachings uncritically. Even those countries, such as Britain, that have set up their own Bhaktivedanta Book Trust, follow the same policy as the parent organisation. Thus, all devotees throughout the world come into contact with the same literature. Lack of contact with other philosophies and books which might be critical of or undermine Prabhupad's teachings has, of course, fostered and helped maintain uniformity of belief in ISKCON, as has the forbidding of criticism of Prabhupad's teachings by devotees. Thus, Prabhupad's teachings and the belief system in general are very strongly insulated against any kind of criticism which might undermine it.

Homogeneity of belief in ISKCON has also been attained by excluding the philosophy of Krishna consciousness from internal politics, the all-consuming passion of many devotees. Since Prabhupad's teachings are considered ultimate truth and criticism of them is forbidden, individual devotees have not been able to use differences in interpretation as a political weapon and as a basis for factionalism. Since Prabhupad's death, this has become an increasingly important factor in helping prevent the fragmentation of the movement.

It is no coincidence that ISKCON has developed so rapidly and attached such importance to such a detailed uniform and all-encompassing world view which covers a wide area of thought and action or that ISKCON governed by a detailed set of rules rather than being a strongly ethical movement. Indeed, it has had significant consequences for the form and role that belief plays in ISKCON.

Moreover, ISKCON's belief system is expressed in a very complex and detailed ritual system, whose development significantly went hand in hand with that of the belief system. As with the belief system, great importance is attached to ritual in the movement, the performance of which takes up a great deal of the devotees' daily routine. Devotees are, in fact, obsessive ritualists. They place greater emphasis on ritual and follow it far more closely than do traditional Hindus. They have expanded and embellished traditional Vaishnava rituals. For instance, the ceremony of bathing and clothing the deities in the morning has been extended from the perfunctory few minutes it takes in the traditional Vaishnava system to over an hour and a half in ISKCON—they have invented new rituals. Devotees invent rituals at the drop of a hat. Anything they do they tend to embellish with ritual. This emphasis on obsessive ritualism in ISKCON, particularly as young people nowadays tend to be extremely antiritualistic and dismissive of it, tends to suggest that there must be some reason for this ritualism and because of its importance in ISKCON any account of the movement to be meaningful, must necessarily attempt to explain this fact. It seems reasonable to conclude, that ISKCON's belief system and concomitant ritual system have developed in the manner they have precisely because they have an important symbolic role and function in the movement.

Beneath the apparent 'gobblygook' superstructure of Krishna Philosophy and mythology, a symbolic world view exists. This symbolic model of the universe and society and social relations provides an interpretive frame of reference for devotees and offers an ideal vehicle for social protest. It is a meaningful frame of reference for the kinds of frustrated people who join ISKCON and it has become a major focus of attention precisely for this reason.

The total homogeneity of the belief system, and the devotees' interpretation of it, have had crucial consequences for the development of the form and content of ISKCON's symbolic model of the world and social relations. Because there is no inbuilt conflict of belief or fragmentation of philosophy, ISKCON has been able to build up within its system of belief and ritual a unitary uniform symbolic system in which the parts are complexly and tightly interwoven in a highly structured and organised manner. The set of detailed rules which govern wide areas of behaviour has also helped foster this highly structured symbolic world views.

In a belief system governed by ethics, there would, because of argument over what is 'right' and what is 'wrong', be fragmentation of philosophy and deviation from the norm and symbolic unity and coherence would be difficult to achieve in the symbolic world view. But in a rule-governed system of belief like ISKCON's, the rules are the same for everybody and everybody is expected to conform to them; this has helped foster coherence and uniformity within the symbolic system.

Uniformity of belief in ISKCON moreover has meant that the symbolic model of the world and social relations is applicable to all devotees and can be utilised by all devotees and applied to a wide variety of occasions and contexts. This symbolic world view, because of its unitary structure and lack of internal conflict, has been able to develop a close correlation with devotees' needs and social situations. As such it offers an ideal basis for action and for solving the problems confronted by them in their daily lives.

To demonstrate this, let us now examine the content of ISKCON's symbolic model of the world and social relations. From the totality of Gaudiya Matha beliefs and practices, ISKCON has extrapolated and laid great weight on one concept which is focused around the individual and interpreted individualistically and personally, namely 'I am not my body, I am spirit-soul'. As with the rest of ISKCON philosophy, it is a common belief shared by all devotees in all temples throughout the world. It is, in fact, the focal concept of the movement and greater weight is attached to it than any other. Moreover, it provides the framework of the symbolic world view embedded in ISKCON philosophy and provides the blueprint for ritual and symbolic action. For devotees, it is fundamental to belonging to the movement to know that 'you are not your body, you are spirit-soul'; and it is one of the first principles of ISKCON philosophy a neophyte learns. It frequently occurs in devotees' conversations. When they talk to visitors, it is soon introduced into the conversation. Whenever leading devotees give public speeches, such as at the Rathyatra Festival held annually in July, a discussion of it always provides an integral part of the speech. Reference is often made to it in ISKCON literature, particularly in *Back to Godhead*.

When devotees were asked for the source of the concept 'I am not my body, I am spirit-soul', they all pointed to the same *shlokas* (verses) Chapter 2 of in the *Bhagavad Gita As It Is* with which they all appeared to be very familiar.

S: 13 As the embodied soul continually passes, in this body, from boyhood to youth, and then to old age, the soul similarly passes into another body at death. The self-realised soul is not bewildered by such a change.

S: 20 For the soul there is never birth nor death. Nor, having once been, does he ever cease to be. He is unborn, eternal, ever-existing, undying and primeval. He is not slain when the body is slain.

S: 22 As a person puts on new garments, giving up old ones, similarly, the soul accepts new material bodies, giving up the old and useless ones.

S: 12 Never was there a time when I did not exist, nor you, nor all these kings; nor in the future shall any of us cease to be.

When devotees say that they are 'spirit-soul', they maintain they are referring to the eternal soul (*atma*) or (*jiva*) which, in Krishna Consciousness, is believed to reside in the heart of man. Some of the more philosophically oriented devotees are aware of the fallacy of identifying *atma* with the western concept of soul. But nevertheless, devotees do think of themselves as 'spirit-soul', as the concept '*I* am spirit-soul' clearly indicates.

Traditional Vaishnavas do not place such emphasis on these body/soul beliefs particularly that of the body/soul dichotomy. They do not play such an important part in their everyday life or conversation as it does in ISKCON. Nor do traditional Vaishnavas focus the body/soul dichotomy around the individual or express it verbally as, 'I am not my body, I am spirit-soul'. In traditional Vaishnavism, the emphasis is more on the devotional, rather than the philosophical side of religion. More emphasis is placed on 'surrender to Krishna and devotional service than on the intricacies of philosophy. Traditionally, the accent is on the manipulative side of worship, the individual asking for and depending on the Godhead for help. But for ISKCON, the body/soul dichotomy 'I am not my body, I am spirit-soul', provides the focal concept and basic framework for the movement's philosophy and is part and parcel of everyday life. Although it may appear only a minor deviation, to emphasise this concept and interpret it in the manner they have, devotees have radically reinterpreted traditional Vaishnava philosophy.

When devotees state that, 'I am not my body, I am spirit-soul', they mean that the body is purely a vehicle for the soul. Krishna Consciousness philosophy maintains that human beings falsely identify themselves with their bodies—they think and act as though their bodies really were their actual selves rather than a covering for their real self, namely their soul. ISKCON views false identification with the body and bodily senses as the root and cause of all man's problems, for the movement holds that it leads to a desire for 'sense gratification' and forces the individual into *maya*. Material life and the body in ISKCON are equated with *maya* and just as material life is considered a disease, so too the body is considered a feature of that disease. Only by controlling bodily desire for sense gratification and overcoming false identification with the body, Krishna Consciousness states, can an individual obtain self-realisation and realise his original God Consciousness and true relationship with the Supreme Personality of Godhead, namely that of servant and loving devotee of Krishna. An examination of a few of the usages of 'I am not my body, I am spirit-soul' and the way the concept is articulated in ISKCON will demonstrate this point.

Back to Godhead is an excellent barometer and indicator of belief and practices that are important to devotees. Unlike Prabhupad's books, *Back to Godhead* is edited and written by devotees themselves. It thus reflects their own points of view and attitudes and what they consider important and significant in Prabhupad's teachings. It is read by devotees throughout the world and, except for the *Bhagavad Gita*, is for some of them, the only direct contact they have with ISKCON philosophy. It is primarily from *Back to Godhead* that they learn about Krishna Consciousness philosophy and *Back to Godhead* therefore has a great deal of influence on devotees' beliefs. *Back to Godhead* thus provides them with knowledge of the philosophy whilst at the same time expressing and articulating their own interpretation of it.

Very often articles in *Back to Godhead* take the form of an interview between Prabhupad and some notable, e.g. Cardinal Danielou, or a discussion with some prominent devotee about the philosophy of some famous philosopher, e.g. Schopenhauer, Plato, or St. Thomas Aquinas. They are either fabricated or resumés of actual interviews and are used for the purpose of providing a vehicle for explaining ISKCON philosophy and for disposing of any point of view which appears to contradict it. Significantly, nearly all of them contain references to the belief, 'I am not my body, I am spirit-soul'. For instance, Prabhupad (BIG UK Vol. I, No 1, p 6) in an interview with Mike Robinson of London Broadcasting maintained:

> The first thing is to understand that you are a spirit-soul. And because you are a spirit-soul, you are changing your body. This is the ABC of spiritual understanding. So, when your body is finished, annihilated, you are not finished. You get another body, just as you may change your coat and shirt. If you come to me

tomorrow wearing a different shirt and a different coat, does that mean you are a different person? No. Similarly, each time you die you change bodies, but *you*, the spirit-soul within the body, remain the same. This point has to be understood: then one can make further progress in the science of Krishna Consciousness. People are suffering because they misunderstand themselves to be their bodies. If you think that you are your coat and shirt, and you very carefully wash the coat and shirt but you forget to eat, but will you be happy?

Secondly, a major point made by Bhaktivedanta Swami in an article he wrote on ISKCON's role in India was:

> We understand from the Vedic literature that the living being is not actually his material body; he is the spiritual soul within the body. That spiritual soul is eternal but because of material desires, he's taking birth in one body after another, in various species of life. The body is temporary and, after the death of the body, according to one's consciousness, he takes a new body. In this way, the living being takes body after body in 8,400,000 species of life, until gradually he comes to the human form. Then in the human form, one gets the opportunity to cultivate spiritual consciousness, or God consciousness, and the perfection of that God consciousness, is to get free from this cycle of birth and death by becoming a pure devotee of Krsna, and going back home to Godhead. But even if one doesn't achieve that perfection, if one makes only partial advancement on the path, he still gets to come back again in another human body and continue from where he left off.

Brahmananda Swami a fat ex-college wrestler and one of the first devotees, said referring to a lecture given by Prabhupad in Nairobi in an article he wrote on ISKCON in Africa:

> Then he spoke about the meaning of human life. He said that the real aim of human life is to understand that we are not this body but pure spirit-soul, and that our duty is to serve the Supreme Lord, Sri Krishna. (BTG. Vol. 10, No. 12, p 14)

Such importance do devotees attach to this belief ('I am not this body, I am spirit-soul') that at the Mind and Body Festival in 1978 where ISKCON had a stall, it was the first point in a precis of their philosophy written on a poster and placed in a prominent place at the back of the stall. 'The ABC of spiritual life is to know that you are not your body you are spirit-soul' it said. Indeed, this belief has been included in the 'Eight basic principles of Krishna Consciousness philosophy', a short precis of ISKCON philosophy, which in the last two years has frequently been published at the front of *Back to Godhead*.

The second point in this short statement of ISKCON philosophy is:

> We are not our bodies but eternal spirit souls, parts and parcels of God (Krishna). As such, we are all brothers and Krishna is ultimately our common father.[1]

Indicating the importance devotees attach to this belief (it is in fact one of the few real references to a philosophical concept made in the eight basic principles). The fact that it is placed second demonstrates the importance attached to it. Indeed, given the greater influence *Back to Godhead* has in the movement (for those who read little else, it *is* ISKCON philosophy), the frequency of the publication of this short statement of ISKCON philosophy in it is, perhaps, a major reason for its all pervasive influence and why all devotees see this concept as central to ISKCON philosophy.

Even the Hare Krishna *mahamantra* is interpreted in the movement in terms of 'I am not my body, I am spirit-soul'. This is clear from the comment (see p. 61) of Jnana dasa, the Oxford graduate

---

[1] The other basic principles are:

(*i*) By sincerely cultivating a bona fide spiritual science, we can be free from anxiety and come to a state of pure, unending, blissful consciousness in this lifetime. (*iii*) Krishna is the eternal, all knowing, omnipresent, all-powerful, and all attractive Personality of Godhead. He is the seed-giving father of all living beings, and he is the sustaining energy of the entire cosmic creation. (*iv*) The Absolute Truth is contained in all the great scriptures of the world. However, the oldest known revealed scriptures in existence are the Vedic scriptures, most notably the *Bhagavad Gita*, which is the literal record of God's actual words. (*v*) We should learn the Vedic knowledge from a genuine spiritual master—one who has no selfish motives and whose mind is firmly fixed on Krishna. (*vi*) Before we eat, we should offer to the Lord the food that sustains us. Then Krishna becomes the offering and purifies us. (*vii*) We should perform all our actions, as offerings to Krishna and do nothing for our own sense gratification. (*viii*) The recommended means for achieving the nature stage of Love of God in this age of Kali, or quarrel, is to chant the holy names of the Lord. The easiest method for most people is to chant the Hare Krishna mantra.

'I Am Not My Body, I Am Spirit-Soul'

mentioned previously at the lecture he gave on the basic principles of ISKCON philosophy at the Mind and Body Festival in 1978. Generally *sat* is translated in English as 'existence', 'being', 'what really is', *chit* as 'consciousness' and *ananda* as 'bliss'. They are terms central to Vaishnava philosophy, but when discussing the Hare Krishna *maha mantra,* Jnana dasa interpreted *sat* as the *'energy by which we realise that we are not these material bodies, we are eternal spirit-souls'* and he went on to interpret *chit* and *ananda* in terms of ISKCON philosophy too.

The concept, 'I am not my body, I am spirit-soul' and the quotations cited make it clear that devotees vehemently reject, and disassociate themselves from, their bodies. In fact, they speak of their bodies as though they are separate from themselves. When I asked Steve, an art college graduate and one time part-time devotee who has since 'blooped', how he knew he was not his body, he replied:

> I don't think I'm my body. It really came home to me in India. I saw this stiff corpse of an old man being buried. He was so stiff—his body obviously wasn't the person he was before he died. The body is always changing. I look at photos of myself when I was seven. I know I'm not the same person. I know I'm spirit soul.

Steve's answer, his pointing to the ageing process of the body to demonstrate that human beings are not their bodies, is one frequently given by devotees when questioned on this point.

So, too, did Prubhupad, so perhaps it originated with him. Whatever the case, emphasising the ageing process of the body is an important focus of attention in ISKCON. It is used to demonstrate the difference between the body and soul.

Visakha and her husband, Yadubhara Dasa have made a film entitled *Spark of Life,* the theme of which (significantly that devotees like best and feel best able to relate to) focuses on the body/soul dichotomy. It attempts to prove that an individual is not his body, he is spirit-soul, and, to demonstrate this point, includes clips of the body at various stages of life from embryo to old age.

This concept is also reflected in ISKCON art. One of ISKCON's most famous artists has painted a picture of the human body at various stages of life from babyhood to old age to skeleton. It is from this picture that the film-makers appear to have got their idea for including clips of the ageing process in their film.

So well known and influential has this picture become that a copy of it, some six feet long, was made by English devotees which was used as the backcloth for ISKCON stall at the Mind and Body Festival in 1978. FATE, in their Los Angeles waxwork exhibition, has reproduced this picture and made it the central waxwork showpiece in the museum.

A major reason perhaps for the quick development of the belief 'I am not my body, I am spirit-soul' and devotees' rapid acceptance of it, lies in the former drug-taking past of the early American devotees. Out-of-body experiences are quite common features of LSD trips. Individuals, whilst 'high' on LSD often feel they are floating outside of their bodies. Thus, the idea that body and self are separate would be perfectly acceptable to an ex-acid head. A concept such as 'I am not my body, I am spirit-soul' would provide

a meaningful frame of reference for interpreting previous drug experiences and the latter would give credence to the concept too. In fact, Judah (1974: 131) carried out a survey in the Haight Ashbury and Los Angeles temple of devotees' drug experiences. Thirteen per cent significantly reported that whilst under the influence of acid they felt that 'they were not a body, but spirit or pure consciousness'. Significantly, they describe their experiences in terms of self-realisation; the focus of Krishna Consciousness. The fact that this concept—'I am not my body, I am spirit-soul'—is used so often and provides an interpretive scheme for such a wide variety of occasions and events, indicates its importance to devotees. Indeed, it provides the basic framework for the total interpretive scheme in ISKCON and the rule of thumb by which all actions are evaluated and expressed.

Although devotees have rejected their bodies and identified with their souls, paradoxically, great emphasis is placed on the body in a wide variety of rituals and actions in the movement. This is evident from my previous examination of the concept 'I am not my body, I am spirit-soul'. In fact, during rituals in the movement devotees appear to be body-fixated and body-obsessed.

Indicating ISKCON's body focus, great emphasis is placed in the movement on appearance—the shaven heads and saffron robes of the men (the standard uniform of the Gaudiya Mission) and the saris of the women are obligatory for full-time devotees within the temple and serve to demarcate the boundary between the devotees and the 'karmi' outside world.

The body is highly ritualised in other ways too. For example, devotees are expected to bathe frequently and afterwards apply *tilaka* (Vaishnava body symbols painted with sandalwood paste). On becoming a devotee, an individual learns a new set of physical movements, including dance forms and bodily taboos.

The body is also emphasised in ISKCON art. Devotees' painting and book illustrations rarely show any abstract forms and the people they depict are always portrayed realistically. The fact that ISKCON has built a high quality waxwork museum costing £100,000 also reflects their obsession with the body. Prabhupad's body is an important focus of attention. It is obviously very highly valued, for when he 'passed over', most temples commissioned the waxwork museum to make them a lifelike (and they are incredibly realistic) wax statue of him.

Clearly this paradox, both rejection of the body and emphasis on it and the philosophical, ritual and action focus on the body as well as its apparent acceptance of Vaishnava culture in toto, suggests that there must be an important reason for this body focus in ISKCON.

CHAPTER NINE

The Role of the Body in Western Society Today

> The contradiction between 'technology' and 'the body' has been faced by man ever since he first began to reflect on his situation in myth, art and philosophy. The experiences and perceptions of the body are to a great extent immune to the objective, analytic description that technology prefers; they can be hinted at in poetry and art, but they always constitute a real and inexhaustible resource against narrow rationality—if often a dangerous, even 'diabolic' resource, for the body is easily sentimentalized.
> —Jonathan Benthall, *The Body Electric*, 1976: 14

To comprehend why ISKCON's belief, ritual and social organisation revolve to such a degree around the body, why devotees reject their bodies and why 'I am not my body, I am spirit-soul' has become a central concept in ISKCON's system of belief, it is necessary to understand the part played by the 'body' and the role of body symbolism in modern western society.

Historically, the West has had an ambivalent attitude to the body. On the one hand, belief in the resurrection of the body, the belief that the body will rise again, has led to a glorification of the body. Whilst on the other, and this theme has tended to be more influential, the body has been undervalued, the soul has been held to be more important than the body and in consequence it was felt necessary for the body to be transcended, punished and mortified. In Christianity, this attitude led also to bodily repression.

Since the turn of the century, however, the body has become a major focus of overt attention. Enhanced bodily awareness and the increasing manipulation of the values and symbols assigned to bodily categories have become all-pervasive in western culture. This abounds in the media. People are bombarded with it all the time, especially with sexual symbolism on television, in advertisements and in the tabloid newspapers.

Much of modern psychoanalysis is also based on and utilises body symbolism to explain social relations. Modern illnesses (like anorexia nervosa) use body symbolism to express themselves. Bodily Liberationists such as Wilhelm Reich, Norman Brown and the 'Human Potential' movement as a whole, with its interest in encounter groups, biorhythms and bionics, all focus on, stress and glorify the body and look to the body for the solution to personal problems. It is no accident either that fashion, sport, dance, physical exercise (e.g. jogging, 'keep fit'), as well as martial arts such as karate and kung fu which all focus on the body, have become increasingly important concerns in the lives of the masses.

In sum, western society is developing what might be called a 'cult of the body'. Horace Miner (1956: 503) humorously ridicules this in an article on the body in American society entitled 'Body Ritual among the Nacirema'!

> Nacirema culture is characterised by a highly developed market economy which has evolved in a rich natural habitat. While much of the people's time is devoted to economic pursuits, a large part of the fruits of these labours and a considerable portion of the day are spent in ritual activity. The focus of this activity is the human body, the appearance and health of which loom as a dominant concern in the ethos of the people. While such a concern is certainly not unusual, its ceremonial aspects and associated philosophy are unique.
>
> The fundamental belief underlying the whole system appears to be that the human body is ugly and that its natural tendency is to debility and disease. Incarcerated in such a body, man's only hope is to avert these characteristics through the use of the powerful influences of ritual and ceremony. Every household has one or more shrines devoted to this purpose. The more powerful individuals in the society have several shrines in their houses, and, in fact, the opulence of a house is often referred to in terms of the number of such ritual centres it possesses. Most houses are of wattle and daub construction, but the shrine rooms of the more wealthy are walled with stone. Poorer families imitate the

rich by applying pottery plaques to their shrine walls.

   While each family has at least one shrine, the rituals associated with it are not family ceremonies, but private and secret. The rites are normally only discussed with children, and then only during the period when they are being initiated into these mysteries: I was able, however, to establish sufficient rapport with the natives to examine these shrines and to have the rituals described to me.

   The body's importance in modern western society is further emphasised by the fact that bodily symbolism has become the focus of attention and research in the social sciences in the last thirty years. This interest is demonstrated in the works of such eminent scholars as Marcel Mauss' *Les Techniques du corps* (1935), Robert Hertz's (1960) perceptive study of the symbolic significance cross culturally of the left and right hand, Victor Turner's studies of the Ndembu (1967) and Mary Douglas' *Natural Symbols* (1970). In fact, a conference was held at the Institute of Contemporary Arts in 1974, whose subject matter was 'the body', and the papers given were later published as a book *The Body as a Medium of Expression* (Eds. Benthall and Polhemus, 1975). The subject of the Association of Social Anthropologists of the Commonwealth's annual conference in 1975 was also *The Body* and the papers given at the conference were later published as *The Anthropology of the Body* (Ed. Blacking, 1977). Ted Polhemus, the doyen of 'body' studies has also recently published *The Body Reader* (1978), a collection of articles on the body drawn from a wide range of disciplines.

   The research interests of the social sciences are an accurate barometer for measuring changes in the system of belief and social patterns in the West. It is to be expected that social scientists, whose field of study is human behaviour, should be sensitive and perceptive to changes in belief and behavioural patterns in their own society. As such, they would be amongst the vanguard and the first to articulate and express them in their own work.

   ISKCON, significantly, is not the only eastern religious cult that emerged during the 1960s which focuses on the body in one way or another, most of them do, for they attempt to find answers to their problems within themselves outside traditional social institutions. The Rajneesh Meditation Group in Chalk Farm is an example of one of these other new groups that centres on the body. It is essentially an encounter group utilising eastern esoteric terminology. Group 'meditation', held twice weekly, involves going through a number of bodily movements which include jumping up and down, dancing and screaming. This is aimed at releasing bodily tensions and thus enabling a greater understanding of the inner consciousness to be obtained. During meditation sessions at group meetings of Swami Muktananda's Siddha Yoga Group, individuals frequently enter into a violent paroxysm as they experience the 'kundalini', the female energy principle rising in their bodies. In fact, the most influential new cults, namely Yoga and Tantra, are almost totally centred on the body. They attempt to unite with the Godhead or Divine using techniques which involve the whole body.

In Christianity also, although the established Protestant and Catholic churches are on the decline, the 1960s witnessed a boom in small fundamentalist sects such as the Pentecostalists who express their relationship with the divine through forms of body symbolism, namely speaking with tongues (glossolalia), shaking and trance.

But perhaps the best indicator of the role of the body in the West, and British society in particular, is the recently established (1977) annual 'Mind and Body Festival' held at Olympia. It is not without significance that the Festival includes the term 'body' in the title. Primarily, fringe groups, and connected commercial enterprises, exhibited at the festival groups which in some way or another were critical to some degree of some, or all, aspects of modern industrial technological society, and offered alternatives which in general either focused on the body, or mind, or a combination of both. Generally they offered either a 'back to nature' ideology or some specific alternative such as vegetarianism (e.g. the Vegetarian Society of Great Britain). Other groups which had stalls there included minority Christian groups such as the Wrekin Foundation and the Quakers, esoteric groups such as the Theosophists, Eastern religious groups such as ISKCON, Siddha Yoga, Raja Yoga and Rajneesh, and the British Buddhist Society, faith healers and the human potential groups with interests in biorhythms, radionics and encounter groups, as well as anti-vivisectionists who are against the use of animal *bodies* in research. Many sold products connected with the body such as 'natural' body lotions and potions, health foods, vegetarian foods, tea, including ginseng, which is believed by many to be stimulant or aphrodisiac or clothes including 'nature' boots, Asian clothing and nylon fur coats acceptable to vegetarian and anti-vivisectionists.

Thus, the Mind and Body Festival indicates that ISKCON is just one of many marginal and fringe groups that interprets the world in terms of mind and body. It is no concidence that marginal groups critical of society should identify with 'body' and 'mind' (which is part and parcel of and an extension of the body any way) and that 'mind' and 'body' should be juxtaposed and considered an alternative to modern technological society. It would appear that there is a direct correlation between criticism of society and interest in mind and body. Certainly the title used by the organisers of the festival indicates their implicit awareness of the importance of mind and body in the everyday lives of marginal groups and that 'mind and body' was the common factor uniting the groups that they were trying to cater for and attract to the festival.

Other minority and marginal groups have used body symbolism as a form of social protest. Tony Jefferson (1976), in his perceptive study of Teddy Boys, demonstrates how unskilled working-class lads in 'dead-end' jobs proletarianised an upper-class style of dress. He describes how they took as their own, modified and parodied the dress of the Edwardian aristocracy as a form of social protest against their dead-end jobs and personal sense of low status. Similarly, Dick Hebdige's (1976) study of the Mods (who made a fetishism of fashion) and Clarke's (1976) study of Skinheads, all show how clothing and appearance were used as a form of social protest by working class youth. Willis (1978), in his study of motorbike boys reports how they are concerned with an enhanced sense of bodily attractiveness. He describes how working-class youths, lacking in verbal sophistication, use their motorbikes as an extension of their bodies and argues that riding their motorbikes enables them to express themselves physically.

The London ICA Conference 'Body as Medium of Expression' explored the speculation that,

> repressed groups will tend to find their most effective and confident expression through the body's wider resources rather than within the enclosure of verbal language, insofar as they opt for

self-assertion rather than for integrating with the norms of the majority! (Benthall, 1976: 137)

This speculation does appear to be borne out by the groups described here. But why, in modern technological society, do marginal and fringe groups, or individuals in general for that matter, focus on their bodies and not on some social phenomenon to express themselves. Why the 'body'?

An important factor influencing the development of the body as an important symbolic metaphor in modern western society, is clearly the traditional dichotomy between spirit and matter, and body and soul in western thought. These four concepts provide the basic framework in traditional Christianity for explaining all phenomena. Traditionally in Christian thought, the concepts 'body' and 'soul' which have been used to describe and explain the nature of man have always been binary opposites. So, too, are 'spirit' and 'matter' which have been used to describe all other phenomena. Usually, 'spirit' and 'soul' have been equated with the heavenly transcendental world and 'body' and 'matter' with this material world. It is no coincidence that from the Reformation onwards, with the decline in religion and increasing secularisation, transcendental explanations of phenomena, including such concepts as 'spirit' and 'soul', should have given way to an emphasis on their opposite, namely 'matter', i.e. scientific explanations, and 'the body'. As the structural study of myth (e.g. Levi-Strauss 1958, 1962, 1964) makes clear, the human mind classifies in terms of binary opposites and tends to go from one opposite and extreme to another. Understandably, therefore, when secularization eroded the belief in spirit and soul, western thought veered towards and emphasised its binary opposite, namely the body, matter and empirical explanation. This was an alternative, moreover, that individuals were already familiar with—being part and parcel of their traditional conceptual schema and as such particularly attractive and easy to assimilate.

In fact, this equation of the body with empirical phenomena and emphasis on the body to explain man's place in the universe and social relationships appears soon after the Reformation, in the late seventeenth century, in the work of Hobbes, one of the earliest empiricist philosophers in his monumental work *Leviathan*. He uses the body as a symbolic metaphor on the cover of *Leviathan*—

in a diagram of the human body are encapsulated a crowd of people. In this picture Hobbes is essentially utilising the body to symbolise society. ISKCON has much in common with Hobbes for, like him, devotees use the body as a symbol of matter, empiricism and, most importantly, society. That ISKCON should have chosen to act out its social protest in terms fundamental to western civilisation, namely body and soul, spirit and matter demonstrates the close integration of ISKCON, in practice, with the wider 'karmi' society. It also further indicates that ISKCON's rejection of western society is on the level of the symbolic rather than actual.

Jonathan Benthall in the *Body Electric* (1976), relates the development of the importance of the body in modern society to the growth of science and technology. He argues that people have, on the one hand, been attracted to the scientific and technological society, seeing it as having beneficial effects—particularly during the eighteenth and nineteenth centuries. This viewpoint he calls, 'the Romance of Technology'. But he maintains that the drawbacks to technology have often soured man's positive attitude to it and have led him to seek an alternative framework for life. One of the alternatives taken has been what he refers to as 'the Recoil to the Body': people turning to the body as a means of expression and glorifying it.

As he maintains, too, the interest in the body is clearly a reaction 'against the dominance in our culture of logic and analytic reason'. There are other reasons, too. The same reasons that made western youth reject society, namely western society's stifling bureaucratic norms, its lack of close ties between people, its impersonalism and the alienation of urban life, its obsessions with quantity rather than quality, its materialism and its turning of mankind into robots, the inhuman scale of society, the rape of the environment and ecology, the very obvious gap between truth and people's everyday lives, all of which have a dehumanising effect and make people look for alternative frameworks within which to conduct their lives—and the body is understandably a very meaningful alternative.

As Broadbent (1975: 304-305) remarks:

> One of our motives for attending to the human body is that the heavenly bodies are now too far away. We can land on the moon but we can't relate it to twins in the little continent of their

mother's womb. We know too much; so much that the truth has become unknowable in its quantity and complexity, and unrelated to anything else. . . There seems nothing left for the imagination to create; our mind 'hath no ends', so we close in on the body, like a tortoise. The cosmos is expanding at the speed of light, and will collapse again. Civilization is growing exponentially, and will collapse again. The scale of quite familiar and diurnal things has suddenly enlarged—even in England, counties have supernova'd into regions; lorries and planes swell into juggernauts, jumbo jets, supertankers; and their noise drowns the churchbells which, as Peter Laslett noted, used to be the loudest noise in England. Unable to register these expansions, we turn into the one thing whose boundaries we can still define, the body.

But, most importantly, as was mentioned in Chapter Two, many of the existential and social problems faced by people in modern society, the youth in particular, can only be solved by a massive reorganisation of society and not on an individual level. The realisation that solutions to personal problems cannot be found in the outside world, in the wider society, has led people to turn to themselves to find answers to them and the body is a particularly appropriate focus and framework for such.

The 'self' is bounded by the physical body and is inextricably bound up with it. One is the natural corollary or extension of the other. When turning to himself for answers to his problems, the individual naturally has to take into account his body since it is the natural focus of his attention. It is the starting point from which he takes his bearing in space and it provides the boundary between himself and the outside world. The body is for the individual, too, the most direct, personal, intimate and the most obvious vehicle of expression. Moreover it is the one feature of his life that the individual does have control over. Being a biological entity the body is not enmeshed in social structure as such, it is therefore less constrained than purely social forms and more easily open to individual manipulation. It is thus an ideal vehicle for cultural and ideological expression.

But, most importantly, it is through his body that an individual attains emotional satisfaction. Modern urban society, however, deprives people on the levels of emotion and experience, especially through its lackey, the inhibiting and inward-looking nuclear family. Deprived of traditional institutional forms for expressing and attaining emotional satisfaction, it is understandable that the individual should turn to his own body, the locus of his experience, for emotional satisfaction denied him by the social structure of western society. By focusing on their bodies, they are able to obtain a direct and personal form of experience. Understandably, people in modern society are turning in vast numbers to bodily expression. It is no accident that the majority of groups focusing on the body that mushroomed in the 1960s cater for the experiential level and focus around 'experience trips' and ISKCON, of course, is the 'emotional experience trip' par excellence.

The collapse of the traditional world view has accelerated since last World War. The man in the street does not know what to believe or whom to believe. Understandably, he rejects them all as being untrue and looks elsewhere than traditional belief for a coherent framework within which to organise his life. The alternative closest at hand is, of course, the experiential framework of his own body, where belief is irrelevant and 'feeling' is all.

In the light of these reasons for the focus on the body in modern society, the emphasis on and use of the body as a metaphor among fringe and marginal groups becomes understandable. Clearly, their criticism of society stems from the inability of society to provide answers to their problems and they have turned to themselves and to their bodies to express and find solutions to the problems that confront them, which otherwise they would not be able to overcome.

Looked at from the point of view of the body focus of western society nowadays, earlier Left-wing interpretations of Teddy Boys, Mods and Rockers and Skinheads, etc., in *Resistance through Rituals—Youth Subcultures in Post War Britain* (Eds. Hall and Jefferson, 1976), whilst perceptive in seeing young people's use of fashion and clothing styles as ritual forms of social protest, do not go far enough as explanations. They do not explain why young people have chosen to express themselves in terms of fashion and clothing styles rather than some other ideological and cultural form of expression. Clearly, they were attracted to clothing and fashion as a vehicle for social protest precisely because they were extensions of their bodies and provided a medium and framework for bodily symbolism. For example skinheads' love of fighting and Punk Rockers' liking for bodily mutilation, (e.g., sticking safety pins into themselves) would appear to be the most extreme form of social protest; namely violation of the body itself.

ISKCON devotees' symbolic emphasis on and rejection of their bodies is clearly part and parcel of the modern western preoccupation with and cult of the body. They appear to be using their bodies like other marginal groups and their youth peer group in particular to express personal existential and social problems and as a form of social protest, namely expressing resistance, through ritual and symbols.

It would appear, if Skinheads and Punk Rockers are anything to go by, that 'recoil to the body', to use Benthall's expression, need not necessarily lead to a positive affirmation of the body and glorification of it. From the style of dress that they have adopted and their predilections it is clear that they hardly glorify theirs. Rather, it suggests that the interpretation and emphasis placed on the body and the way it is encapsulated in an individual's interpretive scheme will vary from social group to social group, from individual to individual, depending on the social situation and social problems the individual faces and wishes to express.

For potential body symbolists, Hinduism is particularly attractive, for it is highly ritualistic and symbolic in orientation—a symbolist religion *par excellence*. Scholars generally have not focused on the eastern religions themselves and their symbolic content as primary reasons for westerners' conversion to them. But Hinduism not only focuses on the individual and the inner man, but it includes within it a whole set of beliefs and practices related to the nature and function of the body, and this is particularly true of the beliefs and practices of the Gaudiya Sect.

Prabhupad himself was a frequent user of bodily metaphors. A major reason why his teachings are so attractive to devotees is because they contain a set of beliefs and practices related to the nature and function of the body, not only the dichotomy between body and soul but also sexual customs and taboos, as well as concepts of pollution and purity. As potential body symbolists, devotees were quick to recognise the body symbolim inherent in Prabhupad's teachings and, rapidly emphasised, assimilated and used it for their own ends. A major reason why so many devotees have remained in the movement for over five years is precisely because ISKCON's focus on the body provides them with a meaningful frame of reference—a vehicle for articulating their frustrations and acting out their social protest.

CHAPTER TEN

Soul as a Symbol of Self—Body as a Symbol of Society

> The social body constrains the way the physical body is perceived. The physical experience of the body, always modified by the social categories through which it is known, sustains a particular view of society. There is a continual exchange of meanings between the two kinds of bodily experience so that each reinforces the categories of the other. As a result of this interaction the body itself is a highly restricted medium of expression. The forms it adopts in movement and repose express social pressures in manifold ways. The care that is given to it, in grooming, feeding and therapy, the theories about what it needs in the way of sleep and exercise, about the stages it should go through, the pains it can stand, its span of life, all the cultural categories in which it is perceived, must correlate closely with the categories in which society is seen in so far as these also draw upon the same culturally processed idea of the body.
>
> —Mary Douglas, *Natural Symbols*, 1970: p. 65

Since symbols are a kind of language and stand for truths which cannot be expressed directly, to understand them it is necessary to decode them and find out what they stand for. If it is accepted that devotees use their bodies, following the general western pattern nowadays, to express personal, existential and social problems and as a form of social protest, one can begin to comprehend the code and underlying meaning of the concept, 'I am not my body, I am spirit-soul'.

Most symbolic systems contain a dominant, epitomizing or condensed symbol which functions as a simple general code and which stands for the totality, such as the cross in Christianity, the lotus or the wheel in Buddhism and the cresent in Islam. Dominant symbols express or evoke in a single set of symbols the array of otherwise apparently disparate symbols and meanings in a culture. They unify seemingly disparate significata and simultaneously express many ideas and relations between things. They state succinctly the common features of the different meanings and the special ways in which they resemble each other. An understanding of the dominant symbol is therefore crucial to an understanding of the total symbolic system of which it is a part.

Devotees' extrapolation from their belief system and emphasis on one concept, namely 'I am not my body, I am spirit-soul', reflects the development and establishment in ISKCON of one such dominant symbol. In a way it is like a chemical formula. It sums up simply in a condensed and succinct way the totality of ISKCON philosophy and the symbolic pattern inherent in it. Its very simplicity facilitates everyday usage, particularly as a weapon for social protest and as a simple code for expressing the devotees' view of reality and their position in it.

Devotees' responses to my usage of 'I am not my body, I am spirit-soul' indicate that the concept does function as a condensed symbol in ISKCON. Leading devotees were very interested in my book and would often ask me what it was going to be called. When I said, 'I Am Not My Body', a look of instant recognition would light up their faces. They would nod in assent and would immediately agree that that was what ISKCON was all about and that the title well summed up the movement.

Symbols are of course, not only expressed verbally, but also in ritual and action too. An examination of the concept, 'I am not my body, I am spirit-soul' and related rituals and how it is articulated in social behaviour, as well as its position in, and relationship to, the total symbolic system used by ISKCON further demonstrates that it does function as a condensed symbol.

Traditional Indian Vaishnavas do not intellectualise and express *shlokas* (verses) 12, 13, 20 and 22 in terms of the phrase, 'I am not my body, I am spirit-soul'. Moreover, they do not generally interpret them personally, in an ego-focused manner or with such a degree of individualistic emphasis as do devotees which suggests that there must be some reason for it developing in this manner in ISKCON. When devotees were asked why they expressed these *shlokas* in terms of this phrase, the answer frequently given was that it was for the sake of simplicity. It was a quick and easy way of saying it. Anyway, as many commented, 'it's true—We are not our bodies, we are spirit-soul'. This cryptic remark of the devotees tends to further suggest that it is no accident that the concept has developed in the manner it has and that such emphasis has been laid on it in the movement.

It became apparent that the concept has been singled out, expressed n this form and developed as the ideological focus of the movement because it was directly related to devotees' needs and social situation. The key to understanding this condensed symbol and the role it plays in the movement lies, in the body/soul dichotomy embedded in it and the underlying beliefs and practices related to both the concept 'spirit-soul' and 'body' in ISKCON. An examination of these demonstrates that the soul/body dichotomy in 'I am not my body, I am spirit-soul' parallels and symbolically stands for the individual and his relationship to society. 'Spirit-soul' stands for the individual 'self' and 'body' for society. Combined with associated rituals, this dichotomy, the way devotees conceptualise 'spirit-soul' and 'body' and the dialogue they carry on between the two all provide the blueprint for devotees' view of the relationship between the individual and society.

The ego-focus of the concept, 'I am not my body, I am spirit-soul' and its interpretation from the point of view of the individual devotee, rather than from the group level or the movement as a whole is functional.

It reflects the individualistic theme that runs throughout ISKCON, and provides a framework for articulating, sustaining, reinforcing and channelling devotees' 'personal trips'. Its individualistic focus offers the devotees the means of expressing personal concerns on the individual level. It provides a personal outlet for social protest and a means of expressing, dealing with and overcoming their problems individually rather than having to look to the movement as a whole for solutions. This concept is a clear example of the way modern youth has turned to the cultural level and to themselves to find answers to their problems.

In fact, the concept, 'I am not my body, I am spirit-soul', through its equation symbolically with the soul and body, provides devotees on the personal level with a substitute for actual social action. In this light, the high degree of ritual in the movement, and the devotees' obsessive preoccupation with their bodies, become apparent. They provide a surrogate for existential and social problems which they are unable to solve in their daily lives. In sum, it is clear that ISKCON devotees have attempted to solve the problems that confront them by projecting them on to and dealing with them on the symbolic level through ritual.

The framework within which this symbolic model of the world and social relations is acted out is the 'Science of Self-Realisation' which is at the heart of ISKCON philosophy. The focus of 'self-realisation' in ISKCON is of course 'spirit-soul', which individuals in the movement identify with their *'self'*. Its aim also is to purify the soul (i.e. the devotees' 'self') so that the individual can obtain his original God consciousness and thus go 'back to Godhead'.

Devotees' identification of themselves with 'spirit-soul' is not coincidental. It has been developed to such an extent because it offers them a very meaningful frame of reference for overcoming alienation and identity problems, as well as for fostering the development of what Cohen (1976) has termed 'selfhood'.

Identity problems (Erikson, 1968), alienation (the Marxists) and anomie (Durkheim) have frequently been put forward as major problems of industrialised western society. They have often been applied to modern youth and have been suggested as some of the reasons for the development of the Counterculture in America in the 1960s. Daner, (1976) in her study of the ISKCON temple in Boston, uses alienation and identity problems as her basic hypothesis to account for the reason devotees join ISKCON. She sees them as key factors in the lives of devotees and views ISKCON as providing a means of reconciling them. She concludes (1976: 12), using Goffman's model of a 'total institution', that:

> The ISKCON temple provides a total-institutional setting which allows its members a well-defined structural and ideological situation into which they can fit themselves. It creates a social situation in which they can realize their identities, thereby eliminating much of the ambiguity which is generated by modern society.

Certainly, for some devotees, alienation and identity problems are factors contributing to their joining the movement. But they are supporting rather than decisive reasons, for not all young people suffering from alienation and identity problems join

ISKCON or similar religious groups. Daner is perhaps saying that ISKCON devotees are more alienated and have greater identity problems than their peers in the outside world who have not joined ISKCON. This may have been the case in the early days when most devotees came from a hippie and drug background, particularly devotees in the Haight Ashbury temple, situated as it was in a especially alienating and identity-destroying environment.

Some devotees do have personality problems, but, as has been mentioned, those with real psychological problems generally cannot cope with the movement's strict regime and soon leave. Many devotees however appear quite 'normal'. This is particularly true of British devotees, most of whom have had little contact with hippy life and have been only marginally involved in the drug subculture. The majority do not appear to have any more alienation and identity problems than their peer group in the outside world.

Alienation, identity problems and anomie in fact are not new concepts. Studies of them have provided social scientists with their bread and butter for the last century. What differentiates modern youth, and ISKCON devotees in particular, from their similarly alienated predecessors is not the fact that they are more alienated (working-class people in industrial slums in northern towns in the 1840s could hardly have been less alienated), but that they have a positive attitude to their alienation and identity problems. Moreover unlike most of their predecessors, they have actively tried to do something about them. They have used groups such as ISKCON to come to terms with their difficulties and overcome them.

ISKCON appears to offer an excellent solution to devotees with identity problems, as well as those with psychological problems with an excellent solution. The movement does indeed offer devotees who are 'spaced out' with the means of straightening themselves out and 'getting their heads together', as devotees put it. Devotees, for instance, frequently point to the concentration needed for *japa* (repetitive chanting) and its rhythm as beneficial for achieving this. As Daner suggests ISKCON also helps by providing devotees with a 'total institutional structure'. However the movement's institutional structure on one level, with its focus and emphasis on individualism, is likely to hinder personality integration. But, most importantly, ISKCON has provided an answer to devotees' feeling of alienation and identity problems by evolving a unified conceptual symbolic framework within which devotees' personality and psyche can be integrated, that is through the concept of spirit-soul and its juxtaposition to the concept of body.

This concept provides devotees with a clear-cut sense of identity and with the means of integrating themselves, not only on the level of personality, but at the level of what Cohen (1977) has called 'self-hood'. Cohen, in a cogently argued and convincing theory, sees the concept of 'self'—'the sheer oneness of man'—as rooted in a deeper level of the psyche beyond what we call personality and he sees it as being expressed and created through symbolic action:

> In our contractual relationships we are essentially involved in roles whose performance formally involves only segments of our personality, not the totality of the person. An engineer is involved in his job only as an engineer not as a father or member of a political party. The relationship is instrumental, in the sense that the parties involved in it use one another as a means to an end and not an end in themselves. In our social life we come to perform different and sometimes discrepant roles of this kind. As a result, our life tends to become compartmentalised and our personality fragmented (p. 122).

Man cannot live a normal life, he maintains, without having a 'self' and it is through the symbolic act, he argues, that self-hood is achieved, for it is through symbolism and symbolic interaction that the totality of roles in which the individual is involved in his daily life is integrated into one unified system. The kinds of daily roles many devotees were involved in prior to joining the movement particularly those in the Haight Ashbury temple where the ISKCON belief system was developed, were essentially disintegrative and of a fragmenting nature and likely to foster the disintegration of self-hood, identity problems and alienation. The strong development of the symbolic level in the movement and the focus on the concept of spirit-soul would appear to be a response to the alienating environment in which the temple was situated and the devotees' own disintegrative and contradictory roles which provided fertile ground for chronic identity and personality problems. Understandably, early devotees latched onto the concept of spirit-soul and developed the movement around it. Nowadays it is through the concept of spirit-soul and related symbols and rituals that 'self-hood' is continually created and recreated and alienation and identity problems are overcome in the movement.

The science of self-realisation and concomitant rituals offer an ideal framework for getting to know, and coming to terms with, devotees' inner self and for attaining internal peace and contentment. Most importantly, the concept of spirit-soul which devotees equate with their 'self', is the focus point of the path of self-realisation, which aims at the purification of the soul. It thus provides an excellent coherent stable framework and reference point for developing a defined sense of identity for those devotees who either do not have one or who have a fragmentary one as well as offering them a frame of reference and basis for action.

ISKCON, by equating spirit-soul with 'self', provides devotees immediately on joining the movement, with a clear-cut sense of identity for it tells them who they are, namely that they are spirit-souls. Devotees often remark that Krishna Consciousness philosophy is an ideal religion because it answers the questions: 'Who am I', 'Where am I going?' In fact, devotees' articulation and emphasis on 'Who am I' etc. in their philosophy clearly indicates that identity problems and their solutions are important issues.

Devotees' identification with their spirit-souls is reinforced when they are initiated into the movement. This generally occurs after they have been in ISKCON about six months. They are given a new name by their guru, usually the name of one of the characters of the Vaishnava scriptures and they tend to equate their new names with their souls.

Moreover, the soul is considered eternal and unchanging. For those devotees who have a very fragmented sense of self-hood and identity and who suffer from thought confusion, tension and anxiety as well as for devotees who appear to find it difficult to cope with the sense of impermanence induced by rapid change in modern society, such a belief is particularly helpful and attractive. It gives them a permanent point of reference, as well as a sense of stability, continuity and permanence. This enables them to combat their feelings.

Most importantly, the traditional Vaishnava concept of soul (*atma*) is a unitary concept. When devotees have attempted to translate *atma* into English, they have translated it using the twin terms 'spirit' and 'soul' and have combined the two together. There is no direct equivalent to *atma* in western thought. The nearest are the Christian concepts of 'soul' and 'spirit', but neither are quite the same as *atma*. Devotees, instead of emphasising the difference between these concepts when attempting to translate *atma*, combine the two together so that they form a unitary concept. This indicates that for devotees it is the unitary nature of the concept of *atma* that is all important rather than a precise definition. This is understandable, for the spirit-soul's unitary nature is an ideal point of reference for integrating their sense of identity and creating and recreating their sense of self-hood. By identifying with a unitary symbolic concept, such as 'soul' they are creating a framework for withstanding the disintegrative and alienating nature of the multiple roles that people, the youth in particular, have to play in modern western society. Moreover the fact that 'spirit' and 'soul' are part of devotees' traditional conceptual framework, has made it easy for them to take over and assimilate the concept of *atma*, albeit in an interpreted form.

Devotees associate their souls and the transcendental spirit world with happiness, peace, contentment, continuity and ideal relations. Moreover it is through their souls that devotees are able to articulate and communicate with the transcendental world and thus with the total symbolic model. By so doing, they are able to cut themselves off from the destructive effects on personalities of their fragmented role relations. Through their identification with their souls, they are able to project themselves onto the transcendental spiritual level; to a world where roles are all ideally integrated and where they can create and manipulate in their minds the ideal social relations which they cannot achieve in their everyday lives.

Moreover ISKCON provides them with a social environment and ritual system which continually reminds them of this identification with their soul and reconfirms it repeatedly throughout the day. This imprints it permanently on their consciousness and strengthens their belief.

In the concept, 'I am not my body, I am spirit-soul', ISKCON has really developed for itself a magnificently useful social symbol, for it enables devotees to rise above their social and existential problems through identifying with their souls.

It is no accident that while devotees identify with their souls they reject their bodies. Moreover, in this phrase they identify their bodies with the exact opposite to that with which they identify their souls, namely with material social relations, unhappiness, anxiety, impermanence, frustration, suffering and matter. This is clearly indicated by the quote at the beginning of the Bhaktivedanta Institute Monograph *What is Matter, What is Life* (1977): To understand the distinction between matter (the field or body) and life (spirit, or the knower of the field) is called knowledge (*Bhagavad-Gita*, 13 : 3).

Bodies exist and operate within a social context and, as my examination of the role of bodies in western society demonstrates, the messages conveyed by bodily expression are about the society itself. ISKCON devotees, in focusing on and emphasising the body, are using their bodies as a form of communication and as a language system to say things about themselves.

Marcel Mauss (1935) pointed out that the human body may be considered as a natural symbol of society. Mary Douglas (1970) too, in her seminal work *Natural Symbols*, demonstrates that the body may be used as a symbol of society and that symbols based on the human body may be used to express different social experiences. The body, she says, is a model which can stand for any bounded social system. Its boundaries can represent any social boundaries which are threatened or precarious. The function of its different parts and their relationship afford a source of symbols for other complex structures. The body may be used, she argues, as a diagram of a social situation, and the powers and dangers accredited to social structure may be reproduced in miniature on the body. Mary Douglas' Durkheimian approach throws a great deal of light on the workings of ISKCON for devotees appear to be natural symbolists par excellence. They emphasise the body and bodily ritual in order to symbolise and represent their social relations and society.

The devotees project all their social problems onto their bodies, which they consider to be the cause of all their misery and suffering. They hold that their bodies, having emotions and physical needs, consequently involve them in social relations with others. Indeed, they believe that it is the bodily need for sense gratification that is the reason for all their problems. Reflecting devotees' body fixation, references to the body are made frequently in conversation. As Atma Atma said, when discussing his relationships prior to joining the movement :

My body was giving me hell. My relationships were falling apart. I knew I was suffering. I am eternal. I am more than this grotty society and its action on me. It is doing it to my body, not to me.

The material body and what happens to it is considered unimportant. Devotees reject it completely and try to break their attachment to it by a life of austerity and the control of their senses and bodily needs. By identifying with their souls by denying that they are their bodies and by projecting their problems onto their bodies, devotees are able to disassociate themselves from their anxieties and social problems. They do not feel that what has happened to them or will happen to them is their own fault or anything to do with them, which makes it easier for them to accept their lot in life.

In symbolically projecting their attitudes to society, onto their bodies, they in fact symbolically identify and equate their bodies with social relations and society, in particular the 'karmi' world outside. It is not they but their bodies that have social relations and interact with society.

This conceptualisation provides them with a rationale for existence and a focus for action since it enables them to they act out their rejection of society through the use of bodily functions and symbols. Devotees' equation of their bodies with social relations and society (particularly their relationships with the 'karmi' world), is apparent from conversations with devotees as well as from Prabhupad's writings and *Back to Godhead*. A few quotations will demonstrate this.

Firstly, there is the final remark made by Mark, a science student in the film *Spark of Life*. He is converted during the film from an atheistic scientific view of the world to a belief in God and the impermanence of the body:

> From a spiritual viewpoint all living things are equal. If we think, I'm a man, I'm a woman, I'm American, I'm Chinese, I'm young, I'm old, I'm black, I'm Christian, I'm Jewish, I'm Hindu. We think we belong to a particular family and country and race and faith. But these names apply only to the body, they have nothing to do with us. Each of us is an anti-material (soul) particle, a pure spirit eternally.

Visakha in her article 'The World We Live In', in *Back to Godhead*, (Vol. 10, No. 2, p. 15) stated:

Our vision now, however, is clouded by false ego, which is the basic principle of material existence. False ego means the acceptance of the body to be oneself. Thus our bodily designations, such as American, Russian, black, white, Christian, Hindu, man, woman, fat, thin, stupid and intelligent, are manifestations of false ego. Our real ego is spiritual, for we are tiny spiritual parts of the supreme living entity, Krishna. Since we are actually spiritual souls, our only connection with our material bodies and minds is that we dwell within them for fifty or a hundred years. Bhagavad-Gita therefore compares the gross or visible body to a coat, and it compares the subtle body—consisting of mind and intelligence—to a shirt. The person within, however, is different from the bodily shirt and coat.

She also went on to say (p 16):

The example of Arjuna (to whom Krishna recounted the Bhagavad Gita) shows how bodily relationships (which are also material interactions) cause material perplexity. Because of bodily designations and mental relationships, Arjuna was averse to fighting his kinsmen in the Battle of Kurukshetra.

Prabhupad himself, for instance, stated in an interview entitled 'Getting to the Soul of Psychology' with a psychologist, Dr. Frazer:

First of all the basic principle of understanding is that you are a spirit-soul—you are not your body. But because you have accepted a body, you have to suffer so many bodily troubles. All our troubles are due to this material body. Therefore, this material body itself is our problem. (BTG, Vol. 11, No. 9, p. 7).

And in the interview with Mike Robinson of London Broadcasting, he also stated:

Similarly, everyone is simply washing the 'coat and shirt' of the body, but forgetting about the soul within the body. They have no information about what is within the 'coat' and 'shirt' of the body. Ask anybody what he is, and he will say, "Yes, I am an Englishman," or, "I am an Indian". And, if, we say, "I can see you have an English or an Indian body, but what are *you*?"—that he cannot say. (BTG, UK, Vol. 1, No. 1, p. 7).

Relating the body and materialism to social relations and status —to Hindu, Jewish, old, young, etc., as appears constantly in the previous quotations, is something that devotees do all the time. Indeed, they are aware that they do it and refer to it as the 'bodily concept' of life.

In sum in rejecting their bodies, devotees are symbolically rejecting society. Their bodies, and bodily functions and rituals, in sum, provide a battlefield for the war with the 'karmi' world; the arena for acting out their rejection, alienation and antagonism to the outside world.

CHAPTER ELEVEN

Bodily Ritual in ISKCON and Devotees' Attitudes to the Body, its Boundaries and Orifices

> This material body is a lump of ignorance and the senses are a network of paths of death. Of all the senses the tongue is the most voracious and uncontrollable. But Krishna has sent us this very nice prasdam to help us conquer the tongue. So let us take this nice prasadam to our full satisfaction, glorifying his lordship.

ISKCON's focus on the body and its utilisation of it to symbolise society and social relations is depicted in devotees' attitudes to their bodies and bodily ritual in general. One of the most noticeable features of the movement is the devotees' obsession with their bodies and the high degree to which bodies are ritualised which leads them to focus their attention on their bodies throughout most of the day.

Although Hinduism is perhaps the foremost bodily symbolist religion, devotees have selected and adhered to only those Gaudiya Matha purity and pollution beliefs and practices that are meaningful in terms of their framework of symbolic protest. For instance, they do not emphasise and adhere to purity and pollution customs related to death, marriage and childbirth, which are very important to Indians. Instead they follow only those beliefs and practices directly related to their own bodies and their relationships with the outside society that is those purity and pollution customs that they can use to express their social protest and their relationship to society and use as a substitute for action.

It is Prabhupad himself perhaps who acted as the catalyst to the development of bodily symbolism in ISKCON. In his own speech Prabhupad appears to have been prone to bodily symbolism; or at least he is made to appear so in *Back to Godhead*. A trait which devotees—since the body is so meaningful a symbol to them—were quick to copy and to quote frequently in *Back to Godhead*. He is reported as saying for example in a discussion with Richard Dalrymple of the *Los Angeles Herald Examiner* (BTG. 11, No. 8, p. 15):

> Just as in my body there are different parts, but the most important part is the brain, so the important section of society is made up of those who are fully God-conscious. You can cut off my hands or my legs and I shall live. But if you cut off my head, I must die. At the present moment there are big scientists and skilled technologists: they are society's hands and legs. But there is no brain. Therefore, in one sense, it is a dead society. So we are trying to bring America back to life by supplying the brain. If America takes Krsna consciousness seriously, other nations will follow. Make a 'United Nations' for God consciousness and all people will be benefitted.

The attitude of devotees to their bodies reflects their attitude to society. Mary Douglas (1970: XII), discussing millennial movements, argues that in a 'grid' type society, where rules relate one person to another on an ego-centred basis, when something goes wrong the dominant symbolic form will draw on bodily symbolism. She says, for millennialists,

> society appears as a system which does not work. The human body is the most readily available image of a system. In these types of social experience, a person feels that his personal relations, so inexplicably unprofitable, are in the sinister grip of a social system. It follows that the body tends to serve as a symbol of evil, as a structured system contrasted with pure spirit which by its nature is free and undifferentiated...The flesh does not suggest temptation to lust and all physical delights. It would more likely represent the corruption of power and organisation.

Western society would fit into her grid-type category, and it is in a situation of crisis. Although ISKCON is not truly millennial, nevertheless, much of what she has to say holds for the devotees' attitudes to their bodies; to them, their bodies represent the society they hate. They hold their bodies in low esteem and in their hatred to their bodies is mirrored their hatred of society. Just as they see society as corrupt, so they see their bodies as bad, evil and contaminating. They both reject and deny their bodies and focus on and show great anxiety about bodily orifices. They draw on Hindu concepts of pollution to express their disgust with their bodies. They frequently remark that bodies are made of 'stool', or that hair is nothing more than 'dried stool'. The movement is often accused of brainwashing its members and devotees frequently quote Prabhupad's comments on the subject. 'I am not brainwashing them', he said, 'I am just washing the stool out of their brains'.

Prabhupad also expressed hippiedom in terms of bodily symbolism. According to many devotees, he used to remark to lazy male devotees who did not keep their heads shaved. 'Sprouting hair on your head reflects the germination of the seeds of hippiedom in your hearts'. Mary Douglas (1970: VIII) maintains that where:

> a man recognises very strong allegiance to a social group, and at the same time does not know how he relates to other members or what his expectation should be. He tends to use the image of the human body to express both the exclusive nature of the allegiance and the confused social experience. The group is likened to the human body; the orifices are to be carefully guarded to prevent unlawful intrusions.

She holds that in a society where group structure is strong the body will be cherished and viewed as vulnerable.

ISKCON is very group-focused, but, as has been pointed out, the body far from being considered vulnerable, susceptible to danger and open to attack is considered bad, corrupt, evil and threatening. Devotees frequently refer to it in terms of stool, blood, urine and mucus. This attitude to their bodies is referred to again and again in the Sri Vyasa Puja Books, e.g.:

> "I was born in the darkness of ignorance, and my spiritual master opened my eyes with the torchlight of knowledge. Therefore, I offer my respectful obeisances unto the lotus feet of my spiritual

master." Only by your grace can one become freed from this false conception of identifying with the material body. We were all so proud of this miserable body, worshipping it and giving it our complete attention, without knowing that it is just a bag of stool, blood, urine, mucus and bile. There is nothing glamorous about it at all. (1977: 235, Paris devotees.)

and:

How can we count the gifts you give us, you are training us all, lions, tigers, dogs, cats, gangsters and cheats, like a lion-tamer in the circus of illusions. Mad men prisoners in the material world, you point out 'who is crazy and who is sane?'. For ten years I meditate on how you try to show us that we are not this body. We still take refuge in this cage of mucus, bile, stool and bone. If we realized this simple fact there would not be any fighting. (1976: 122, Gurudasa Swami.)

Indeed, devotees view their bodies prior to joining the movement as being dead.

We were without life before we met your Grace; simply dead bodies, not being able to distinguish reality from illusion. You have taken these dead bodies and given them life through devotional service. We can only bow at your lotus feet. (1975: 72, Costa Rica devotees.)

The person who has not at any time received the dust of the feet of a pure devotee of the Lord upon his head is certainly a dead body. (1973: 108, Bhagavatam.)

Since in ISKCON, the body is used not to symbolise their own groupings but the outside 'karmi' society and their relations with it bodily orifices, far from being guarded, are considered polluting and contaminating. As would tend to be expected from a group who are very antagonistic to society and have developed a very strong 'them/us' attitude, devotees' strong sense of social boundaries is reflected in an equally strong sense of bodily boundaries. They show a preoccupation with bodily entries and exits which they emphasise and highly ritualise. In fact, the bodily model of entries and exits is used to represent points of entry and exit to social units and to represent their rejection of society and to play out society's ills. Since both society and the body are considered bad and contaminating, in ISKCON it is to be expected that bodily orifices should become important and that bodily excretions should be considered polluting. For example, ISKCON's rejection of lavatory paper in favour of the Asian custom of washing the bottom with the left hand after defecating. It is a rejection loaded with symbolic significance. Bearing in mind that ISKCON temples in Britain are situated in urban areas where Asian-style plumbing is not normally obtainable, this may appear to an outsider to be carrying things to an extreme and rather ridiculous degree. Nevertheless, the devotees make a great fuss about this ritual and place great emphasis on it. Understandably so, since it is directly related to a bodily orifice from which impurities come. It is one of the ways they use their bodies to express social protest. They are using lavatory paper as a symbol of rejection, for in rejecting it they are making a social protest and rejecting society.

Hindu concepts of pollution, to which all devotees attach great importance and to which they adhere strictly, also provide them with apt symbols to express this attitude. The body and mouth as in Hinduism, are considered particularly polluting and contaminating. Devotees symbolically have to be protected from the polluting aspects of the body in the same way that they have to be protected from the pollution and dangers of society. For instance, any devotee who touches the mouth or anus is expected to wash immediately, and this involves most devotees bathing several times a day. Devotees gleefully state that the soul of people in the outside 'karmi' world will leave at death from the anus, whilst the souls of yogis will leave from the top of the head.

Devotees constantly associate their minds with stool and urine too. 'Our minds, which have bathed in stool and urine, are factually being washed clean in the transcendental ocean of devotional service.' (V.P.B. 1973: 50, Buffalo temple devotees.)

Devotees' rejection of their bodies and their view of their bodies and concomitantly, society as being corrupt, is reflected thus in the way they treat their bodies. They project the frustrations and aggression which they cannot externalise socially onto their bodies. They abuse their bodies and treat them badly. They deprive them of sleep, take cold baths, sleep on hard floors, put up with little heating in winter, accept a poor diet, and repress their sexual urges. Often devotees are very tired and not infrequently ill, particularly in winter. But they accept this with equanimity as the norm. A number of bodily degradation rituals are also included in ISKCON's ritual system. Devotees are expected to totally prostrate themselves (an act which is generally considered a humiliating position and unacceptable to westerners) in front of the guru, deities, *sannyasins*, and other devotees they have not met for a long time. Devotees appear to enjoy prostrating themselves. These degradation rituals therefore appear to be an assault on, and symbolically aimed at degrading society.

While in India devotees often get very ill. The commonest disease is dysentery which is generally caused by drinking local polluted water and eating *prasad* (consecrated offerings) which is often contaminated. The Ganges and the Yamuna are sacred rivers for the Hindus and are considered to have purifying powers. It is customary to drink from and bathe in these rivers despite the high level of pollution in them. ISKCON devotees also follow this custom, even though they are fully aware of the consequences. This gesture has to be understood in terms of ISKCON's symbolic framework. For, for them the water of the Ganges or the Yamuna as well as the *prasad* is, by definition, non-different from Krishna and hence purifying. When they get dysentery they view it, in terms of the transcendental. They believe it has a purifying effect, purging the impurities and bad 'karma'. For them it is almost like a symbolic purification of society. Impermanence of the body as a focal concept is essentially a projection by devotees onto cosmology through the mediation of their bodies, of the states they experience as well as their relationships in society. This concern is not common amongst young people who are more interested in the 'here and now' and the enjoyment of life rather than in the hereafter and in 'birth, sickness, old age and death', as devotees refer to the aging process and the impermanency of the body. The sense of impermanence thus stressed seems to have germinated from the devotees' social relations prior to joining ISKCON. These young people have grown up in a rapidly changing world where everything is in a state of flux. Their relationships have been unstructured and impermanent, full of emotional crises and social problems of all kinds. Devotees appear to feel this impermanence more acutely than the average young person and many admitted to a feeling of mental chaos prior to joining the movement. ISKCON's stress on the impermanence and the aging process of the body thus provides devotees with the symbolism to express the impermanence in their relationships and their inner chaos.

Body symbolism, not only human but that of the animal is employed to criticise and symbolise what the devotees consider to be the main problems and ills of the outside 'karmi' world. Although Krishna Consciousness is conceived of as a 'science' and the Bhaktivedanta Institute has been set up to prove the truth of Krishna Consciousness 'scientifically', devotees view science as the bogey of the modern technological society which they detest. Science, they maintain, is 'puffed up' because it denies the existence of God and falsely thinks that it can explain all phenomena. What the devotees consider as the real miseries and problems of modern society are again expressed in terms of bodily stages and ills namely 'birth, sickness, old age and death'. When attacking modern society and science, devotees tend to use the same metaphorical argument to prove that science does not have all the answers. Science, they frequently point out, cannot cure 'birth, old age, disease and death'. Devotees also use animal bodily symbolism and often compare modern society to the existence of dogs. All that 'karmis' are interested in, they say, is 'eating, sleeping, mating and defending'. They are like dogs. And their society is little better than a dog civilisation!

Tara dasa for instance in an article 'Farming with Krishna in mind' when discussing the ideal social structure, is quoted as saying (BTG 1977, 12, No. 11 p. 21):

> Interwoven into the social fabric (caste system) are the four spiritual orders—student life (*brahmachari*), married life (*grihastha*), retired life (*vanaprastha*), and renounced life (sannyasa). These orders provide the necessary spiritual discipline to keep society from descending to the animal platform—simply worrying about the problems of eating, sleeping, mating and defending. No matter how sophisticated their technology, men who concern themselves only with these four problems are no better than polished animals. And any amount of philosophy which does not solve life's *real* problems—birth, death, disease and old age—is merely intellectual *animalism.*

Prabhupad himself is also stated as saying in *Back to Godhead* (Vol. 12, No. 3/4 p. 6):

> Owing to ignorance, one does not know that this material world is a miserable place where there are dangers at every step. Out of ignorance only, less intelligent persons try to adjust to the situation by fruitive activities, thinking that resultant actions will make them happy. They do not know that no kind of material body anywhere within the universe can give life without miseries. The miseries of life—namely birth, death, old age and diseases—are present everywhere within the material world. But one who understands his real constitutional position as the eternal servitor of the Lord, and thus knows the position of the Personality of Godhead, engages himself in the transcendental loving service of the Lord. Consequently, he becomes qualified to enter into the Vaikuntha planets, where there is neither material, miserable life, nor the influence of time and death...

In a later volume of *Back to Godhead* (Vol. 12, No 5, p. 14) Prabhupad remarks:

> Of course, scientists, journalists and politicians are not known for considering things in the philosophical light of transcendental knowledge, but a sober fact to consider is this: if, even after all the scientist's achievements, we must still die and suffer the miseries of repeated birth and death, then what is the benefit of that science?

In the same issue in an article entitled 'Beyond Animal Technology' p. 4-6, Prabhupad also uses animal habits as a metaphor for criticising scientists and society:

> Though today's scientist has devised a lofty technology, essentially he knows about as much as his dog: how to eat well, how to sleep peacefully, how to have an enjoyable sex life, and how to defend against enemies. But what about *human* technology? How is a living body different from a dead body? Who are we really? Where have we come from? Where are we going at death? We can find out all these things from someone who knows... When I spoke before some students and faculty members at the Massachussetts Institute of Technology, the first question I raised was: 'Where is the technological department which is investigating the difference between a dead man and a living man?' When a man dies, something is lost. Where is the technology to replace it? Why don't scientists try to solve this

problem? Because this is a very difficult subject matter, they set it aside and busily engage in the technology of eating, sleeping, mating and defending. However, Vedic literature informs us that this is animal technology. Animals are also trying to do their best to eat well, to have an enjoyable sex life, to sleep peacefully, and to defend themselves. What, then, is the difference between man's knowledge and the animal's knowledge? The fact is that man's knowledge should be developed to explore that difference between a living body and a dead body.

Devotees spend much of their time trying to purify their bodies by frequent ritual baths. They also eat large quantities of 'prasad' in order to purify themselves. They adhere to strict cleanliness. British devotees must be amongst the cleanest people in London. They are expected to bathe, in cold water on rising at 3 a.m., and always after defecating. Those who deal with food, such as the cooks and servers, are expected to wash if they come into contact with any kind of dirt or when they touch their mouths, since the mouth is considered one of the most polluting parts of the body.

Devotees' attitude to food apears to contradict the basic stress on asceticism, self-control and renunciation in ISKCON. Food seems to be an obsession and a major focus of concern in the movement. Devotees tend to eat large amounts of it and some of the women are quite fat.

Offerings of 'prasad' are made daily to Krishna at the *arati* ceremonies. This food, once offered to Krishna becomes indivisible from Krishna and is thus sanctified. In India visitors to temples are given token amounts of 'prasad'. But in the West, those who visit the temple at lunchtime and at the evening meal before the evening *arati* ceremony, are given large meals of 'prasad' and the devotees generally partake of the same themselves.

Devotees are well aware that the offer of a free meal is an attraction, particularly amongst the kinds of people who are likely to be potential converts (for example those on the dole) and it is for this reason that they give out free meal vouchers to passers-by in the street. Getting visitors into the temple is all important, for it brings them into contact with Krishna's potency.

Devotees also believe in the purifying effect of the 'prasad'. Feeding the body with 'prasad' is perceived as a means of controlling and purifying it and planting Krishna in the heart. 'Prasad' is considered particularly important for neophyte devotees. The greater the quantity of 'prasad' eaten, the greater its purifying potency is held to be; a useful piece of rationalisation for young westerners with healthy appetites. This endeavour to purify their own bodies and those of others would seem to be a symbolic attempt to control and cleanse society. The great weight attached to food in ISKCON and the all-pervading influence of 'prasad' on devotees finds a clear example in the case of Radha. She expressed her psychological problems and alienation in terms of 'prasad'. Radha was lucid enough to be aware of and able to explain her own problems. She saw her illness as due to being 'run down' and she felt that drinking large quantities of milk would give her 'the strength' to become well. Milk is of course considered the most important food by devotees, being a product of the sacred cow. She became obsessed by milk and food and grew enormously fat. Once again here we see an attempt to express and reconcile social problems in bodily terms.

Devotees also use their diet as a form of social protest and as a means of controlling the outside society. They follow orthodox Gaudiya teachings and are strict vegetarians—'Krishnatarians' they call themselves—having given up meat, fish, eggs, cheese and even onions and garlic. Many people critical of modern society and seeking an alternative lifestyle have become vegetarians. Food in general is highly ritualised in western society and a major focus of attention and concern. It is not so surprising either in a society which focused body symbolism, particularly as a form of social protest, that people, including ISKCON devotees, should use this basic bodily need as symbol of social protest. In their rejection of the meat-eating norm of western society and by emphasising a bodily orifice, namely the mouth they are rejecting western society. Vegetarianism, and this is true too of the general obsession with, and over-ritualisation of food, has become something of a cult phenomenon in western society because of its relationship to the body.

Food is believed by devotees to be the factor determining human qualities in general and, hence, the basis of social relations. Meat-eating is believed to foster aggression. According to Prabhupad, meat contains poisons and cholesterol that dull the mind and debilitate the body. Meat, for the devotees, is also, a symbol of confrontation and agression vis-a-vis the outside 'karmi' society. When beginning a discussion with a visitor, to determine whether they are sympathetic and have a similar outlook on life to that of their own devotees will ask them whether they eat meat or not. If there is an argument with visitors, devotees will bring up the subject of meat-eating, particularly when they are losing, and if the visitor is not a vegetarian they will use it as a means of attack and as an insult. In fact, 'meat-eater' is a general term of abuse implying that the person thus referred to does not value life. It is frequently used by devotees to characterise 'karmis'; 'meat-eaters!' they say with scorn.

Devotees' attitude to Prabhupad's body is of particular interest. The way it is articulated and the ideas associated with it indicate that in ISKCON, Prabhupad's body symbolises ISKCON's model of the ideal society, namely Vedic culture, which is uncorrupted by the evils of western civilisation. As Atreya Rishi (1977: 50) remarked in his Sri Vyasa Puja eulogy to Prabhupad:

> And this is the birth of your MOVEMENT—ISKCON. It is a precious gift, a golden carriage to carry your words. It is your divine body, it is devotional service, it is Krishna personified in this day on this planet. It is the path, the gate and the home.

Whilst the Bhaktivedanta Book Trust Travelling Sankirtan party (1974: 11) in India claimed in their eulogy: "Your body is the manifestation of Gauranga's (Krishna's) mercy, and by seeing you spiritual sight is restored. What sunrise can match the gleam of your smile."

Prabhupad had led such a pure life that, unlike devotees' bodies, which are seen as corrupt and contaminating, his body was viewed by devotees as being totally purified. He was not considered a material body, but pure 'spirit-soul':

> One who thinks that the spiritual master is a common man certainly possesses hellish intelligence and his eternal captivity in illusion is a certainty. Srila Prabhupada, your body is completely spiritual and your every breath is a prayer to Krishna. Your smile and shining teeth are a gateway to the spiritual world, and from your mouth there is a constant cascade of golden Vaikuntha nectar. May I always bathe myself in the Krishna-katha which flows from your lotus mouth. Your

eyes are like a window to Goloka, and if one steadily gazes into your lotus eyes he becomes melted in ecstasy, for they twinkle with pure love of Godhead. (VPB. 1977: 129 Bogota Devotees.)

The power and spirituality of Prabhupad's body is also reflected in two more Sri Vyasa Puja eulogies:

Oh devotee of the Lord, the purpose of the visual sense is fulfilled simply by seeing you, and to touch your body is the fulfilment of this bodily touch. The tongue is meant for glorifying your qualities because in this world it is very difficult to find a pure devotee of the Lord. (1975: 170.)

and

Oh divine spiritual master, we pray that we who have no qualification to serve you, may be able to meditate upon your *body*, words and deeds from which Krishna *prema* shines forth, destroying our lust, anger and greed. (1974-147 Stockholm devotees.)

The way devotees articulate Prabhupad's body in terms of their own social relations further demonstrates that his body is viewed as the ideal society in the movement. The ISKCON belief system postulates that Prabhupad's pure body was vulnerable to the corrupting influence of the devotees themselves. It was held that when a devotee joined the movement, Prabhupad took on all their bad karma himself. If he became sick, it was attributed to devotees' 'bad karma', as happened when he became ill immediately before he died. The British temple authorities at the time exhorted devotees to behave properly so that Prabhupad would become well and not have to suffer their sins. Continuous chanting of the holy names was carried on for several days to help foster better karma too.

Prabhupad's body also functions to promote the ideal society within the movement and helps foster conformity to ISKCON's norms. Devotees are held to be to some extent at the mercy of their own bodies and bodily need for sense gratification and 'lust'. Meditating on Prabhupad's body is viewed in ISKCON as a means of controlling devotees' 'passions'.

Devotees claim that it was not old age and disease that killed Prabhupad but that he decided that it was time he 'left his body'. This suggests that devotees saw Prabhupad as being in complete control of his own body. It was also a symbolic claim that Prabhupad was in direct disciplic succession from Krishna. In controlling his body—the symbol of the ideal society—was able to control 'karmi' society.

In sum, bodily control and control of the senses such as sex and food, which are seen as the chief causes of the desire for sense gratification and hence of falling into *maya*, provide a major focus of the movement. Also the emphasis on controlling the senses is a surrogate for and a symbolic attempt to control the wider society which, in their everyday lives, they are unable to influence.

CHAPTER TWELVE

Appearance: ISKCON Dress and its Relationship to Internal and External Relations

> The soul does not have any material qualities. The soul is pure, but because of his contact with the different qualities of material nature, he is dressed in various ways. The Krishna Consciousness movement aims at removing this material dress. Our first instruction is: "You are not this body." It appears that in his practical understanding Plato identified the soul with the bodily dress, and that does not show very good intelligence.
> —Vol. 11, no 5., p. 5

ISKCON's focus on the body and utilisatian of it as a symbol for society is expressed in the movement's attitude to dress and appearance. Clothes and other accessories are a major medium through which body symbolism is articulated in the movement. In fact, they, too, are used as a surrogate for action and as a vehicle for social protest.

ISKCON devotees are perhaps best known to outsiders for their eccentric appearance—the shaven heads and saffron robes of the men (which ISKCON claims is the customary clothing of the Gaudiya Matha) and the saris of the women which, devotees maintain, Indian women wore in 'Vedic' times.

Unlike ISKCON, few of the other new eastern religions, expect their members to don a specific type of dress and to wear them most of the time. Significantly, those that do—the western Sikhs and the Sufis—have, like ISKCON, totally rejected their own culture. In ISKCON, devotees are expected to wear Indian dress when they are within the temple confines and it is obligatory for them to do so if they enter the deity room and during daily ritual. Only if they go on 'sankirtan' or 'business' is the rule relaxed. Such importance is attached to Indian dress that as soon as a new devotee joins the movement, he is given saffron to wear or if a woman a sari. They are shown how to wear them and are expected to put them on immediately. Even visitors, if they stay on in a temple for a long time are expected to don Indian dress as well.

ISKCON attaches such importance to dress chiefly because of the symbolic significance with which it has endowed it. Since ISKCON is dependent on urban life and interacts a great deal with it and its rejection of western society is essentially symbolic rather than real, it has been necessary for the movement to forge for itself a separate identity to symbolise its rejection of western society. This precisely is what its costume does. Besides the group affiliation and solidarity that it provides, ISKCON's distinctive dress also defines the movement's boundaries, and strengthens the devotee's identification with and commitment to the movement.

Dress and appearance have always played a particularly important role in the British political arena, for they have traditionally been used symbolically to define group affiliation, status and position. One may cite the umbrella and the bowler hat of the 'city gent', the cloth cap of the pre-war worker and recently, the gaily coloured mix 'n' match casual clothes and beads of the Hippies, to mention but a few. Any change in appearance is assumed either to be an expression of social deviancy, or as indicating a change in factional or group allegiance, or as signalling an attempt at political change. As such, it is considered suspect and feared by both the man in the street and the ruling elite.

Since young people have started earning big salaries appearance, particularly fashion has acquired an even more dominant role. Fashion has become not only a form of expression but also a political weapon. Young people have made it their own, as the boom in the fashion industry in the last two decades bears witness. Fashion and appearance, more than most social phenomena are to some extent independent of social structural constraints and lend themselves to individual variation. They are a means of individual self-expression and social protest. Dress also provide a substitute for action for young people in dead-end existences who have no way of influencing the social structure to their advantage and of getting themselves out of the boring rut of their everyday lives. There have been for example the unskilled working-class Teddy Boys who parodied Edwardian aristocratic clothes, Hell's Angels who made a fetish of leather and masculine garments, and Mods who made a fetishism of fashion itself. These are clearly

Appearance: ISKCON Dress

examples of under-privileged groups who have used fashion as a form of self-expression and social protest and ISKCON utilises dress similarly.

Devotees appear to enjoy wearing Indian dress very much, partly because of its underlying symbolism. If it is accepted that members of ISKCON conceive the human body as a symbol of society and social relations, the emphasis on dress in ISKCON becomes understandable and further illuminates devotees' use of the body itself as a symbol. Bearing in mind that devotees see their bodies, like western society, as corrupt and contaminated, it seems reasonable to conclude that Indian dress is used by devotees to turn their corrupt bodies, symbolic of western society, into pure bodies, symbolic of the ideal Vaishnava society embodied in the movement.

The most significant factor when a new devotee joins the movement is 'body stripping'. It is a ritual surrender in which the external signs of his previous 'karmi' identity are totally given up. Dress is also expressive of social relations and in shedding his garments, a new devotee is symbolically divesting himself of the symbols of his former social relations as well. Here the Indian dress of the renunciate that the new devotee is given to wear adds to the significance of the ritual for it represents the movement's ideal of renunciation. Thus, when devotees divest themselves of their 'karmi' clothes and give up the symbols of 'karmi' society, they superimpose on their corrupt bodies the symbols of the ideal society which ISKCON embodies. In sum, ISKCON devotees are attempting, through dress, to change western society which they are, in practice, unable to do themselves, into the ideal Vaishnava society based on the principle of renunciation. In particular, they are attempting to express and create through their dress ideal male-female relations—based on renunciation.

The use of *tilaka* (sacred Vaishnava symbols made of sandalwood paste) serve the same function. It is obligatory for devotees in ISKCON to anoint their bodies, as do Indian Gaudiya *sadhus*, in nine different places after washing. Devotees appear to keep to this rule. In fact they seem quite compulsive about it. *Tilakas* are sacred and pure symbols. The U-shaped symbol above the nose which all devotees wear represents Vishnu's foot, for instance. In the light of the symbolism underlying clothes, devotees' liberal and obligatory use of *tilakas* appears to be a further attempt to purify the body and thus symbolically cleanse western society. Applying *tilaka* gives devotees satisfaction because it provides them with a means of symbolically controlling society through their bodies.

Outsiders tend to be extremely antagonistic and condescending to ISKCON 'sankirtan' devotees in Indian dress. They are frequently abused and ridiculed in the street and are also witch-hunted by the police. Individual quirks in dress are acceptable in western society. They are deemed merely 'eccentric'. But because of the traditional role of clothing as a political weapon and identifying symbol, any major change in dress is viewed as threatening. Since most antagonistic outsiders know nothing about ISKCON, it would seem reasonable to assume that it is some overt symbol which makes them react against the movement. Given western attitudes to changes in dress, it seems likely that it is ISKCON's dress that upsets them and frequently provokes them into making derogatory remarks. In short, ISKCON's dress is to outsiders what a red rag is to a bull.

Devotees aware as they are of the reactions they thus generate continue to wear their dress deliberately. In a sense, they play what might best be described as a clothes game. They use dress as a political weapon for 'cocking a snook' at 'karmi's. When they go out as a group on public chanting parties in Oxford Street, it is obligatory to wear Indian dress. This suggests that such dress is of social significance and great importance to them on public occasions when they interact as a group with 'karmi' society. Wearing their Indian dress in public clearly functions as a form of public social protest. They are intentionally making a public display of it. They are talking to the world they reject through the medium of their bodies and their clothes. Well aware of 'karmi's' attitudes to their clothing, by wearing them in public they are thumbing their noses at the outside world. Moreover, they present to the world their bodies clothed in the symbols of the ideal Vaishnava society. They flaunt their bodies to the 'karmi' public, wrapping them in pure clothing which symbolically represents the ideal pattern of social relations which they cannot find in the outside society.

However, aware of the effect their appearance had on outsiders, they modify their dress accordingly and wear 'karmi' clothes when they want to make a favourable impression. 'Sankirtan' devotees discovered early on that their Indian dress created antagonism, hindered book distribution and made money-making and 'doing business' difficult. Devotees, when they do 'sankirtan' or 'business', are now allowed to wear 'karmi' clothes. The kinds of 'karmi' clothes they wear, however, are of symbolic significance in themselves. It may seem surprising to outsiders that they do not wear the casual dress of Hippies. Instead, the men wear very 'straight' conventional clothes—jackets, ties and even three-piece suits. At one time too, 'squire' type cloth caps were also fashionable in the movement. The transformation from Hippie or casual wear to three-piece suits is perhaps one of the most spectacular transformations of all that the devotee undergoes when he joins the movement. Until recently, in Britain ISKCON women have been dressing up in what can only be described as very respectable 'country lady clothes'—long skirts and jackets and felt hats with brims. In summer in recent years they have been wearing very pretty flowered frocks which in themselves attract large donations from men.

Devotees on the whole tend to be inherently conservative. This attitude is reflected in their traditional capitalist economic structure as well as in the attitude of those devotees who led a hippie life earlier. Although many of them, particularly American devotees, indulged in promiscuity before joining the movement, they appear to have been never quite at ease with it and often appear to have felt guilty about it. Indeed, they were never really comfortable with their hippie life and were often ashamed of it. They have espoused the extreme puritanism of ISKCON with alacrity, finding its ethical system more suited to their true nature. In fact devotees are people who find it difficult to cope with the permissiveness of modern society in general and this is expressed and acted out in the movement. Their 'karmi clothes' demonstrate that beneath devotees' bizarre exteriors beat the hearts of traditional 'super-straights'.

Lastly, whilst on one level Indian dress fosters allegiance to the group and identification with the movement, nevertheless each devotee wears his dress in a very idiosyncratic manner. Outsiders often complain that devotees look a 'shambles' and don't know how to wear Indian dress properly. Few devotees are spick and span in their appearance. They tend to dress in a rather individualistic slipshod manner. ISKCON has adapted Indian dress to fit in with the exigencies of the western climate and western clothing pattern. Devotees have included in their dress a wide variety of western items of clothing which they dye saffron, such as jumpers, long-johns, knitted hats and sweat shirts with Krishna pictures stamped on them, combining such items in an idiosyncratic manner. Thus, whilst all male devotees wear saffron and women wear saris there is, in practice, a great diversity of dress in the movement. Dress, like everything else in ISKCON provides a backcloth for and is expressive of devotees' innate individualism.

CHAPTER THIRTEEN

The Sexual Rites of ISKCON—Devotees' Attitudes to Sexuality and Their Use of Sexuality as a Means of Social Protest

> Dear Srila Prabhupad, there is no love in the material world. We have searched and searched, destroying our minds and defiling our bodies, seeking the pure experience. There was nothing so pure or so absorbing that it could help us to forget the anxieties of birth, death, old age and disease. We were so uneasy before we met your mercy, and so puffed up, thinking we had found happiness. You are so kind that you have given us the supremely lovable object, Krishna, but you haven't asked us for anything in return. As a result, we are obliged to try to give you everything— our bodies, our senses, our minds and our hearts.
>
> —S.V.P.B. (1975)

Indian society, like many other societies and groups which utilise body symbolism to express social relations, uses sexuality as a basis for symbolism. This is also true of ISKCON, where devotees use their sexuality symbolically as a means of articulating their social protest, as well as coming to terms with both personal problems and relationships with the opposite sex.

The majority of devotees are young when they join the movement. ISKCON thus largely consists of an age group whose main interest normally would be sex, marriage and children. As a result sexuality and male-female relations have become focal concerns in the movement.

ISKCON is no hippie commune with lax sexual morals. On the contrary, devotees have totally renounced the sexual mores of the Permissive Society. As with other features of ISKCON, they have sought an alternative in the exact opposite to that which is acceptable in the Permissive Society, namely in the renunciation of their sexuality. Sexual renunciation in fact has become a 'trade mark' and symbol of the movement, and is seen as such by the devotees themselves.

ISKCON adheres to a set of sexual beliefs and practices which incorporate an extreme form of sexual renunciation, which they claim were the practice in 'Vedic' times. Some would be considered very orthodox and extreme even by conservative Gaudiya standards and the details of practice would not be accepted by many modern Gaudiyas.

Ideally male devotees are expected, following Gaudiya custom, to be celibate for life. The highest status in the movement is that of the sanyasin who renounces sex for life. Men may marry however if they think it will help in their service for Krishna. Women, on the other hand, are expected to marry and have children, remaining chaste before marriage. Married couples, however, are supposed to have sex only if they want to have children and then only once a month.

Any other sexual relationship is looked upon and referred to as 'illicit sex' and is viewed derogatorily as 'lust' and equated with the behaviour of 'dogs' and 'hogs'. Romantic love of course is considered an illusion and a misplaced substitute for love of Krishna. Sex is equated with and seen as 'sense gratification' and *maya*. Individuals are expected to learn to detach themselves from this bodily urge. A remark made by Prabhupad (BTG Vol. 13: no 1-2, p. 5) clearly sums up the movement's attitude to sex.

> Here in this world we are experiencing frustration. Here we love—a man loves a woman, or a woman loves a man—but there is frustration. After some time they are divorced, because their love is a perverted reflection. There is no real love in this world. It is simply lust. Real love is in the spiritual world, between Radha and Krishna. Real love is there between Krishna and the *gopis*. Real love is there in the friendship between Krishna and His cowherd boys. Real love is there—between the trees, the flowers and water. Real love is there between the trees, flowers and water. In the spiritual world, everything is love. But within this material world, we are satisfied merely by the reflection of the things in the spiritual world.

Paradoxically, however, although devotees reject their sexuality they appear to be obsessed by sex. Far from sex being a taboo subject, it frequently crops up in devotees' conversations. The need for sexual renunciation, references to 'illicit sex', 'lust' and

The Sexual Rites of ISKCON

the animal-like behaviour of 'karmis' are frequent topics of conversation. Sex is also a common subject for sermons and is often referred to in the ISKCON literature. So overtly is this subject articulated in the movement and so obsessed are devotees by sexual renunciation, that in the Los Angeles temple guest-house book of rules and regulations is included the injunction that couples staying in the guest-house may only have sex if they chant 58 rounds of *japa* first. As one neophyte Asian devotee perceptively remarked 'they spend more time talking about sex than doing it'.

Whilst sexual renunciation is a pivotal ideal, most of those who join ISKCON and are under thirty, like their peers in the outside world, do get married and nearly all have children. Some temples have a number of children, including Bhaktivedanta Manor which has some twenty. There are several hundred children in the movement, a figure which is difficult to explain given ISKCON rules governing sexual intercourse. Married females are allowed to have intercourse only on the seventh day after they begin menstruating, which they say is a Vedic custom. This seventh day, however, falls in what Catholics refer to as the 'safe period'. As such if devotees followed the rule they would be unlikely to conceive. But as devotees say, conception is 'Krishna's mercy'.

The movement has set up a number of schools (in Vrindaban, Gita Nagari in Philadelphia and France) to cope with the increasing number of children. There are so many children at Bhaktivedanta Manor that it appears more like a children's nursery than a monastery. It has a secular atmosphere rather than an ascetic one.

Marriage and family life of devotees and the movement's ideal of celibacy might well appear contradictory and mutually exclusive. But in practice they reflect a progression in the devotee's life cycle. Renunciation of sex provides young adolescents and devotees in their early twenties in ISKCON, most of whom would not want to marry at this age anyway, with a blueprint and channel for social protest. It also provides them with the means of dealing with their adolescent sexual problems and relationships with the opposite sex, as well as their problems in general. But in the process of growing out of their adolescent problems, they generally react like their peer group in the outside world and the natural desire to marry and have children finds expression. It was a necessary and particularly shrewd move on Prabhupad's part to have allowed devotees to marry, for the majority of devotees are young and appear to be heterosexual. Without the companionship of members of the opposite sex and the possibility of marriage open to them, it is unlikely that devotees would remain long in the movement.

Prabhupad, taking into account the sexual egalitarianism of western society, has founded the tradition of having both single women (*brahmacharinis*) and married couples (*grihasthas*) to live in ISKCON temples where celibates reside. Devotees are also allowed to take a marriage partner from within their temple. These are seen as deviations by Asian critics of ISKCON. They maintain celibates should live only with celibates as is the traditional custom. These are amongst the few clear-cut deviations from Gaudiya teachings made by ISKCON. Though seemingly minor, they have had far-reaching consequences. They have led to the development of a radically different institutional structure in ISKCON from that found in traditional Gaudiya temples and sect organisations; namely an organisation that revolves around sexuality. Where you have a group of predominantly young people such as in ISKCON, living in close proximity as they do, sex understandably becomes a major interest and focus of attention. This situation has led to the preoccupation with, and the establishment of, a highly developed system of sexual role differentiation, to a stress on male and female roles and their interrelationship. In particular, this has led to an emphasis on sexual symbolism.

It may seem strange that people brought up in the Permissive Society should willingly reject sex. The lives that the earliest devotees led prior to joining the movement however, sheds light on this phenomenon. The ideal of sexual renunciation appears to have originated in the Haight Ashbury temple. Many of the young people who joined the movement in Haight Ashbury, had been promiscuous and had become deeply disillusioned with and even ashamed of their lifestyle. Sita, for example had run away from home at the age of fourteen and had many lovers. Seven years after she gave up her hippy life she still felt guilt-ridden. She felt her former life had marred her whole life and personality. For such young people, essentially conservative at heart, Prabhupad's emphasis on sexual abstinence and strict regulation of sexual life was highly appealing.

Having men who are expected to be celibate and women who may marry in the same ashram provides devotees with a framework and weapon for expressing their social protest and for dealing with their own personal sexual problems. In ISKCON, the sexual role confusion created by the Permissive Society is writ in microcosm. Renunciation of sex is, for devotees, a means of articulating and coming to terms with fundamental contradictions inherent in male/female sexual roles in western society.

Given the ideal of celibacy, having men and women living in the same ashram has created a fundamental contradiction and problem for ISKCON. On the one hand it has made the 'Vedic' ideal of non-association with women impossible. At the same time, if the women are to obtain husbands from within the movement, as is the preferred rule, then they must come from the very group which is expected to be celibate. The whole institutional structure that has developed in ISKCON is an expression of the incompatibility of these two conflicting ideals. It attempts, often in a highly farcical way, to reconcile male celibacy on the one hand with women devotees' desire for marriage. In some temples it has in fact led to a battle of the sexes with the result that much of the politics of the movement revolves around sex and asceticism.

ISKCON has rejected the Permissive Society's egalitarianism in male/female relations and instead has accepted the Hindu traditional pattern. The archetypal dominant male is the decision maker and the breadwinner, and a woman is expected to be faithful, submissive and devoted to her husband and children. Women are not allowed to hold any position of authority or office in the movement. Also it is considered unnecessary to educate women as their role is in the home. They are expected to learn at home from their mothers how to look after a house, to cook, sew etc. and the jobs considered particularly appropriate for them in the movement if they do not want to do 'Sankirtan' are making clothes and garlands for the deities. According to Prabhupad who held extremely conservative views himself on the subject of women (BTG, Vol. 11, No. 6, p. 7):

> Socalled equal rights for women means that the men cheat the women. Suppose a woman and a man meet, they become lovers, they have sex, the woman becomes pregnant, and the man goes away. The woman has to take charge of the child and beg alms from the government, or else she kills the child by having an abortion. This is the woman's independence. In India, although

a woman may be poverty-stricken, she stays under the care of her husband, and he takes responsibility for her. When she becomes pregnant, she is not forced to kill the child or maintain him by begging. So, which is real independence—to remain under the care of the husband or to be enjoyed by everyone?

However, continuous external criticism of ISKCON's attitude to women has, over the years, had its influence. In recent years, when ISKCON is criticised for its chauvinistic attitude to women, devotees are quick to point out in their defence that although male and female material bodies are different, those of women being inferior, all souls are of equal status at the spiritual level. But any attempt by women, even now, to try and attain formal power and status is always quickly thwarted by the men.

Most women have no desire to hold positions of authority anyway. But for the few who do—they tend to be the more educated, generally ex-college students—it is particularly frustrating. The experience of Yadurani, the first American female devotee, is a typical case. Yadurani, now in her early thirties, is an ex-art student and runs the Art Department in Los Angeles. She is generally recognised as an 'advanced' devotee, with a deep knowledge of the scriptures, who is both outstanding and saintly. She wanted to be a preacher. Since she was one of the first devotees, she was very close to Prabhupad and got his permission to conduct the daily *Bhagavad Gita* classes where the philosophy is taught. So as not to excite the men, she made herself as unattractive as possible. Resorting to body symbolism she shaved her head, dressed in white and wore no jewellery. Even so she did not last long. The men in the class rebelled, saying that she 'agitated' them and in consequence she was forced to give up the classes. Gaudiya teaching does allow women to be gurus and Yadurani was well qualified to be one, but when Prabhupad passed over in 1977, she was not appointed to be one, a fact which appeared to disappoint her.

Nevertheless, some women, such as Yadurani, do have informal influence and power. Much of her influence is derived from her saintliness and the fact that she is one of the movement's most famous artists, and book illustrators. She is looked up to and admired by the other women. In practice she functions as the informal leader of the women in the movement. Those female devotees who do have informal influence and power in the movement tend to be the older ones. Also they appear to have either been in the movement from its earliest days, or to have been close to Prabhupad, or to have led very ascetic lives, or else to have come from rich background or to have held *pujari* (priestly) roles in the same temple for a number of years. Those who have husbands in positions of power and influence in the movement also tend to acquire influence and power themselves. In fact Manjvali, the wife of Jayatirtha Maharaj, acts as his informal deputy. When he is away she keeps an eye on things for him.

Since celibacy is the ideal for males and even those who are married abstain from sex most of the time, their sexual awareness is naturally heightened and increased; living as they do in close confines with women, most of whom are on the lookout for a husband. This appears to be the main factor responsible for overt emphasis on sex, the ample references to 'lust' and 'illicit sex' and so on. Such emphasis in turn, tends to further arouse and exacerbate devotees' sexuality rather than cool it down, as is the usual aim of asceticism.

In an attempt to reconcile male celibacy with having women living in the temple, ISKCON has developed a system of avoidance rituals. Celibate men are not supposed to have any association with women. To maintain this non-association, ISKCON has resorted to segregation of the sexes. As in Indian religious institutions, men and women are not supposed to talk to each other except on temple business. They are not even supposed to look each other in the eye. As a mark of their modesty, women have to cover their heads with their saris and lower their eyes so as not to 'agitate' or arouse the men. Such behaviour has of course the exact opposite effect to that intended—it exacerbates and heightens devotees' awareness of each other.

Some of the *sannyasins* and *brahmacharins* are extremely committed to the celibate ideal and carry rituals of non-association and avoidance of women to an extreme. They see all women as *maya* and the prime cause of temptation, ever ready to make them fall from their celibate ideal. Hence they reject women totally and go out of their way to demonstrate their avoidance of them. For instance, when they come into contact with women they make a point of making it obvious that they are avoiding them and are often extremely rude to female devotees. These devotees are referred to as 'heavies' in the movement.

They justify their attitude and reaction to women by pointing to

Chaitanya. They maintain that from the age of 24 onwards he had no association with women. Yet, traditionally, the Gaudiya and Hindu ascetics' attitude in general to women has been that they are all to be considered either as 'mothers' or 'sisters'. As such they are to be treated with courtesy and respect. Prabhupad himself had a great deal of association with women. One of his favourite devotees was a girl. As one middleaged Indian *brahmacharin* said when discussing the subject—"They say women are 'hellers', women are poison, but, for us, all women are like our mothers and sisters and we treat them as such". He then went on to say that he couldn't talk to me in public because the western devotees would think we were having an affair. He arranged for us to meet clandestinely and when we met in public from then on, he overtly avoided me.

The 'heavies' are often devotees who have difficulty coping with their enforced celibacy and are frustrated or have psychological problems and/or they are misogynists: ISKCON's male dominance ideology is, of course, attractive to such types. They attempt to force their opinions on other devotees and make them follow their example. One of the most famous and powerful *sannyasins* in the movement, the former Swami Govinda who was in his late twenties, was, perhaps, the most notorious 'heavy' and women-hater in the movement. When he preached, one of his favourite sermon topics was 'women are *maya*'. His followers were all 'heavies' too.

Some of the women who are very committed to the celibate ideal and have renounced marriage and their sexuality for life, play similar avoidance games as the men. They utilise body symbolism too. Referred to as 'Vedic widows', they emphasise their status vis-a-vis the male celibates and the other women, by wearing white robes, shaving their heads, and ostentatiously avoiding the men.

Perhaps two of my own encounters with ISKCON 'heavies' will demonstrate how extreme their attitude to women is in practice and how far some of them take non-association with women. One day in Vrindaban in 1977, just before Prabhupad's death, I was waiting with others outside his house for his arrival from Bombay and was passing the time chatting to a fifteen year old male devotee who was standing beside me. On Prabhupad's arrival, one of the *brahmacharins* who accompanied him, a 'heavy', on seeing me talking to the boy, rushed up and without a word dragged him off unceremoniously and gave him a dressing down on the evils of speaking to women.

On another occasion, at Bhaktivedanta Manor, I was talking to a neophyte *brahmacharin*. A leading American devotee and a 'heavy', on seeing me talk to the new devotee, rushed up and with his back towards me deliberately placed himself between me and the new devotee. He engaged him in conversation and on the pretext of wanting to talk to him, led him away.

In some temples, the 'heavies'' attitude and behaviour towards women leads to a great deal of tension, and conflict. They tend to take on women 'pujaris' who have remained in the same temple over a number of years and in so doing have attained informal influence. They are the ones who tend to bear the brunt of the 'heavies'' attack. At one point, in the New York temple the 'heavies' actually took over and threw out all the women including the 'pujaris' who had been there a long time.

It is difficult to understand how in the Permissive Society, women accept such bad treatment from men or even join ISKCON in the first place. For many of the women, ISKCON obviously provides a genuine and meaningful religious experience and because of the satisfaction they derive from participation in the movement, they put up with the men's treatment. Some women pay lip service to 'female inferiority' and avoid the men, or just go their own way. Still others find they are fulfilled through motherhood. They know, because of the scarcity of women, that, ultimately, if they want to they can marry and very probably the husband may become a leader in the movement and as such, the 'heavies' will leave them alone for fear of annoying their husbands. Some, however, get hurt and frustrated at the male devotees' treatment of them, as in the case of Yadurani. One devotee said it sometimes made her feel very 'unloved'.

But, in general, the kind of girls who join ISKCON in Britain are not 'Women's Lib' types. They are still very traditional and see their futures in terms of motherhood and family, particularly those who come from the lower status groups. It is the more educated ones who find the movement's attitude to women irksome. The kind of women who join ISKCON are not the kind who are going to set the world on fire and they would not expect to hold positions of power and authority in or out of ISKCON. Most are content with their role of mothers, and do not feel frustrated at not being in positions of formal authority. In fact they have a very easy life once they have children, for the temple looks after their needs and they have nothing to do but look after their babies. Ironically, most of the temple chores are done by the *brahmacharins*. Such a situation is very appealing to lazy female devotees.

Very few girls join the movement, which indicates that most women who visit the temple are put off by the rules governing women's behaviour in ISKCON. ISKCON men get the women they deserve. Although ISKCON attracts some very pretty girls (often after unhappy love affairs) the majority are plain. Many of them, especially the married women, are lazy and slovenly. Many ISKCON men themselves have a low opinion of the type of women that ISKCON attracts and some either prefer not to marry at all or try to find a wife outside the movement.

Lastly and most importantly, body symbolism itself offers a justification and rationalisation of women's position in the movement. It provides women devotees with the means of rationalising and reconciling their position. They see their femaleness as a bodily attribute and not part of themselves. Women devotees talk about 'the inferior body of a woman', as though it was separate from themselves. When the men treat them as inferior and are rude, the women believe they are doing it only to their bodies and not to their soul or character and as such, making it one step distant, such treatment becomes acceptable.

As one American devotee said:

> You're protected and given instruction, and you don't have to make the decision: it's really pleasant... The boys really have propensities for administration—that we just don't have. So it must be my female body, but I'm very pleased not to have to make very many decisions anymore. (*Judah*, 1974: 87.)

For the majority of *brahmacharins*, this emphasis on celibacy and non-association with women is essentially symbolic, since the majority of them do become householders. Nevertheless, although marriage is allowed in ISKCON, once again the movement inverts the custom of free choice, followed in the outside 'karmi' world, for in ISKCON, at least in theory, marriages are arranged. If a *brahmacharin* wants to marry, he asks his temple to find him a wife.

In many cases, because of the rules of non-association with women, a couple will have had little contact and will not know each other prior to the proposal. However, because of the close confines of temple living and small numbers of devotees in a temple, they may have seen each other around the temple. In other cases in temples where conformity to non-association with women is minimal couples will have had some contact and interaction, particularly if they are 'pujaris' and serving the deity. Not infrequently, 'pujaris' marry each other.

The rules governing non-association with women foster the development of relationships focused on body symbolism. Individuals who are attracted to each other develop their relationship through eye contact, meaningful looks, and dress. When a man decides that this is the girl for him, he goes to the temple President and gets him to arrange the marriage.

Female dress takes on a new significance in the marriage stakes. Taking an interest in personal appearance and dress is frowned on and viewed as succumbing to *'maya'* and sense gratification. But those female devotees who want to marry, tend to dress well and wear pretty saris and jewellery to attract the men, frequently to the amusement of other devotees who are quick to read the symbolism. In fact, if it is done too obviously, the temple President will ask the girl if she wants to marry and all things beings equal, he will try to arrange it. In a temple where the 'heavies' hold power, if a girl dresses too attractively she will be asked to leave. This happened at Vrindaban, where a pretty young French girl dressed very attractively all the time. She was asked to leave because she 'excited' and 'agitated' the men.

Unfortunately, relationships where spouses have had little or no communication, particularly those based on eye communication, however erotically they may develop, are essentially unreal and lack substance and, generally, they are not a sound basis for a permanent relationship. The inherent brittleness in ISKCON marriages reflects this. Couples frequently find soon after marriage that they are incompatible and the marriage rapidly breaks up. Serial monogamy is not uncommon. The ISKCON marriage pattern, therefore, far from transcending the 'karmi' marriage pattern with its high divorce rate which devotees despise, reflects it.

Marriage which is celebrated by a traditional fire sacrifice, a ritual that focuses around a sacred fire, is also used within ISKCON as a means of social control. As men outnumber women by more than two to one and since most of the devotees do eventually marry, clearly there are not enough women to go round. The majority of women tend to marry sooner than the men, reflecting their scarcity. Generally, marriages are only arranged for devotee males who have been in the movement for at least two or three years, are well established and hold positions of influence and/or power. Partners are not found for devotees who are 'maverick', have psychological problems or are considered unstable. Those that do not find wives tend to leave, for there are few devotees over thirty unmarried who joined the movement under the age of twenty-five.

After about five years in the movement most devotees tend to become restless and bored. This appears to be a crucial stage. If the devotee is unmarried and a useful acquisition to the temple and in a position of power and influence, to prevent him 'blooping' the temple authorities may offer to find him a marriage partner.

The degree of tension between the sexes, the amount of influence the 'heavies' have, and, the degree to which the rules governing non-association with women are actually conformed to, varies from temple to temple and country to country. Some temples, such as New York, Vrindaban and Mayapur in India are very 'heavy' and conform to the rules of non-association with women to a high degree. Others such as Hawaii, are very easy-going and relaxed and there is very little tension between the sexes. Likewise, in Britain where there is a lot of contact between men and women devotees, avoidance rituals are conformed to minimally and the atmosphere is relatively free and easy.

This variation is, to a great extent, determined by whether the President of a temple and or the local Governing Body Commissioner is a *sannyasin* or *grihastha* (householder). *Sannyasins*, having renounced their sexuality for life, tend to be highly committed to the celibate ideal. If they have the power, particularly if there are other like-minded males in the temple to support them (and where there is a big 'heavy' in power they tend to attract the same kind to live in the temple too) they will enforce segregation of the sexes and the non-association with women. Some of the more extremist 'heavies' will not allow unmarried women, and, in some cases householders too, to live in their temples at all, as at one time was the case in New York. In Vrindaban, too, where the woman-hating

Swami Govinda gained power on Prabhupad's death and immediately put his likeminded followers in positions of authority, all the unmarried women were expelled. On the other hand, if the president or GBC is a householder, then the atmosphere in a temple will tend to be more relaxed and the relationship between men and women easy-going and the avoidance of women rules will only be minimally enforced.

It is therefore no accident that in Bhaktivedanta Manor, Bury Place and more recently Soho Street the atmosphere is relaxed and easy-going because Jayatirtha Maharaj is a householder. He and his wife Manjvali reside at the Manor with their small son. Their influence is all pervasive. Another reason for the easy-going atmosphere there is that nearly twenty married couples reside at the Manor too.

In temples where householders are in power or where their numbers give them a lot of influence, they are able to control the 'heavies'' extremism. In fact in these temples if a *brahmacharin* acts too 'heavy' and annoys or upsets the girls, they marry him off. Devotees justify this action with a superb piece of logic. They say a really renounced *brahmacharin* should not be affected by the presence of women—an overreaction indicates they are not really detached. Such devotees, they argue, are not cut out for a life of celibacy and can serve Krishna better if they marry, and so they marry.

To understand the dynamics of the relationship between householders and celibates it is necessary to examine the concept of celibacy; that is, the *sannyasin* and *brahmacharin* roles on the one hand and that of householders (*grihastha*) on the other. Their patterns of behaviour and orientation to life are fundamentally different and opposed.

In the Vedic system, which ISKCON maintains is their ideal, *sannyasa* was the fourth and last stage in the *varnashramadharma*. The term *sannyasin* is used very loosely in India now to refer to any *sadhu*. In traditional Hinduism, by the time a man took *sannyasa* at the age of sixty, he had already had a family and performed his expected sexual role. Therefore, sexual renunciation, although part of the *sannyasin* role, was not a particularly important factor and, as such, was not emphasised. Thus, when Indians are asked the meaning of *sannyasin*, they tend to refer to renunciation in general, rather than specifically to sexuality and sexual renunciation. But most of the ISKCON devotees who have become *sannyasin* are young men still at their sexual peak. Their renunciation of sexuality is therefore an all important factor and this is reflected in the emphasis laid on it in the movement and the focus of the *sannyasin's* role around it. Once having taken *sannyasa*, these young men feel a great commitment to, and need to over-perform the *sannyasin* role and to emphasise sexual renunciation, and in this lies much of the basis of the 'heavy' extremeness in the movement.

Sannyasins are treated with great respect. Using bodily symbolism, devotees kneel and touch their foreheads on the ground as a sign of respect when they walk by. To set themselves apart from the other devotees they utilise bodily symbolism too. They wear the saffron robes of a Gaudiya Matha *sannyasin* and carry a *sannyasin's* staff (*tridandi*) at all times, even to *Bhagavad Gita* classes; much to the amusement of the more humorous devotees.

But in practice, however, there is little difference between *sannyasins* and other devotees in terms of degree of asceticism. Devotees, when asked to define *sannyasin*, often state that they are the movement's preachers, but so, too, are leading householders. Indeed, some of them are, of course, the richest and most influential devotees in the movement. Swami Govinda for instance was considered so worldly that he was not made a guru. Because generally, power, position and influence go hand in hand with being *sannyasin*, *sannyasins* tend in ISKCON to be far more materialistic and worldly than the average rank-and-file devotee.

Because of the prestige, power and status, the position automatically confers, not just anybody can renounce the world and become a *sannyasin*. Only the leaders are allowed to do so. Moreover it is only *sannyasins*' focus on their sexuality and renunciation of it for life that differentiates them from the rest of the devotees. Thus, given ISKCON's focus on sexuality, it may be argued, that the *sannyasin*, the ideal in ISKCON, since it is essentially conceptualised in sexual terms is a sexual symbol. This is clearly no accident, nor for that matter whilst the movement follows Gaudiya Matha teachings remarkably closely, it is in the sexual realm that ISKCON deviates the most. How, therefore, do we explain ISKCON's interpretation of the *sannyasin's* role in terms of sexuality, or, their extremist interpretation of Gaudiya sexual mores, which is far more extreme than that followed by traditional Gaudiyas or Hindus in general? In fact, how do we explain the movement's obsession with, and focus on sex in general? For the average westerner, the sexual pattern of ISKCON must appear extremely strange. What attracts predominantly healthy young men and women brought up in the Permissive Society, particularly those from a Hippy 'hang loose' background, to accept as normal and to take part in such practices? It is not insignificant that another group, the Moonies, also practise self-imposed restrictions on sex, and similarly reject western society.

Sexual freedom is an all pervading theme in the Permissive Society. Modern man is told that his basic motivations are sexual and the media and the arts continually bombard him with this awareness. Permissive sexuality in other words, has become the symbol of the Permissive Society. In this light, the focus on sexuality in ISKCON becomes explicable. It is a reflection of the importance and focal role of sexuality in western society. It is a projection onto religion and the symbolic level of this importance. In symbolically using their bodies as the medium of expression— as the symbol of society—in rejecting their sexuality which is a major body function, devotees are, in essence, rejecting the focal symbol of western society, and hence western society itself. Thus, this emphasis on celibacy as the ideal is an expression of social protest and rejection of western society. Most importantly since body control in ISKCON is symbolically equated with control over society, devotees in controlling their sexuality, are attempting, through control over western society's major symbol, to demonstrate their power over society.

Also on one level the emphasis on celibacy is the acting out, and reconciliation in microcosm of sexual role contradiction and conflict between the sexes in western society. Since the introduction of the Pill, a catalyst to the permissiveness of the 1960s, sex has been easily obtainable. But many people find permissiveness makes them feel insecure. Female emancipation and 'Women's Lib' have undermined the traditional dominant male role, particularly as far as sex is concerned. Women demand and demand more from their sexual lives than in the past and expect more say in decision making too. Many men find this particularly threatening. Even those who cling to the old dominant male role, find it difficult to live up to in the face of the emancipated female. Understandably, a philosophy such as ISKCON's, which offers a safe archetypal male dominant role is attractive to men who find liberated females threatening. For them, ISKCON is, an ego-trip and many of the woman-haters certainly appear to enjoy their roles. Looked at from the point of view of its sexual mores, it is easy to see why men out-number women by two to one in ISKCON.

But men also outnumber women because they are far more socially frustrated than women who can find fulfilment in a wife and mother role alone. Looked at from this perspective, it is significant that the movement's celibate ideal, that of *sannyasin* is a male role. Indeed, focusing as it does around male ideals and male interests, it is to be expected that the movement's ideal, the *sannyasin*, should be expressed in terms of a male role. It represents, particularly as it goes hand in hand with political power in the movement, the aspirations, and frustrations of males. In the celibate ideal, and the *sannyasin* role in particular, male devotees are expressing not only sexual but social frustration in general, and the rejection of their sexuality is an expression of their frustration. Social frustration is directly correlated with the heavies' extremism and emphasis on avoidance of women. The stronger the sense of social frustration the greater the 'heavy' emphasis and the greater the avoidance of women.

The majority of *brahmacharins* and *sannyasins* and the heavies in general for that matter, appear genuine and sincere in their desire to raise their consciousness level and go back to Godhead. They are genuine too in their renunciation of sexuality as the means to this end. But it must be borne in mind that the celibate role in ISKCON is a symbolic one since the majority of devotees do marry. Even amongst the *sannyasin* who number some twenty in the movement, the rate of 'falling down' is high and marriages are quite common. Devotees know they may marry if they want to and that the majority of their peers in the movement actually do marry as they get older. Some devotees are honest about their attitude to marriage. The 22 year old Atma Atma when asked about celibacy, said that he did not consider himself a celibate; he had just not yet married and did not feel ready for marriage. Even so whilst male devotees remain *brahmacharins* they act out this sexual renunciation role and avoid all contact with women.

However, there are clearly social, economic and political reasons for devotees' commitment to the celibate ideal and the 'heavies' extremist attitude. Celibate roles and asceticism in ISKCON provide the basic framework, channel, and incentive for individualism.

In particular, they sanction individualism in a wide variety of ISKCON's social, economic and political institutions. Moreover, it is within the ascetic roles in ISKCON that *bhakti yoga* and the movement's all pervasive rampant individualism come together and is legitimized.

This is particularly true of the role of *brahmacharins*. Traditionally, they were students of philosophy, who, when they attained the age of 25, were allowed to marry if they wanted. This role is a very attractive one for those young men not yet ready for marriage. In fact, *brahmacharin* is the liminal role par excellence, for it provides and sanctions young male devotees with a pleasant way of life.

By renouncing their rights to marriage, *brahmacharins* free themselves from family responsibilities and social encumbrances in general. This allows them to go where they choose or do what they like. They are looked after by their temple which provides their needs so they do not have to worry about board and lodgings. Although their existence and standard of living tends to be spartan, like most young people, devotees do not mind roughing it. In fact, they often appear to enjoy doing so.

Many devotees, particularly Americans, manage to 'see the world on ISKCON'. They travel all round the world, including India, via the world-wide ISKCON temple network, in so doing providing themselves with an enjoyable and varied life. Within the States mobility between temples is also high. If devotees get bored with one temple they can move to another. Since most temples suffer from a chronic manpower shortage devotees willing to work are welcome anywhere. If they have no skill to offer they can always offer their services for 'sankirtan'.

The aim of the movement—to preach Krishna Consciousness to the world—also sanctions and allows devotees to do much as they choose. In particular they can travel wherever they want to go because they can go anywhere on the pretext of preaching Krishna Consciousness. Swami Brahmananda for instance, who took ISKCON to Africa and opened the Nairobi temple in 1973, decided to get up an expedition to go up the Congo to preach Krishna Consciousness to the local population there. Clearly such an expedition, though unlikely to increase the size of the Krishna Consciousness population in the area nevertheless provided him with a great adventure.

The development of the world-wide network of ISKCON temples demonstrates the devotees' individualism and desire to travel. The movement has temples in such attractive, far-away and romantic places as Fiji, Mauritius and Hawaii. Generally a new temple would be started by one or two devotees deciding they would like to visit some country, as was the case with the devotees who started the movement in Britain. On the pretext of spreading Krishna Consciousness, they would go and stay in the country of their choice and would turn their initial living accommodation, often a flat, into a shrine and small temple.

Most temples of course, including the British, have single sex 'travelling sankirtan parties'. Since these small groups of like-minded young men, freed of all responsibilities and having their basic wants provided for, have a very stimulating and varied life and often a great deal of fun, it is understandable that once 'travelling sankirtan parties' were introduced they mushroomed rapidly throughout the movement. They are particularly important in Britain, and the British movement bought a fleet of buses as soon as they could afford to since devotees do not have the advantage of large networks of temples to move to when they get bored as they do in the States.

Moreover *brahmacharins*, by rejecting and ruling out their sexuality, are able to maintain group harmony and cohesion. If they were allowed to develop relationships with women, very likely competition and conflict over women would soon appear, especially in such close knit groups as travelling sankirtan parties, this would which threaten the harmony of the movement and perhaps lead to its disintegration. By renouncing their sexuality altogether they can enjoy themselves, unencumbered with all the problems that relationships with women would entail. Such a life is appealing to frustrated young men in the liminal stage of life prior to marriage, particularly to young Britons who were either on the dole or in dead-end jobs prior to joining the movement. The attractive life of the *brahmacharins* is an important reason why ISKCON is still doing very well in Britain. Far from 'copping out' for the young men who become *brahmacharins* joining the movement is a reasonable and logical decision to make.

The *sannyasin* role allows for the greatest individualism of all in the movement and has even more advantages to it than the *brahmacharins* as is clear from the leading roles *sannyasins* play in social, economic, political spheres in ISKCON. Once a devotee becomes a *sannyasin* the need to fill the vacuum created by renouncing his right to marriage and a family permanenty provides a *sannyasin* with an incentive and motivation to carve himself out an even greater political and economic role in the movement. Moreover, since it is a high ascetic standard which sanctions and justifies power in the movement, becoming a *sannyasin* further legitimises this increased economic and political activity in ISKCON.

Having no family responsibilities, *sannyasins* are free to go anywhere or embark on any enterprise they choose to further their interests. Also being able to travel widely and frequently they can have a wider sphere of economic and political influence and can keep in contact with their followers regularly; a necessity if they are to retain their allegiance over the long term.

Sannyasins may genuinely believe in the celibate ideal, but it is in their interests particularly the extremely political ones with large bands of followers, such as the former 'heavy' Swami Govinda, to maintain that women are *'maya'* and to emphasise the celibate ideal and to hold more extremist views on asceticism than do traditional Gaudiyas for their followers are generally *brahmacharins* and it is the celibacy rule which provides them with these followers.

Celibate devotees attitudes and behaviour however change radically if they marry and have children, and most do; though a small proportion of *brahmacharins* become so institutionalised in their footloose existence after a few years and so used to relying on the temple for their basic needs that they cannot face the responsibilities and social ties that marriage brings with it. They often shy away from marriage. In some cases the marriage is arranged and they back out before the wedding day. The philosophy of celibacy also takes its toll. It makes some long term advanced devotees so insecure and uptight about sex that they avoid marriage. However for the majority of devotees who marry, there is a change of attitude and lifestyle on marriage for they are forced to give up their footloose fancy-free existence for a sedentary one. Marriage infact leads to a beginning of the of reintegration of devotees into society and the defusing of their social protest which in turn is expressed in terms of bodily symbolism.

The way of life of *brahmacharins* or *sannyasins* is directly opposed to the lifestyle of the *grihasthas*. *Grihasthas* since they have renounced the celibate ideal and are to some degree 'into maya' have a much more relaxed and easygoing attitude towards asceticism which is referred to in the movement as being 'mellow'. *Grihasthas* place less emphasis on conformity to norms associated with celibacy because it is to their economic, political and social advantage to do so. The anti-materialism, footloose existence, geographic mobility and general ascetic renunciation of the *brahmacharins* and *sannyasins* existence which sanctions a comfortable life for them is irrelevant to and threatens the way of life of *grihasthas*. Instead, a *grihastha* is pulled towards his family and its economic and social needs rather than towards celibacy and to the movement as a whole. Although some temples, as does the British, make a token contribution to supporting families, married devotees generally are expected to fend for themselves and financially support their own families and children. This includes the fees for their children if the children happen to attend any of the movement's schools. The husband is supposed to get a job either in ISKCON e.g. restaurant work, Spiritual Sky or a paid administrative position etc., or a 'karmi' job; in the States it is not uncommon for a married male devotee to take one up in order to support his family. Good, steady, well-paid jobs are few and far between in the movement and once a householder gets one, he tries to keep it and this leads to his staying on in the same place for some time.

Their childrens' needs also limit *grihasthas* mobility. Once devotees have a family, they tend to stay in one place or at least not move around quite so frequently. Accomodation and play facilities are important factors—determining where devotee families live. The New York temple, a drab twelve-storey block near Central Park, has poor facilities for children and no place for them to play, and so couples with children generally prefer to live elsewhere. In the States many couples have moved to Los Angeles, where ISKCON has bought the majority of houses and flats in Wanseka Avenue which they rent out to devotee families. There the climate as well as environment is ideal and the temple complex has better facilities for bringing up children. Also, the Los Angeles temple is the home of Fate Studios and the headquarters of BBT, both of which give employment to a large number of householder devotees.

Since most devotees marry after a few years of being in the movement, householders tend to be older than the *brahmacharins*. Some householders are now in their mid-thirties. Their age also contributes to the change in onlook on life and lifestyle. As they get older, they become like their married peers in 'karmi' society and desire a higher standard of living. Unlike the *brahmcharins*, they are unwilling to put up with lack of possessions, and are unwilling to rough it. They wish to get away from the spartan communal sleeping quarters of the unmarried devotees and have their own living accommodation, preferably self-contained and of a reasonable standard. Their family responsibilities, particularly the need to financially support their family, helps to foster and develop their materialistic attitude.

Los Angeles is the epitome of an ISKCON householder community and its two hundred householder families represent the most developed stage in the movement's growth and reflect how other temples are likely to develop in the future. The London temples, with some 30 householders have only just begun to develop along this path. In fact, the Los Angeles temple has a suburban atmosphere; some of the women devotees live like suburban housewives and keep neat, well-furnished and brightly decorated flats. As the wife of the Vrindaban Guest House Manager said when attempting to justify the householder's materialist attitude:

> You need somewhere nice to bring people. Its nice to be able to invite 'karmis' back to supper and discuss Krishna Consciousnes with them. A nice home gives them a good impression of Krishna Consciousness, and is good publicity for the movement.

Only two British devotees, have really become economically successful. But in America it is common to find materially successful devotees. One devotee in Los Angeles is in real estate and runs a Mercedes Benz for instance.

Grihasthas' residence patterns also foster mellowness. Few temples have facilities for *Grihasthas* with families however except Los Angeles, and, where they do they tend to be of poor quality. As is the case at Bhaktivedanta Manor, where the numbers have increased so much that it is overcrowded. Until recently some devotees were living in rooms the size of cupboards whilst others did not have their own rooms. In America because of lack of facilities many married couples prefer to live out and never move into the temple complex at all, whilst in Britain all devotees until recently lived in the temple and were actively discouraged from living out. Now, because of lack of space they are also being asked to live out.

A number of *grihasthas* have recently moved into flats and houses in and around the Watford area. One or two have even got themselves council accommodation.

Once devotees move out of full-time association and interaction with other devotees they become more mellow, as has happened in Los Angeles and is clearly about to happen in London too. Often devotees who live outside find it difficult to attend the temple regularly, particularly the pre-dawn *mangala arati* ceremony. Transport is frequently a problem. Although they generally start off with good intentions devotees often soon become lax in attendance and this fosters a more relaxed and easygoing attitude for they do not have the constant association of other devotees to help them keep their minds on Krishna the whole time and to pressure them into adhering closely to the movement rules. Also *grihasthas* who live outside, particularly if they hold 'karmi' jobs usually interact a great deal with the outside world, and come under its influence. This leads them to modify their views and behaviour and become more mellow too.

In sum, *grihastha* status leads to married devotees emulating to a great extent the pattern followed by their married peers in the outside world. It leads to a gradual reintegration with the wider 'karmi' society for many devotees and a decline in their social protest expressed in the movement through the celibate roles. Except for those in the administrative and managerial positions *grihasthas* and *sannyasins* and *brahmacharins* have little to do with each other. Where they do, they often come into conflict for *grihasthas* mellowness is a direct threat to the renunciation which underpins and sustains the *sannyasin*, *brahmacharins* way of life whilst the celibates renunciation is a direct threat to the economic and social needs of the *grihasthas*. It is to be expected, therefore where they are in positions of power that the *grihasthas* will attempt to control the 'heavies' and vice versa. Indeed the former Swami Govinda on taking over the Vrindaban temple expelled all the householder's viewing them as a threat to his position.

Householders, for obvious reasons, prefer to live in temples where there are other like-minded householders and congregate together as has happened in Los Angeles. Where their numbers are large enough as is the case in Los Angeles, even though the GBC is a *sannyasin* they are, through sheer force of numbers, able to influence and determine the prevailing ethic. Moreover, constant association with like-minded householders, fosters and sustains their belief in the validity of their own mellow interpretation of Krishna Consciousness and their belief that materialism in the service of Krishna, is acceptable.

Householders in ISKCON, in general, reflect the movement at its best. Most householders have either grown out of their adolescent problems if they had any and the responsibilities of marriage have enabled them to contain them. They tend to be amongst the most sincere and genuine devotees and the most hardworking. 'I am not my body I am spirit-soul' is the focal concept also for householders, who, however tend to be less dogmatic and have a more thoughtful attitude towards Krishna Consciousness. They are on the whole more ethical and more socially aware. They usually make a favourable impression on outsiders and their living outside the temple is good for ISKCON image. However, like devotees in general they express their reintegration into society in terms of body symbolism not only through clothes and appearance but, in terms of hairstyles as well.

CHAPTER FOURTEEN

Hair Symbolism in ISKCON

> The struggle of the early seventeenth century between the Cavaliers and Roundheads is an interesting representation of the conflict between sexual libido and super-ego. The Cavaliers, who wore their hair long, indulged in women and wine and generally expressed their libidinous impulses. The Roundheads, who cut their hair short, were Puritans—symbolically and mentally they cut off their penis—albeit they assumed a substitutive and compensatory aggression.
>
> Charles Berg, 1951, *The Unconscious Significance of Hair*

In the West, hairdressing and hairstyles, like dress, have always been an important focus of attention. This is reflected in ISKCON too, where great emphasis is placed on hair style and hair rituals. Unmarried devotees are expected at all times to keep their heads shaven; except for a tuft of hair at the crown, referred to as a *sikha*. Married men may grow their hair if they wish, but they are expected to keep it in a short, back and sides style. Women on the other hand, following Indian tradition, grow their hair long and tie it at the back, preferably in a bun.

Devotees' shaven heads, like their dress, provoke strong reactions and antagonism from outsiders. In the West, to shave one's head is an outrageous and bizarre act; in consequence the bald heads of ISKCON men are the source of frequent comment and ribald remarks by outsiders. In the context of western culture, therefore, it is a drastic step for a man to shave his head. To understand why devotees do so and why they place such emphasis on hair styles and rituals, it is necessary to examine hairstyles in the light of the role and function of hair in western society.

Western society is infact a hair symbolist society par excellence. Westerners are extremely conscious about hair and hair length, as outsiders' reactions to ISKCON hairstyles indicates.

Hair styles and rituals in western culture, like dress, are used to articulate and express social relations, including defining and denoting people's social status and group affiliation. They are also used as symbols of identity and of political and social protest in general. During the Civil War, for instance, Cavaliers had long hair, whilst the Puritans cut their hair short. Nowadays, long hair on men is associated with hippies, left-wingers, effeminacy and the unconventional, whilst 'short, back and sides', is viewed as 'straight', conservative and conventional. This focus on hair is part of the increasing emphasis placed on the body. In modern society particularly amongst young people who use hairstyles to symbolise group affiliation and as a form of social protest, e.g., Teddy Boys, Mods and Rockers, Skinheads and so forth, ISKCON appear to be following the pattern of their secular youth peer group in their use of hairstyles as a form of social protest.

Hairstyle, just as dress, offers devotees a means of being different. It provides a strong symbolic boundary between the devotees and the 'karmi' world. It helps foster a strong sense of 'them/us', as well as solidarity and identification with the group. In fact, 'shaving up', as devotees refer to the custom of shaving their heads, is, in itself, a sign of strong commitment to the movement. Since a bald head would be a source not only of ridicule but of embarrassment in 'karmi' society, a devotee only shaves his head when he feels strongly committed to the movement, or at least intends to stay.

Hair being an outgrowth of the body, is a particularly appropriate symbol for a group which focuses on the body and uses bodily symbolism as a form of social expression. Shaven heads, like saffron robes, are part of the uniform of ascetics. In ISKCON the ascetic is the symbol of the ideal society and of the movement's rejection of society whilst the body represents the corruptness of society. As with their distinctive dress, so with their shaven heads too, devotees attempt to represent the ideal Vaishnava ascetic society embodied in ISKCON. In essence, through the medium of their bodies they attempt to superimpose their own ideal society onto western society.

Hair styles in ISKCON also reflect and articulate fundamental role contradictions between men and women in western society, as well as the problems that confront individuals in their daily lives, particularly male devotees. In ISKCON hair symbolism centres largely on males and reflects their interests and concerns.

According to Hallpike (1969: 260) who relates hair length to social structure, cutting hair represents social control. 'Long hair is associated with being outside society and the cutting of hair symbolises re-entering society, or living under a particular disciplinary regime within society.' Thus he sees the tonsuring of candidates for admission to a religious order as a symbolic submission to social control. Just as in recent years the long hair of hippies and 'freaks' was an affirmation of a wish to be free from social control.

In ISKCON male devotees do both shave their heads and enter a highly disciplined and controlled life when they join the movement. This custom however does not symbolise an entry into society but, on the contrary, is based on a rejection of society and is an expression of individualism. Anyone who joins the movement is essentially moving into the fringes of society. If Hallpike's theory were applicable to the movement, then male devotees would grow their hair, not cut it, on entry.

On a superficial level, ISKCON hair styles are rooted in Hindu custom and can be explained as following the traditional Indian pattern. But, overlaying Hindu custom ISKCON uses hair style as a symbol of sexual status. The movement's use of hair styles moreover reflects and is an expression of, the inherent contradiction in male/female roles in western society. The contradiction between the traditional western submissive female role and the liberated egalitarian female role of the Permissive Society is played out, as is generally the case in ISKCON, using inversion as the medium of expression. The male domination of ISKCON, its focus around male concerns and interests and the return to the traditional male dominant role in the movement is reflected in female hair styles. It is no accident that the traditional long hair of Hindu women is the same as that worn by western women when they acted out the submissive female role prior to the First World War. Clearly, the long hair of female devotees in ISKCON is symbolic too of traditional western custom and is used to express symbolically their inferior status in the movement.

Those female devotees who become *Sannyasinis* however emulate the men and either crop their hair an inch all over, or shave it off completely. By rejecting marriage these women liberate themselves from a husband's domination and authority. As they get older, although theoretically under the control of the temple authorities they are allowed to do much as the choose. Many of them travel extensively and one or two hold positions of informal authority. As such *sannyasinis* shaven heads would appear to symbolise their liberation from male domination in the movement and their positions of power. It suggests that in the movement they are symbolically equated with men.

Looking at male devotees' shaven heads in the context of sexual relations is also illuminating. It indicates that male shaven heads are directly related to male problems, including sexual problems. It is significant that unmarried male devotees in ISKCON not only deny and reject their sexuality, but they shave their heads as well. Berg (1951), a Freudian, in his classic study of hair symbolism and the psychological significance of hair, maintains that there is a correlation and direct relationship between hair style and sexuality. He puts forward a rather ingenuous argument to explain the custom of shaving the head, which he relates to the Freudian theory of the unconscious. He argues that there is a basic symbolic equivalence between head hair and male genitals in the unconscious, in which hair cutting is equal to castration. He cites the example of wandering Hindu ascetics who renounce their sexuality and shave their heads.

ISKCON devotees' celibacy and their custom of shaving their heads is, of course, derived from this Hindu ascetic ideal. Yet obviously, not all devotees suffer from castration complexes. Whilst a small minority do seem to have overt sexual hangups, the majority appear to be normal. Since most devotees marry, marriage rather than celibacy is the norm in ISKCON. Thus Berg's hypothesis would not be applicable to ISKCON.

Leach (1958: 147-64) has argued against Berg too that hair symbolism is not unconscious but is often the exact reverse. It is used he maintains precisely because hair behaviour embraces a widely understood set of conscious, sexual symbols. He criticises Berg's assumption that 'the *sannyasin* ascetic's behaviour is a compulsive one welling up from hidden springs in the individual unconsciousness'. In the Indian context, he says the ascetic's detachment from sexual interests, and his shaven head which symbolises this detachment, are both conscious elements in the same religious doctrine. Although Leach does appear to be right about the conscious sexual symbolism of cutting the hair, his assumption that conscious sexual symbolism underlies the *sannyasins*' custom of shaving their heads is not borne out by Burghart (1978: In communication), a specialist on Hindu ascetics who maintains that *sannyasins* cut their hair not for any sexual reason but because hair is associated with bone marrow excreta and the act of cutting the hair is therefore a rite of purification.

In ISKCON, too, devotees in general do not appear to be consciously aware of any sexual symbolism underlying their custom of shaving their heads. Only one devotee, when asked why devotees shaved their heads, specifically referred to celibacy. In general, they either refer to austerities, saying that it is a symbol of a life of renunciation or just it is the custom. It is cleaner they say, and besides making them unattractive to women, it helps people to immediately recognise them in the street. Thus, in ISKCON shaving of the head either has nothing to do with sexuality or else, as would appear to be the case, devotees are operating a form of sexual symbolism of which they are not aware, and this is related to the unconscious in some other way than as reflecting an individual castration complex.

Like sexuality, hair is put to symbolic use in ISKCON's rejection of western society. In a society so obsessed by hair symbolism it seems reasonable to see ISKCON's use of hair styles as following the traditional pattern of usage in western society, as a vehicle to express protest against society. By shaving off their hair altogether, devotees are stating symbolically that they are completely rejecting the 'hair game' and that they are unwilling to play society's games and follow its rules. Variation in hair length is acceptable in western society as a political statement—shaven heads are not. In sum, the devotees' shaven heads symbolise a total rejection of society.

This interpretation is supported by a number of factors. Firstly, the devotees themselves recognise that they are playing a 'hair game'. They are well aware of the antagonism their shaven heads attract from outsiders and they do it deliberately. Moreover indicating devotees' awareness of their use of hair style, the degree to which they keep their heads shaved varies with the degree to which they reject or interact with 'karmi' society. Recognising that their hairstyles attract animosity when they interact with 'karmi' society, they wear hats or wigs, particularly if they want anything or are selling literature on the streets or 'doing business'. The wigs, significantly, like their 'karmi' dress, reflect their conservative orientation to life. They are usually 'short back and sides' in style or 1960s 'college boy' cut.

Devotees who hold positions of authority, such as Governing Board Commissioners, temple presidents, or managers, frequently grow their hair. They are generally older devotees who have usually been in the movement a number of years. Identifying with it closely, they have a strong desire for Krishna Consciousness to be accepted by the outside world as a 'genuine bonafide religion', they overtly reject the outside world less and are most willing to adapt to it. Thus, their hair length parallels a greater acceptance of society's norms.

There appears to be in ISKCON a direct correlation between sexuality and shaven heads and rejection of society. Shaven heads and celibacy vary together, and they both vary according to the degree that western society is rejected by a devotee.

Shaven heads actually do go hand in hand with celibacy, for it is generally only *sannyasins* and *brahmacharins* who 'shave up'. Householders in general grow their hair, usually in a 'short, back and sides' style symbolic of their conservative, 'straight' attitude to life.

The reason given for so doing is financial. Householders need to support their families and so 'do business' which leads them to interact a great deal in 'karmi' society. In consequence, so as not to antagonise outsiders, they are allowed to grow their hair. Yet many *brahmacharins* and *sannyasins* also 'do business' and interact extensively with the outside world. In fact, some of the most successful businessmen in the movement are *sannyasins*, but they tend to keep their hair shaved.

In practice, the growing of hair in the movement is correlated with marital status. *Brahmacharins* when they are about to marry, whether they have a job that necessitates interacting frequently with the outside world or not, usually grow their hair as a symbol of their new married status. Celibates, who keep their heads closely shaven at all times, tend to be the 'heavies' who place most emphasis on sexual renunciation and who are the most rejective of western society. The more easygoing a *brahmacharin* is in his relationship with women devotees the less strict he tends to be about keeping his head shaved all the time.

In those temples where celibates and 'heavies' in particular predominate or where the President and/or Governing Board Commissioner is a *sannyasin* and is in control and celibacy is idealised as the norm, the rules about 'shaving up' are enforced. As is the case in the New York temple where the GBC is a 'heavy', and the majority of devotees are 'brahmacharins'. But in Los Angeles, the largest temple in the movement, although the GBC is a *sannyasin*, it is the easygoing ethic of the householder majority that prevails and the atmosphere is much more relaxed. Rules about 'shaving up' are not so strictly enforced, partly because most of the members are householders and are therefore allowed to grow their hair. Because British ISKCON is run by a householder and has a fair proportion of householders as well as celibates, it also is easygoing. It is left up to the individual whether he shaves or not.

The Hawaii temple is another interesting example. Devotees refer to it as the 'bloop capital' of ISKCON. They view other members of the movement who go and stay in the Hawaii temple as not very sincere and committed and into '*maya*'. They maintain they go to Hawaii to have a good time, and to enjoy the sun and the beaches. Very often devotees soon succumb to the attractions of the beach, surfing, and the easygoing way of life. The Hawaii temple, run by a householder, has been subverted by and influenced by its surrounding environment. The atmosphere is very relaxed. Devotees do as they choose, which, in most cases, is not much. Even the Hare Krishna Mantra is sung in a more relaxed and easygoing way than in the western 'heavy' urban temples—at a slower tempo reminiscent of Polynesian songs. This easygoing atmosphere is reflected in hair length. Devotees, especially those who have come just for a short holiday, tend to keep their hair rather long.

However, the temple authorities, well aware of Hawaii's reputation in the movement occasionally try to get the lacksadaisical devotees into shape and conforming to the norms. One of the main means they use to achieve this end is to emphasise the body. They force devotees to dress more correctly and make them shave their heads. Thus, in Hawaii, 'shaving up' is a symbolic attempt to demonstrate control. This also happens sometimes in other temples. If a President feels that the devotees in the temple are getting lax, are falling into *maya* and 'karmi ways' he will order a tightening up of the rules. Generally, one of the first commands will be 'get your hair cut'.

It is interesting to see how devotees use both sexuality and shaven heads to represent symbolically their rejection of society and how their attitudes to both sexuality and hair vary with the degree to which they conform and adjust to the outside society's norms. There appears to be a parallel and link between the explanation put forward here and the Freudian psychological explanation of hair shaving. Leach himself (1958) remarked that often social and psychological interpretations are interrelated. The custom of shaving the head in ISKCON parallels the fact that most devotees are people who, prior to joining the movement, were unable to solve their problems socially and were frustrated and fed up with material life and had only a dead end future ahead of them in the outside world. The devotees were people who, to rephrase a sexual metaphor, could well be described as 'socially impotent', particularly the males, around whose frustrations, interests and concerns, the movement focuses. With one or two exceptions the female *sannyasins* who have renounced their rights to marriage and children and who shave their heads, and have become symbolic males in the movement appear to suffer from psychological problems and tend to be the most 'socially impotent' of the women. The custom of shaving the head in ISKCON would seem therefore to be an expression of devotees' social frustration. In the same way that shaving the head symbolises, in Freudian terms, castration of the body, so, for devotees who use the body as a symbol of society, the act of shaving their heads is an expression of their social impotence. Symbolically, they are socially castrating themselves and making a symbolic statement that they view society as castrated. An understandable view of society and a symbolic statement from individuals who view society as unable to provide them with a meaningful existence and as corrupt— 'the society of the cheaters and the cheated'.

CHAPTER FIFTEEN

Bodily Movement and Dance in ISKCON

> One reason for the inseparability of dance and culture, except for analytical purposes, is the inseparability of dance from its creator and instrument of expression- The creators and instruments live in a cultural context that shapes them and their dance. Dance does not exist apart from dancers. We must, therefore, not only look at the form of the dance, but consider as well the meanings it has for the people who create it, do it and watch it (1977: 214-215).
>
> <div align="right">Anya Peterson Royce, <i>The Anthropology of Dance</i></div>

ISKCON places more emphasis on bodily movement than any other of the new eastern religious groups that emerged during the 1960s. For people who dissociate themselves from their bodies, devotees paradoxically focus a great deal of daily activity and ritual around body movement of various kinds. Although this may seem inconsistent, ISKCON's rejection of the body and emphasis on bodily movement are directly related. The movement has developed this emphasis on bodily movement because it has an important symbolic role and function.

Devotees learn a totally new set of bodily movements, and a completely new orientation to their bodies when they join the movement. These new movements are used to articulate and express social relations both towards other devotees and to the 'karmi' world outside. They function in many cases to define the boudaries between ISKCON and the external world. Like their distinctive dress and hair style, they provide devotees with a further symbolic means of differentiating themselves from the outside world.

For instance, new devotees are taught to sit cross-legged on the floor rather than use a chair, and learn to sleep on the floor as well. As is the custom in Indian temples, they are expected, and expect all visitors, to take off their shoes when they enter the temple and walk inside either bare footed or in their stockinged feet. If visitors do not, they are asked to leave or are forcibly ejected. Many devotees cultivate a new type of walk that of a humble ascetic. Women attempt to imitate the walk of chaste Hindu ladies and keep their heads down.

A great deal of communication between devotees is expressed through symbolic bodily movement. Eye avoidance for example is used to articulate the non-association with women rules. Also when devotees meet fellow devotees whom they have never seen before or whom they have not seen for a long time, they are expected to prostrate themselves in front of the other person as they do when they meet a *sannyasin* or guru.

Prostration is perhaps the most important new body movement that a neophyte devotee learns. It is a frequently performed act, for devotees are also expected to prostrate themselves on entering and leaving the temple room and during *arati* ceremonies. Some devotees on entering the temple room lie prostrate on the floor for several minutes whilst they say their prayers. For proud westerners, 'bowing the knee' is an alien and unacceptable custom and one which in normal circumstances they would find repugnant. Yet devotees often appear to enjoy humbling themselves, which tends to suggest that the emphasis on prostration should be interpreted as another example in ISKCON of social protest through inversion. Devotees get satisfaction out of doing it precisely because it provides them with another means of 'cocking a snook' at the values of Western society.

No analysis of ISKCON's bodily movement patterns would be complete, however, without an explanation of its ecstatic and spontaneous dance expressive of love of Godhead which is one of the most distinctive features of ISKCON known to outsiders. Dancing, of course, features prominently in both the daily *arati* ceremonies and in the public congregational chanting parties.

However, ISKCON has made significant changes to traditional *vaishnava* ecstatic dancing making it the centre of attention in the movement and the focus of group and public rituals, indicating that it has taken on a new function and role in the movement to that which it had in India.

As is clear from Royce (1977) and Lange's (1976) study of the anthropology of dance, dance is a universal practice which subtly mirrors social conditions and evolves according to social change and social needs. Lomax (1968), a leading exponent of choreometrics, argues that culture and dance are directly related. Religious and social upheavals and dance appear to go hand in hand, medieval dance manias being but one example. In the latter half of the nineteenth century and the beginning of the twentieth century too, the prophet/ghost dance of the Peyote of the North West Plains area and the dream dance which appeared amongst the Potawatomi, Menominie and Chippewa (Kurath, 1949: 281) offered a vehicle for social protest. They provided Indians with a sense of their own identity and fostered resistance against the incursions upon and destruction of the Indian way of life and identity. In the light of these examples, it would appear to be significant that from the First World War onwards, a period of rapid social change in the West, dance should have developed as a form of mass recreation, one moreover which has been taken up and adopted by young people, especially during the 1950s and 'Swinging Sixties'. The emphasis on dance in western society would appear to be a direct reaction to social constraints and the existential vacuum created by the scientific and technological society of the West. Dance and the music which goes hand in hand with it have become a major medium of expression for young people nowadays. The pop music industry which has developed into a major industry catering for young people bears witness to this. The forms of dance favoured by young people clearly are an extension of the pop scene. They are as Melly (1972) says of early pop music a form of self-expression and a vehicle for social protest, and a substitute for action for working-class kids in dead-end jobs, unable to change the humdrum routine of their daily lives. Although, as with pop music, these dance forms have gradually percolated up the social scale, becoming embourgeised in the process. Dance in ISKCON appears to perform a similar role and function.

But why has youth in modern western society, and ISKCON in particular, as well as people in other cultures from times past such as the Amerindians, chosen dance as a means of expression and as a counter-reaction to rapid social change and structural constraints? What is it about dance that gives it impact and which can be expressed in no other way?

Man biologically has emotional needs. Societies channel and cater for human emotions in various ways. Some provide better channels for emotional satisfaction than others. Modern Western society, and urban society in particular, is one that does not. Modern man, looking to his body as a means of overcoming the emotional sterility of western society, focuses on body movement, particularly dancing, as an ideal vehicle for channelling and expressing emotions, since it is the most immediate and primary form of emotional expression. Dance, like all human movement being directly related to the inner psyche offers the most direct expression of human sentiments and feelings and of the inner being of man. Dance provides the primary means by which individuals can express their emotions and how they feel about themselves and their relationships with others. In no other way can man express himself so directly and completely as in dance.

Ecstatic dancing in ISKCON is viewed as expressive of love of Godhead. According to Krishna Consciousness a devotee dances because his soul is active and when it comes into contact with the Hare Krishna *mantra*, the sound vibration of the Lord, it feels an ecstasy which it expresses through the medium of the devotee's body by making him dance. Since it is performed every morning and evening, ecstatic dancing has become to some extent, routinised. Unless a devotee is really in the mood for an emotional experience, it is often little more than recreational activity. However, when a large number of devotees dance together on a big occasion such as the Sunday afternoon *arati* at Bhaktivedanta Manor or when participating in chanting parties in Condon's West End on Saturday evenings, devotees often get worked up and induce in themselves highly-charged emotions, which they describe as 'bliss' and 'happiness'.

Generally, 'kirtan' is started by a 'kirtan' leader, a male devotee who leads off the *mantra* which is then repeated by other devotees to the accompaniment of cymbals and drums. When there is a large group of devotees dancing and chanting together, 'kirtan' is much more dynamic. Devotees' emotions and feelings soon get swayed and whipped up. Gradually, the tempo of the music increases, the 'kirtan' leader's singing gets faster and faster and the cymbals, drums and clapping get louder and louder. The dancing becomes more frenzied, devotees jump up and down energetically, sweat pouring down their faces. The sound is deafening and has the overall effect of a total assault on the senses. The deafening sound of the drums and cymbals, the singing, the pulsating and increase in tempo soon produce heightened states of awareness which appear to generate what devotees refer to as an 'electric atmosphere'. Devotees rapidly get worked up into a frenzy. Watching them there is no doubt that they really do sometimes experience real emotional 'highs' and feelings of ecstasy, as well as intense mystical experiences. One devotee described a large-scale public 'kirtan' in India in which he and Prabhupad himself participated. He said Prabhupad danced so ecstatically he was obviously a 'pure devotee'. The whole atmosphere, he said, became charged and electric. He felt completely overwhelmed with feelings of transcendental ecstasy and bliss, and for him it confirmed his belief in Krishna.

Dance is a particularly appropriate form of self-expression in western society for it focuses on the individual and is thus only minimally constrained by social structure. As such it provides a wide repertoire for self-expression and enables individuals to express through dance those things that are important to them and which they are unable to do socially.

Dance is also a non-verbal form of communication. Devotees, being generally people confused by and ill at ease with the multiple theories of existence presented to them by western society, have turned to that which they know to be truly real and theirs, namely their bodies and the experiential level. Dance, because it combines both bodily movement and a non-verbal level of communication, is a total experience, and is thus an ideal vehicle for this expression.

ISKCON, by linking dance to the Godhead and seeing it as expressive of love of God, has maximised the emotional potential of the dance and has provided a broad framework for emotional expression. Moreover, since ecstatic dancing is performed twice daily, devotees are able to derive regular emotional satisfaction. Being a regular stimulus, it helps sustain devotees' commitment to the movement. Devotees say you can always tell whether visitors are potential devotees by whether they join in 'kirtan' and dance. If they join in the dance, then they say they know they are emotional types looking for a bodily experience and are thus potential devotees.

Dance is a powerful symbol. It is a language of communication, conveying in ISKCON information about the movement's system of belief and social relations. There is a direct correlation between the form the dance takes and ISKCON's view of the nature of the relationship between the individual and society. Dance in ISKCON is intricately bound up with their focal concept 'I am not my body, I am spirit-soul'.

Douglas in *Natural Symbols* (1970) argues that bodily control is an expression of social control and 'the full possibilities of abandoning conscious control are only available to the extent that the social system relaxes its control on the individual.' She contends that where role structure is strongly defined, formal behaviour will be valued. A social structure which requires a high degree of formal conscious control will find its style in ritualism and the shunning of experience in which control of consciousness is lost. She argues that where the favoured patterns of religious worship include trance, glossolalia and trembling or other expressions of incoherence and dissociation—and she cites (p. 79-80) revivalist movements, e.g. West Indian Pentecostalist soul sects in London—they will tend to be found in 'grid' type societies where relationships are ego-focused and where concomitantly the level of social organisation is low and the patterns of roles unstructured.

ISKCON would appear to fit in with Douglas' hypothesis, involving as it does dissociation, spontaneity, lack of control etc. Also, western society has relaxed its control over the individual. Having been liberated from the traditional constraints of social structure the individual has, in theory, a wide choice of behaviour open to him. Western society is a prime example of a 'grid' type society and prior to joining the movement, devotees were involved in ego focused relationships. Being in the 'betwixt and between' stage of life, the level of devotees' social relations was low and their relationships fluid and ever shifting, particularly among those in Britain who were on the dole prior to joining the movement, and in the States, those who were involved in Haight Ashbury. Devotees' social patterns thus fit in with Douglas' hypothesis. Devotees' type of social life prior to joining would seem to correlate with their form of dancing. Their spontaneous ecstatic dancing expressive of love of Godhead would appear to be an expression of personal liberation, as the product of the relaxing of social structural constraints and devotees' encapsulation in a low level of social organisation.

But usually since devotees' behaviour prior to joining the movement was generally constrained, as is the case with young people, their liberation from the constraints of social structure is more apparent than real. It is for this reason perhaps, rather than Douglas' hypothesis, that devotees have taken to this ritualistic and expressive form of dance. When Douglas applies her theory to modern youth she is referring to hippie types. Devotees, of course, are essentially conservative types who are ill at ease with the new liberated roles forced on them by the Permissive Society. Also, devotees' daily lives in the movement, far from being minimally organised, loosely structured and fluid, are highly regulated, and their daily routine is spelt out in detail. Dance in ISKCON therefore reflects the strong constraints that social structure places on devotees and the aridity and poverty of the world view and quality of life offered to youth in the urban West, rather than lack of social control as Douglas contends.

ISKCON's ecstatic dancing bears a striking resemblance to the dance forms favoured by young westerners in the 1960s and 1970s. The limited variety of steps used in both the dances of modern youth and ISKCON's dance form, their repetitiveness, their rhythms which are out of keeping with the natural pattern of the body, as is the increase in the pace of the dance as it progresses, as well as the tendency to dance alone and the deafening singing and music which accompany dancing, are all clearly a response to and an expression of the dehumanising machine-like and alienating nature of urban life in the West.

Dance form in ISKCON is to some extent controlled and reflects and symbolises the constraints under which devotees live too. Not only has the dance become part of every morning and evening routine, there are also limits placed on the degree to which spontaneous dancing is acceptable. Real ecstasy is believed to be a sign of a 'pure' devotee, the sign of someone who is in actual contact with the Supreme Personality of Godhead. To show signs of extreme ecstasy, such as rolling on the ground or becoming hysterical, as did Chaitanya, would be to imply that the person was a 'pure' devotee. Any devotee who attempted to show such signs would be considered boastful and would be thought bogus and get short shrift from other devotees. This constraint has clearly contributed to the mechanical, stunted and poverty-stricken form dance has come to take in ISKCON.

The movement also uses dance symbolically to express its philosophy. It is through 'kirtan', which has been developed as the focus of group ritual in ISKCON, that the philosophical dichotomy between body and soul is expressed and the slogan 'I am not my body, I am spirit-soul' is articulated. Dance has been developed as a major symbol of the transcendental world in ISKCON. Devotees frequently say that in the spiritual world, in Vaikuntha, 'every word is a song' and 'nobody walks, everyone dances'. 'Everybody dances for joy in the spiritual world', devotees say, 'everbody feels so happy they want to dance. But in the material world dance becomes perverted. Dance is used as a means of satisfying lusty desires and to attract the opposite sex.'

Dhananjaya replied when asked why devotees danced—'Dance is the natural activity of the active soul. It is an expression of the joyful and ecstatic state of the soul within the heart of men. The soul is eternally active and when it comes into contact with the *mantra* (the sound vibration of the Lord) then it immediately feels bliss and naturally expresses it in ecstatic dancing.'

Devotees' interpretation of their ecstatic dancing is a symbolic statement of the nature of the individual and his relationship to society. Since devotees identify themselves with their souls and their bodies with society, in saying that it is their souls (themselves) that are controlling and manipulating their bodies (society) and making them dance, they are stating symbolically that they are able to control and manipulate society. Moreover, since, in ISKCON, dance has been developed as a major symbol of the transcendental world, devotees are attempting through the medium of ecstatic dance both to express the ideal spiritual society and to superimpose it on their bodies which for them represent a society which they have no control over and which they see as the cause of all their problems and frustrations. Dance thus symbolically provides them with a substitute for the problems of everyday life to which there are no solutions. Understandably therefore devotees enjoy dancing and have developed it as the central focus of their ritual system.

Ecstatic dancing also provides devotees with an ideal vehicle for expressing social protest. In jumping up and down and shaking their bodies, at an ever increasing tempo, whilst singing the *mantra* increasingly vigorously and loudly, devotees are metaphorically shaking off the society which has frustrated them and reduced them to social impotence.

It is no accident either that ISKCON has revitalised the traditional public congregational chanting parties in the street, introduced by Lord Chaitanya, which are becoming less common in India. The devotees are playing here the political 'body' game in public. Both in Britain and America, public displays of the body and emotions have always been traditionally frowned upon and shunned, and anyone who dances like the devotees do would be considered either mad or inebriated. Often on Saturday nights when devotees hold 'kirtan' in Londons' West End, the more 'upright' onlookers tend to gawp or look askance. The devotees' use of dance in public is deliberate. They are well aware of 'karmi' attitudes to their bodies and their dancing. They aim to shock. In its use of public dance, ISKCON is operating its normal symbolic pattern of behaviour: social protest against society by means of inversion.

CHAPTER SIXTEEN

West Meets East: ISKCON and India

> True, for centuries Westerners have come to India to teach that economic development is the path to success. But we're teaching Indians a different lesson—that materialism isn't what human life is all about, and, therefore that industrialisation isn't the answer to their problems. Only Westerners can teach this lesson to India because only Westerners have experienced the emptiness and frustrations of gross materialism. The present generation of Indians hasn't been through this yet so they're easily led to believe that large-scale industry will solve all their problems.
>
> Dhananjaya Dasa
> BTG Vol. 11, No. 3/4 p. 17

India and its culture provide a backcloth against which devotees act out their symbolic individualistically-orientated, body-focused world view. Devotees revere India as the 'Holy Dham', the place where Krishna lived on earth. Devotees, too, frequently compare India's long history of spirituality favourably with the materialism of western society, which they reject. But the nature of ISKCON's actual relationship and degree of interaction with India and Indian culture reflects the essentially symbolic and ritualistic nature of both the movement's rejection of western society and its espousal of India's culture and way of life.

At the behest of some of his earliest devotees, Prabhupad took a group of them to visit the 'holy places' in 1969. A decision was then made to preach Prabhupad's message in India too, and, for this purpose, ISKCON temples were established there. The temple at Mayapur was completed in 1972 and the Krishna Balaram Mandir at Vrindaban in 1973. Since then, an International Guest House and a *gurukula* (school) have been added to the temple complex at Vrindaban. ISKCON also has small preaching centres at New Delhi, Calcutta, Hyderabad and Chandigarh, as well as a large, new temple complex and International Guest House in Bombay which was opened in 1978. Architecturally, ISKCON temples in India are a western interpretation in the 1960's psychedelic style of the traditional Indian temple. By Indian standards, with their marble floors, glass chandeliers and oil paintings on the wall, they are opulent.

All devotees have expectations of going to India to visit the holy places. Most long-term devotees have been, some of them several times. When the majority of devotees go to India, it is usually to attend the festival which ISKCON holds every March at Mayapur and Vrindaban. This is usually attended by several hundred devotees from all over the world. Whilst in India, utilising the ISKCON temple network there, most devotees manage to tour much of the country on the pretext of visiting Vaishnava religious centres.

Visiting India gives Krishna Consciousness credence and legitimacy in their eyes. Prior to going to India, devotees' knowledge of Krishna since it was derived from Prabhupad and books only was one step removed from the real living religion. But in India their beliefs come alive. There Krishna is a traditional God and worship of him is part and parcel of daily life, which gives devotees self-confidence and reinforces their belief. As one devotee said:

> At home we are in the minority. People see us with shaven heads and think we are a load of freaks and weirdos. But here everybody worships Krishna. Here we are in the majority. Here we are normal. No-one thinks us freaks. Here they are the freaks.

Most devotees, however, only stay in India a short time, usually for a few weeks or months only. They frequently fall sick and rejecting western medicine, they often become so ill that they are only too willing to return home, have such unpleasant memories of India that they have no desire to return. Also some devotees, having been brought up in the affluent West, are so shocked and put off by the squalor and poverty there, that they find it impossible to adapt to conditions in India. Whilst most devotees pay lip service to Indian spiritual values, in practice a high proportion of devotees who have visited India end up disliking the country and not infrequently tend to develop a disparaging attitude towards India and Indians.

Indian reaction to the 'white *sadhus*' on the other hand, tends to be mixed, and varies generally according to an individual's wealth, education and actual degree of contact with devotees. Westernised, wealthy and educated Indians, tend to find anything western attractive and enjoy the association of westerners. ISKCON tends to be well liked and respected by them precisely because it is a western movement. Also, Prabhupad, being an Indian, gave the movement legitimacy in their eyes. As one middle class Indian said when discussing the movement's attraction for him, 'It's the meeting of two cultures—East meets West.'

Devotees were quick to perceive that middle-class, rich and educated Indians were attracted to the movement. The devotees themselves were faced with the problem of financing ISKCON temples in India. Since devotees generally do not speak any Indian language obtaining an income to finance themselves from book distribution was impossible in India. In addition, the majority of devotees found 'sankirtan' too debilitating in the hot Indian climate. Moreover a fact to which ISKCON temple authorities have long since resigned themselves is that devotees visit India primarily to see the holy places and go sightseeing. Most have no intention of working hard while they are there.

ISKCON realised that the Indian temples would have to be financed primarily from the West. However it saw a source of financial support for them in the wealthy and educated section of Indian society, particularly in the Indian business community and especially amongst the immensely wealthy Marwari merchants who traditionally give generously to Krishna-orientated projects. Devotees actively solicited support and financial help from this group. The millionaire Marwari Birla family from Bombay made a large donation for the building of the Vrindaban temple, for example.

ISKCON has also introduced its Life Membership Scheme into India, charging the same price as in the West. Some 2,500 Indians in Bombay and a similar number in Calcutta have become Life Members. The movement is becoming entrenched in the business community. Because it is so expensive by Indian standards to join, Life Membership of ISKCON has become an attractive status symbol and as a result, membership has snowballed amongst Indian businessmen. Life Membership in India also offers the same privileges as Life Membership in the West. They are an attraction in themselves. Members receive a selection of Prabhupad's books which are far superior in quality to books published in India. They use them as status symbols and display them prominently in their houses. Life Members are entitled to stay too in any ISKCON temple anywhere in the world for three days for free, and at a reduced rate for longer periods. ISKCON temples are usually in the centre of cities and have reasonably comfortable guest rooms. With the soaring cost of hotels, this privilege is attractive to Indian businessmen who intend travelling abroad.

Nearer home, it means that members can stay for free at the ISKCON International Guest House in Vrindaban, which has amongst the best accommodation facilities in the town. Because of the quality of the accommodation, it is not unknown for members of the Indian elite such as maharajahs, musicians and film stars, when visiting Krishna's birthplace, to stay there too. The devotees themselves, well aware that wealthy, educated and westernised Indians are a potential source of income, go out of their way to make a good impression on them, and treat them well.

But wealthy, educated and westernised Indians who like and respect ISKCON do not usually have close ties with devotees or interact with them a great deal. In general, their relationships with devotees are ritualistic and lack substance. At the local level however where devotees have a great deal of contact with the local inhabitants, the situation is different. Relationships with the local people frequently tend to be tense and strained. The relationship in Mayapur between devotees and Muslim villagers became so bad in 1977-78 that at one point a fight broke out between them. Devotees allege that 200 Muslims attacked the temple complex with *lathis* (sticks) and in consequence they used guns to defend themselves. In the ensuing fight, 14 devotees were arrested and prosecuted by the local police. In Vrindaban (in 1978), relations with the local inhabitants became so tense that a fight between a devotee and a rickshaw driver led to the rickshaw drivers' union prohibiting its members from taking devotees as passengers. The whole town was up in arms. It took a fortnight and a number of conciliating moves on the part of the ISKCON temple President before the ban was lifted and relations with the local community were normalised. In Bombay tension between the local community and ISKCON led to the murder of an Indian on temple premises.

Many devotees, when they come to India in March and buy religious paraphernalia and clothes both for their temples and themselves appear to throw their money around, especially in Vrindaban, where there is a large bazaar. Seeing such displays of wealth naturally creates envy and resentment on the part of the local population many of whom live on the poverty line. They frequently attempt to overcharge and swindle the devotees, who in turn become rude and antagonistic. Often fights ensue. Being swindled and cheated constantly is a major reason for devotees' dislike of the Indian population and the short duration of their visits to India.

But conflict and tension between the devotees and the local Indian population is also a reflection and outcome of the symbolic and ritualistic nature of devotees' relationship with Indian culture. In practice, although the alternative life-style offered by ISKCON is based on an Indian model, few devotees are interested in India for its own sake. Relationships with the Indian population tend to be ritualistic and for economic purposes only.

The type of devotees recruited in India indicates that western devotees see ISKCON as essentially an American dominated, western movement, and aim to keep it that way. With the low standard of living and unemployment problem in India, many Indian peasants would be only too pleased to join a movement such as ISKCON which appears to be so rich. ISKCON, however, does not actively encourage ordinary Indian peasants to join the movement, since they are regarded as having nothing to contribute. Those that do join are given menial jobs, few privileges and are made to work hard. In consequence those who do join, seeing that there is no advantage in being a member soon leave. Only in Mayapur have the devotees actively recruited from the local peasantry. Mayapur has a farm and manpower problems, and the climate there is particularly debilitating. Since few devotees stay there for long, and even fewer have any inclination to work hard farming, ISKCON has recruited 'devotees' from amongst the local Hindu Bangladeshi refugee population, who are only too eager to get work. But even they do not seem to stay for any length of time.

The only Indians encouraged to join the movement are educated and English-speaking ones with some degree of westernisation. In 1978 there were about 15-20 educated Indian devotees of both sexes in the movement ranging in age from about 18 to old age. They included two women, both ex-secretaries in their thirties who had never married. One young Bengali boy joined the movement straight from school when ISKCON was first established in India. Another was a middle-aged ex-Rama Krishna Mission Brahmacharin, another a retired accountant, and two were a married couple—the husband being a book-keeper. Two other male devotees were ex-college students, of whom one had been a student drop-out in Europe. None of the Indian devotees appear to have come from very well-off backgrounds, but all seem to have been attracted to the movement because of a liking for associating with Westerners. Many complained, however, that the devotees treated them like second-class citizens. Most rank and file Indian devotees maintained that they were about to leave or would leave were it not for lack of funds to support themselves or because they had nowwhere to go.

Educated and English speaking Indians play a crucial role in ISKCON in India. Indeed, they are a necessity for the movement to function properly. Since, in general, the devotees do not speak any Indian language, they are totally dependent on them to act as interpreters and as a link, not only with the wider Indian society, but also internally for those Indians employed by the movement who do domestic work and do not speak English. One or two Indians have been made *sannyasins* so that they can perform this role properly and another, Krsna a Governing Board Commissioner. But, having no real power or influence in ISKCON, none of them were made gurus when Prabhupad 'passed over'.

Wherever ISKCON has temples, devotees' treatment of the Indians in the movement is well known to the local Indian community and this has contributed towards strained relations with the local inhabitants and fostered resentment. The devotees' own attitude to the ordinary local Indian population is also a major reason for the tension and strain. Male devotees in particular, tend to be extremely rude to the local population. They do not appear to feel that the canon of good manners that operates in the West is applicable to them. One young devotee, after he had his camera stolen, went so far as to suggest that the Indian population should 'be pushed into the sea'.

Devotees' rudeness and dislike of the local Indian population are also a product of the symbolic and ritualistic nature of devotees' relationships with Indian people and culture. Although Vedic culture, ISKCON's model of the ideal society derived from Indian culture, ISKCON has not attempted to become 'Indian' or to assimilate into Indian society. Rather in India the movement tends to be temple focused inward looking and socially isolated from the wider Indian society. Although ISKCON is dependent on the Indian population for its support structure, few devotees have developed close ties with Indians outside the movement and even fewer within. In three years only three marriages between western devotees and Indians took place which in itself is significant, since inter-ethnic marriages amongst young people in the West are quite common. Also, devotees in general do not allow their children to play with the local Indian children. Although ISKCON has started a school in Mayapur for the children of the Indian devotees, there is very little interaction between these children and those of the *gurukula* in Vrindaban. The latter has only two Indian pupils.

The limited duration of most devotees visits to India reflects their lack of real interest and involvement in Indian culture. Few attempt to familiarise themselves with Indian culture as a whole or learn a local language, a necessity for any real involvement in a local culture. Moreover, since Prabhupad 'passed over', the movement appears to be increasingly less involved and less interested in India. Whilst he was alive, he spent a fair amount of time there and much of the movement's Indian focus was due to him. But since his death and the splitting of the movement into 'fiefdoms', India has not been really important or politically relevant to Western devotees, except for those who have political interests in the temples there. This decline in interest is reflected in the decrease in the number of devotees, particularly in the number of leaders who have attended the annual Mayapur and Vrindaban festival in India since Prabhupad's death.

ISKCON really only considers relevant and significant those features of India and Indian culture which provide the movement with roots, legitimacy and a framework for acting out its symbolic body-focused view of the world and social relations. Devotees are only interested in India in so far as it sanctions, makes meaningful and relates to their own Krishna Consciousness world-view.

ISKCON in fact superimposes its own 'Vedic culture' symbolic body-focused world view onto Indian society and culture. It accepts as relevant, meaningful and legitimate only those aspects which support and confirm this viewpoint. For instance, devotees look down on modern Indian society in the same way that they do the West. They see it as almost equally degraded and corrupt. They point to 'Vedic culture', the blueprint for their own society, as the ideal towards which modern India should aim. Moreover, since devotees are only interested in those features of Indian culture which articulate and sanction their own philosophy, generally when they visit India particularly the 'heavies', they tend to visit only those sites which are revered by the Gaudiya sect. Other sites and other aspects of Indian culture they tend to ignore and dismiss as 'sense gratification' or 'nonsense', including the Taj Mahal which is only one hour's drive by car from Vrindaban.

For devotees India is of no real interest in itself, but exists as a backcloth for acting out their symbolic real-life drama. Because they are not relevant and intrisically meaningful to them devotees do not feel the need to treat ordinary Indians as though they were real people or to act towards them as they would individuals whom they do include within their symbolic frame of reference. In sum, ISKCON in India, as in the West, is highly selective in its usage and assimilation of Indian culture and society. It only utilises and interacts with those features which provide devotees with a meaningful frame of reference for dealing with their social and existential problems and acting out their social protest.

Although devotees relationships with the Asian community in the West tend to be just as symbolic, nevertheless the economics of the situation make devotees respond to Asian immigrants in the West differently, and lead to a very different level of interaction.

CHAPTER SEVENTEEN

East Meets West: ISKCON and the Asian Community in Britain

> There is increasing concern by Indian parents that their children have no knowledge or inclination to acquire knowledge of their parents' culture, language or religion and it seems that the young people are becoming more and more absorbed and addicted to materialistic values of western society.
> Krishna Consciousness can save your children. At this particular moment, ISKCON is working to establish a very important, far-reaching new programme—to instigate Hare Krishna Youth Clubs in each area of a substantial Asian community. We are arranging that the community in these areas will provide facilities for Hare Krishna devotees to occupy a hall or similar facility on a regular basis each week to present a Krishna Consciousness programme for the young people. . . . A recent survey of young Hindu children shows that almost unanimously these children prefer to visit the Hare Krishna temple because of the life and gaiety they find there. Thus, although children show reluctance to go to other Indian temples, we are confident that we can attract large numbers to such a Youth Club.
> *Hare Krishna Explosion*, Vol. 4, No. 1, 1979.

Surprising as it may seem to outsiders who view the devotees as hippie dropouts, the movement is well-known and widely respected by large sections of the Asian community in Britain. Soho Street and Bhaktivedanta Manor are frequently visited by members of the Asian community. It is not uncommon for instance for several hundred Asians to visit Bhaktivedanta Manor each weekend and at Diwali (Festival of Lights) in 1978 some ten thousand of them visited for the festivities held there.

Wherever ISKCON temples are situated in countries with large Asian populations, such as South Africa, East Africa and Mauritius, the local Asian communities have tended to develop close ties with the movement. But it is in Britain, with its large Asian community, that ISKCON has developed the closest links and has had the most impact on the Asian community. A highly complex and symbiotic relationship appears to be developing between them. ISKCON fills a vacuum in the Asian community and the movement in turn needs Asian support and assistance.

The common denominator of course is Krishna. Many of the Asians wao live in Britain are worshippers of Krishna and followers of *bhakti yoga*, especially those who live in the Southeast and West Midlands who came originally from Gujarat, Bengal and the Punjab, areas where traditionally the worship of Krishna has always been strong. Krishna worship is also the religion of the East African Gujaratis who now reside in Britain. They visit ISKCON in large numbers.

Asians from all castes in Britain frequent ISKCON temples. The great majority are *vaishyas* (merchant caste) as are most Asian Hindus in Britain. However brahmins are not uncommon and *kshatriyas*, (warrior caste), *shudras* (workers) and even untouchables go too. They come from all social classes as well—from doctors, lawyers and accountants to factory workers and railway guards. But because the Gaudiya sect is essentially a Bengali movement and relatively few Asians in Britain come from Bengal or Vrindaban, most had never heard of the Gaudiyas, Lord Chaitanya or Prabhupad prior to coming into contact with ISKCON.

The stage in development and position that the Hindu Asian community had reached vis-à-vis the British host society by the 1970s are important reasons why Hindu Asians participate so actively in ISKCON. The main influx of Asian immigrants into Britain began in the late 1950s. Originally, men tended to come alone seeking work. But, by the 1970s, they had been joined by their wives, children and other relatives. Moreover they had begun to develop their own community life in Britain which focuses, predominatly around caste, cultural associations and *mandirs* (temples).

It has frequently been noted that minority groups encapsulated in a host society with a different culture tend to become very religious as happened with the Gujaratis who migrated to East Africa at the end of the last century. Cut off from their cultural roots in an alien environment, they turned to religion and used it as a means of expressing their cultural identity and differentiating themselves from the wider host society. Through commerce, the community became wealthy. Individuals frequently through the giving of donations channelled surplus wealth into religious activities. The women, having servants and time and money on their hands, became the focus of these religious activities. East African Gujaratis nowadays are considered far more pious and generous to religious institutions than Indians in India.

Hindu Asians from India in Britain, seem to be following a similar pattern. They, too do not have their traditional Indian social way of life to fall back on for their emotional and social needs. They live in an alien and uninviting culture, which considers them second class citizens, a society, moreover, which they barely understand and which radically conflicts with their own. In such an environment they feel isolated and cut off from their cultural roots. They appear to be turning to traditional religious faith too, as a form of solace and comfort.

Personal traditional religious beliefs are one of the few real features of their traditional culture that Asian immigrants have been able to bring with them to Britain. In Britain these beliefs provide them not only a sense of continuity and a means of tapping their cultural roots, but also with a means of identifying with and taking part in the culture that they left behind. Coming to the West fosters an identity and value crisis amongst many Asians, for they are faced with a western value system which totally contradicts all that they believe in. Becoming pious gives confidence and protects their sense of traditional identity giving it coherence as well as legitimacy. Indeed, Asian visitors to ISKCON often admit themselves that they are more pious in Britain than they were in India.

For East African Gujaratis who attend ISKCON proportionately in far greater numbers than do any of the other Hindu immigrant groups in Britain, Britain is just as much an alien environment as East Africa. East Africans in general both rich and poor, since they came to England appear to be more religiously active and to give more generously to relegous activities and to ISKCON in particular than other Asian immigrant groups. This is partly a continuation of their traditional pattern of giving generously to religious activities. But their involvement in religious activity in general in Britain and ISKCON in particular would also appear to be a reaction to the social upheaval of being expelled from East Africa. Involvement in religious activity in Britain, as it did in East Africa, provides them with a sense of identity in their new country. It also provides them with a sense of continuity and stability which helps them withstand the feelings of disturbance and social upheaval engendered by being thrown out of East Africa.

Those Asians who visit ISKCON who lost their wealth when they left Uganda frequently refer to the 'good old days' in East Africa when they were rich and had their own business and servants. They find compensation in religious faith for their lower standard of living and the drab existence of their daily lives in Britain. An East African who visits ISKCON regularly used to have his own business in Uganda, but lost all when he fled the country. He had been forced to send his family to India and he himself took a job with a West End electrical shop. He mended the devotees electrical equipment for free. He said openly that he was only too willing to do so since he was lonely and enjoyed the company of devotees.

The Hindu Asian communities' rapidly developing interest in their natal religion has developed not only around the traditional *mandirs* which they have established but also around ISKCON for a number of reasons. Most Asians actually appear genuinely to like and respect the devotees. Asians frequently remark, like the majority of outsiders who have close, long-term contact with the devotees, how impressed they are by devotees' genuineness and sincerity. Far from rejecting devotees' interest in their religion, they tend to be impressed and flattered that westerners, whom they generally assume to be racist and dismissive of their culture, should convert to their religion, particularly such an orthodox and ascetic branch. Moreover ISKCON provides them with a means of interacting with westerners on an equal basis. Since they are Krishna Conscious by birth it actually puts them in a superior position—an attraction in itself. Not are they put off by ISKCON's dress since it is part of their own cultural tradition. On the contrary they are rather pleased that westerners should want to wear their dress.

ISKCON's close adherence to Gaudiya teachings also makes the movement acceptable to the Asian community. Although ISKCON's symbolic emphasis on the concept 'I am not my body, I am spirit-soul' is a modification of traditional Gaudiya philosophy, nevertheless it is within the traditional Gaudiya belief system and thus accepted by the Asians. Also the devotees accept that Asians, being worshippers of Krishna, are Krishna Conscious already. As such they do not attempt to preach or discuss philosophy with them, in consequence Asians usually do not know enough about devotees' beliefs to be aware of the differences.

Those that do appear to have no objections to them, justify them by saying that such differences are to be expected in the West.

What is really important to the Asians as far as ISKCON is concerned, is not the movement itself, or the way it conducts itself, but the deities. A major reason why Asians visit ISKCON temples is to have 'darshan' (audience) and to worship the Radha-Krishna deities. ISKCON's Radha Krishna deities are traditional Indian images. They are made of marble and imported from Jaipur, a famous image making centre in India. The devotees garland them with flowers and dress them splendidly in fancy jewellery and brightly coloured silks and satins, overlaid with sequins, spangles and tinsel. Asians are extremely impressed with ISKCON's deities which are far more splendid than those in the other Asian *mandirs* in London, which are often small and shabby.

The movement has kept closely to the traditional pattern of deity worship. Any changes which have been made are generally embellishments rather than deviations from tradition. To make devotees particularly 'pujaris' who work on the altar aware of and to enable them to conform to traditional custom, the movement has published an edited and abridged translation by Jayatirtha Maharaj of a famous text, the *Hari Bhakti Vilasa* by Gopalabhatta which includes descriptions of the rules governing deity worship. Asians seeing this willingness to conform to tradition, willingly accept ISKCON's deities as their own.

Asians believe that the deities come down into their status and can be seen by worshippers who can pray to them and ask them for their help. However, whether an individual is able to see and communicate with the deities is determined by the individual's faith, it is not influenced by the institution which owns the deities. Since the onus is on the worshipper, Asians are willing to tolerate deviation from traditional Hinduism as long as there are deities and the rituals surrounding them are followed according to traditional custom, the way the devotees conduct themselves is not of primary importance to them.

ISKCON's close adherence to traditional Hinduism in most spheres also makes Asians feel that they are participating at ISKCON in their own religion not a western copy of it, they are impressed by the devotees' orthodoxy, their renunciation of sex, alcohol and meat, and by the spartan life they appear to lead. They frequently comment on it, saying that the devotees lead far more saintly lives than they do. Also, as is true of the laity of most religions, the majority of Asians who visit ISKCON know little about their own religion and in consequence they are impressed by the devotees apparent knowledge of the scriptures especially their ability to quote Sanskrit *shlokas* by heart. Sanskrit being a language they themselves do not know and of which they are somewhat in awe. When asked questions about Hinduism, Asian visitors to London temples would often reply 'You ask these boys, they know more than we do.'

Asians tend to be strict with their daughters and generally except them to stay at home until they marry. But, reflecting the esteem in which the Asian community holds ISKCON, one Asian, a leading light in a Midlands *mandir*, was so impressed by the devotees that he let his English born daughter join as a full member. They are willing to let their children interact with the devotees because they know that the devotees won't lead them astray. They won't let them drink, take drugs or have sex outside marriage, which the Asian Community sees as part and parcel of western decadence and to be avoided at all costs.

Prabhupad's Indian origin has also given the movement authenticity in Asian eyes as it has in India. His role and leadership in the movement helps foster their view of ISKCON as just an overseas branch of their own religion. Prabhupad's charm and charisma were felt too by Asians who speak highly of him. Some of them even became his disciples. However, the new gurus, including Jayatirtha Maharaj are still unknown entities to the majority of Asians. Their youth is against them, for in the Asian community, age and status go hand in hand. But in their relationships with the Asians they have shrewdly kept a low profile and remained in the background and so far they have not alienated them.

The Asians, whatever reservations they may have about the new gurus and whatever drawbacks and irregularities they may see in the movement, they are willing to put up with them, because ISKCON fills a real need in the Asian community. Soho Street and Bury Place's position in the heart of London's West End has helped foster Asian involvement. There are only a handful of traditional Asians controlled *mandirs* (temples) in London. They tend to be in the suburbs and difficult to get too. Bury Place and Soho Street are easily accessible to Asians who work in the city and the West End. They have taken advantage of this proximity and often visit ISKCON during the day or after work. Most of them come alone. They make their obeisances in front of the deities and partake of 'prasad'. Some of the Asians who attend Bury Place and Soho Street are regular visitors and have been frequenting ISKCON since it opened in 1968. They include a Bengali school teacher with an Oxford degree, a statistician with a Ph. D. from the L.S.E., a bachelor Tamil brahmin who studied mathematics part time, at another London University college, an East African lawyer and a porter from a well known department store as well as ordinary office workers of both sexes.

Bhaktivedanta Manor, however, gets most of its Asian visitors at weekends. Traditionally in India, there is no fixed day for general temple worship, but on coming to Britian Asians have had to modify their religious activity to fit in with the exigencies of the western working week. They have adapted to western custom and become 'Sunday worshippers' like their Christian counterparts. Also many prefer to visit Bhaktivedanta Manor at weekends because it is situated in Letchmore Heath village in the suburbs of London. It is rather inacessible and it is time-consuming to get to during the working week, particularly for those who do not have their own transport.

On Sundays, the devotees' own day of rest, when they themselves converge on Bhaktivedanta Manor to enjoy the festivities held there, the Manor comes alive and is a hive of activity. Often in summer on Sunday when the weather is fine, several hundred Asians, mostly families, but also couples and single people, visit Bhaktivedanta Manor. They come from London suburbs such as Harrow, Wembley, Cricklewood, Hendon and Southall as well as further afield from areas such as Luton, Leicester and even Bradford. Some even stay the weekend in a room set aside for guests. On summer Sundays too, usually one or two coachloads of Asians arrive at Bhaktivedanta Manor, often from the Midlands, organised by a local Hindu *mandir* (temple) or Hindu association.

A major attraction of ISCKON is the facilities it offers. The few traditional Indian *mandirs* in London tend to be shabby. The Leytonstone *mandir* is a converted run-down church hall for example, whilst the Golders Green *mandir* is a room in a private house. Nor do these *mandirs* have full time 'pujaris'. According to Asian critics they are still traditionally Hindu and parochial in orientation and hot beds of local gossip, politics and intrigue.

Asian involvement with ISKCON really took off and increased rapidly after the movement moved into Bhaktivedanta Manor in 1973, indicating that Bhaktivedanta Manor itself and the facilities that it has to offer are one of ISKCON's major attractions for the Asian community. In comparison with the traditional Asian *mandirs*, Bhaktivedanta Manor is what the devotees would call 'opulent'. A mock Tudor monstrosity built in the 1930s, it has been decorated in a combination of 1960's psychedelic and a rather tasteful bourgeois style. Most Asians have come to Britain to better their standard of living. They tend, especially the East African Gujaratis to have strong capitalist materialist values, and place great value on outward wealth and splendour, and conspiciuos display. ISKCON's ownership of such a large and ostentatious country house and the Manor's opulence and general appearance of wealth Asians find very appealing. The movement is also attractive because it has its own fulltime 'pujaris' who can officiate for visitors. Also it is not involved in the whole local *mandir* scene of which the more westernised and more educated Asians tend to be highly critical.

ISKCON also provides the Asian community with a means of bridging the gap between their own and western culture. Both the well educated westernised Asians and the less educated, with little experience of westernisation prior to coming to Britain, were faced with the problem of having to integrate into western culture and reconcile their own worldview with that of the West. This has created for many a strain and value crisis. ISKCON's attraction is that it has its feet in both camps—both eastern and western culture. It thus provides the Asian community with a link and a means of reconciling incompatibilities between their own religion and values and those of the West. Asians are not only flattered by Western devotees' conversion to their own religion but their confidence in their own religious beliefs and values is reinforced and legitmised by it. If westerners believe in it then it must have value, and frequent visits to ISKCON continually ratify this sense of legitimacy and confidence. The movement combines the best of both worlds for Asians who aspire to the superficialities of westernisation: a western framework and an Asian content.

The more educated, westernised and affluent—the doctors, lawyers, accountants and so on, feel the strain of attempting to reconcile their traditional values with those of the West even more acutely than their peers lower down the social scale. Many find their traditional cultures an embarrassment and difficult to justify and attempt to reconcile these incompatabilities of values by becoming more inward looking and religious in orientation.

But many Asians have little affinity with their traditional *mandirs* which they identity with traditional culture and in consequence tend to look down on. Being orientated to western values and culture they can better identify with a western movement such as ISKCON which has a foot in both camps. Most importantly, it appears to be not only wealthy and successful but to have pretensions to intellectualism, all of which Asian immigrants value highly particularly the East African Gujaratis. They are already one step removed from Indian culture having been brought up in East Africa. The majority of them are extremely westernised, and have difficulty identifying with traditional Asian culture. They can much more easily identify with a western movement such as ISKCON.

The Asian community's rapidly developing participation in ISKCON is also due to the stage the Asian family structure has reached in Britain. Traditionally, religious activity within the Asian family focuses on and receives its impetus from women. By the 1970's large numbers of Asian women were resident in Britain. Many by this time had reached middle and old age, when their families no longer needed their full time attention and they traditionally begin to take an active part in religion. Their families were often beginning to accumulate surplus wealth by the 1970s and they were looking for ways to express their religiosity and involve themselves in religious activity. It was only a matter of time before their influence was felt and reflected in the Asian community's participation in religion.

It is estimated that a large percentage of Asian women speak little or no English and this has provided as extra incentive for involving themselves in religious activities. Being unable to speak English and communicate well with the host society, and cut off from their joint families and traditional social environment too, they appear to be turning to religion for solace. Asians have altars in their homes. It is not obligatory for them to worship at *mandirs*. Cooped up within the confines of their homes during the week, visiting the *mandirs*, particularly ISKCON, offers these women an outing and entertainment as well as the company of other people. Knowledge about ISKCON's activities appears to have spread through the Asian community by word of mouth, in particular through female gossip. It is frequently the women of the household, who have been told by a female friend about the movement who provide the initial impetus and suggest a trip to the Manor to see what it is like. Asians often say, when asked why they have come to visit ISKCON, 'Oh, my mother wanted to come'.

By the early 1970s too the children of the Asian community had begun to reach adolescence. On Sundays it is predominantly families with young children who visit Bhaktivedanta Manor. Asians in Britain are faced with a cultural gap between themselves and their children. Their children have been brought up and educated in Britain, in an alien culture and are often unable to speak their parents native tongue properly. Frequently, too, the children are uninterested in, if not totally rejective of their parents' natal culture. Asians not uncommonly have little in common with their children. Yet traditionally they are expected to keep tight control over their children, especially over their daughters. But with their children reared in the Permissive Society and expecting some degree of freedom of choice, Asian parents are finding it increasingly difficult to exercise this traditional control. ISKCON, because it provides a link between Eastern and Western culture, is viewed by Asian parents as a means of providing their children with knowledge of, and interesting them in, their Asian heritage. In taking them to ISKCON they hope to legitimise their traditional parental authority.

Asian children themselves find the traditional *mandirs* shabby. Also, their activities are conducted in Sanskrit or some other language which the children, generally only familiar with their parents' dialect, usually cannot understand. Consequently they find the ceremonies and activities at the traditional *mandirs* uninteresting and boring and learn little from attending them. But at ISKCON Asian children are presented with an outwardly rather grand and splendid version of Hinduism which they find attractive. Since everything is in English, they can understand what is being said too. Moreover because Asian children are western in outlook, they can identify better with ISKCON precisely because it is western, than with the traditional *mandirs* which appear alien to them. Most of the devotees are young like themselves and share with them a common language and culture. Moreover, it is the devotees who teach them about Asian religion and culture rather than their parents which legitimises it in their eyes and they appear to be extremely receptive to devotees' teaching. Asian children seem to enjoy interacting with the devotees very much. They also find attractive Bhaktivedanta Manor with its psychedelic decor and its extensive grounds which they are allowed to play in, and its cows they are allowed to touch as well as the Sunday festivities which they find fascinating.

Asian parents, quickly seeing their childrens' liking for ISKCON and the devotees, are only too willing to bring their children regularly to Bhaktivedanta Manor. Mr and Mrs Patel are typical Asian parents. Originally from Uttar Predesh they now live in Leytonstone. They have lived in Britain for sixteen years. Both are office workers. They have two very intelligent and anglicised children, Ravi a boy aged ten and Jyoti a girl aged 16. They visit the Manor regularly on Sundays and attend all the festivities. Jyoti is going through a religious phase. She finds ISKCON glamorous and is attracted to the devotees. Mrs Patel often complains that working during the week she would prefer to stay at home and do her chores during the week ends. But she is only too willing to forgo them, so keen is her desire to foster her daughter's interest in Indian religion and culture.

The participation of adolescent and young adult Asians in ISKCON is of particular interest. Most Asian adolescents brought up in Britain generally show little interest in their parents' religion and are very materialistically orientated, but the small proportion that are often tend to be the more thinking Asians and usually the better educated. One 17 year old, very sophisticated Brahmin girl student from Southall said she was searching for her 'roots'. The new generation of young immigrants are having as much trouble reconciling the East with the West as their parents. For some of them, ISKCON, with its foot in both camps, provides a means of bridging this gap.

Few Asians however actually join the movement full time in Britain. In 1978 there were some five in all, two women and three men. One, was a teacher in Jaipur before coming to England, but in England he experienced a great deal of frustration. The British Ministry of Education would not recognise his Indian degree and he was forced to take a job as a store man in a factory which he found very frustrating. He subsequently joined ISKCON and has made for himself an enjoyable life there. Another is an ex-psychiatric nurse from Malaysia, married to an English devotee, whilst another is a young university dropout whose mother is a teacher and whose father is dead. All the male Indian devotees appear to come from the better-educated section of Asian society. Most seem to have had some problem, frustration or loneliness prior to joining the movement which contributed to their joining.

Few Asians in Britain join the movement fulltime, since those that come to Britain usually come because they want to better their standard of living, and thus are not orientated towards asceticism. Asians in Britain are more interested in manipulating the movement to their own advantage socially.

The factors which foster Asian involvement in ISKCON appear to cut across the whole Asian community, since all castes, ages, classes and ethnic groups visit ISKCON temples, even ethnic groups such as Sikhs who are not traditionally worshippers of Krishna. All Asians in a British milieu, regardless of who they are, appear to have very similar needs. ISKCON has been able to take advantage of this cross-community need because of the nature of its belief structure which allows for universal membership. Unlike many Indian religious sects or movements which only allow certain castes or classes to belong to them, the Gaudiyas traditionally have always been open to all castes. This rule initiated by Chaitanya himself has proved very advantageous for ISKCON, allowing the movement to infiltrate the total spectrum of the Asian community.

The devotees themselves, however, reflecting the symbolic nature of ISKCON adherence to Vaishnava culture, are not intrinsically interested in the Asian community. But they were quick to see in the Asian community in Britain a source of revenue and a means of attaining not only legitimacy for the movement, but one of the movement's major goals, namely its desire to be considered a 'bona fide religion'.

With one or two exceptions in Britain, British ISKCON devotees have not proved to be successful entrepreneurs. Until Asian involvement in the movement British ISKCON had to rely mainly on book and record distribution for its income. With rapidly increasing overheads, the possibility of an alternative source of income from the Asian community was an attraction in itself. In fact ISKCON in consequence, particularly since 1974, actively set out to attract the Asian community to the movement. It quickly adapted and developed its institutional structure to fit in with the Asian community's interests and needs. It has involved the Asian community as much as possible in its activities and has a extracted as much money as possible from it. Where the Asian community has need of them and where they can be manipulated to provide the movement with a source of income ISKCON has reintroduced and revitalised traditional Indian religious activities. It has also reintroduced western institutional forms where they fulfil a need in the Asian community. Unlike in India devotees always try to present a good image to the Asian community for fear of alienating them and they treat them with respect at all times.

The Asian community infact provides ISKCON with a great deal of financial support. Gifts of food and clothes for the female devotees are frequent. Following Indian custom, money donations are put into the offertory box in the deity room or are made direct to the temple authorities. The house in Clapham which the *brahmacharinis* moved into in 1978, was donated by an East African Gujarati. ISKCON decided to build a tarmac drive and car park for the use of the Asian weekend visitors and asked for 200 donations of £51 to cover the cost. Reflecting the degree to which the Asian community is willing to support the movement, the necessary donations were rapidly received from them.

Asians also supply ISKCON with financial advice. Their accountant, for instance, is an Asian, and an Asian solicitor acted for them when they bought Soho Street. They also provide the movement with a service infrastructure. Leading members of the Asian community, such as the editor of one of the Hindu newspapers, frequently gets bail for them when they get into trouble with the police and get involved in court cases. An East African Asian repairs their radios and electrical equipment for free, whilst an Ayurvedic doctor provides them with free medical treatment. When on 'sankirtan' in the Midlands, devotees usually stay in Asian houses, often in the homes of the leaders of the Hindu Associations and *mandirs*. In fact, ISKCON appears to opperate under the umbrella of the Hindu associations and *mandirs* in the Midlands.

Although the Life Membership Scheme is open to everybody, in practice the majority of Life Members in Britain are Asians. By 1979 ISKCON had 3000 Asian life members in Britain. A number of devotees were working fulltime on the Life Membership programme. Their job is to socialise with the Asian visitors, answer their questions and deal with their problems. The role of the Director who is an Asian devotee is particularly crucial. He acts as a middleman and interpreter for the Asians who do not speak English well, in particular for the women. At one or two of the Asians' request and also as a means of involving the Asians in the movement, a Life Membership Committee was set up in 1979, which gives advice and helps set up projects. ISKCON publishes a newspaper—*The Hare Krishna Explosion*—which focuses on the interests of the Asian community and includes puzzles and competitions for the children.

Moreover, ISKCON celebrates all the major Krishna festivals, including Rathayatra, which are attended by Asians in large numbers. Rathayatra festivals are held for the Asian community not only in London, but in Leicester and Birmingham where there are large Asian populations. The devotees also perform 'kirtan' and *bhajans* at Hindu *mandirs* and Hindu association cultural evenings, and on request in the houses of Asian devotees. They perform quite regularly in the Midlands. Often they are invited to sing at weddings. To encourage the Asian community to visit the Manor and participate in its activities, ISKCON has started its own Sunday afternoon bus service starting at Wembley and winding its way through the North London Asian area.

The movement has also encouraged financial donations from the Asian community by reintroducing traditional Hindu forms of offerings, particularly support of religious institutions and donations to temples and ascetics. Asian devotees believe that Krishna is always watching and that if they support and look after Him, He will repay them many times more and provide them with health, wealth and happiness.

The wealthier an Asian becomes, the more he feels the need to make religious offerings, since wealth is seen as a sign of Krishna's favour. Hence the wealthy generally contribute generously. As the Asians in Britain become financially better off, they appear to be following this custom and contributing to religious activities similarly.

In India, religious offerings have always been directly related to traditional forms of status and prestige. Anyone who made a large donation to a temple usually was given public recognition and rewarded by having their name put on public display, either engraved on a wall or on a plaque so that everyone would be aware of their donation. ISKCON has introduced this custom too. Devotees are getting rather sophisticated ideas for financially milking the Asian community. ISKCON decided to build new cow sheds at the cost of £5,000. At Diwali in 1978, in order to raise this sum from the Asian community and to involve them in the actual building, bricks were sold for £10 each. The name of the buyer was placed on each brick and they were built up to form a wall which was put on public display.

ISKCON provides a social life for the lonely, especially for the Asian regulars who visited Bury Place and now Soho Street. But as yet, Asians who visit the movement have not developed close ties with other visitors or developed these ties outside ISKCON, which is to be expected as the Manor has been opened only a few years. But the seeds of an Asian community life developing around ISKCON are already there, as is clear from the Asians' willingness to give donations which receive public recognition. Also they are beginning to see ISKCON as a means by which they can attain status and prestige in the Asian community as a whole. Since Asians from all areas and all castes and classes visit ISKCON temples, many Asians prefer now to donate to ISKCON because it reaches a wider audience than do the traditional *mandirs* and so enables them to play their traditional status-prestige games on a community-wide basis.

Moreover, the Asian business community has begun to utilise ISKCON. To involve the business community, particularly the enterprising East Africans, in ISKCON and to tap their finances, the movement published its own desk diary in 1978, and ISKCON sold advertising space in it. It is full of advertisements for Asian businesses, for Asian businessmen, realising that it would be read throughout the immigrant community and would thus give them publicity in the community as a whole, were quick to see its financial usefulness. So successful was it, that ISKCON even produced an East African edition, which advertised businesses in East Africa. Reflecting the movement's willingness to adapt to the Asians, ISKCON, when designing this diary designed it to fit in with East African Gujarati religious beliefs. They traditionally belong to the Vallabha sect in which Krishna is worshipped in his child form. To accommodate to them ISKCON put a picture of Krishna in child form on the diary's psychedelically designed cover. If Asian involvement in ISKCON continues at the same rate as now, then in the next few years, a solid Asian community life based on the Asian business community will revolve around ISKCON.

But it is on the Asian children that ISKCON has focussed most of its attention, knowing that if it can attract the children it can attract the parents. The movement has gone out of its way to encourage their interest and to provide facilities for them, especially on Sundays. Utilising traditional western social forms to do so the devotees also teach them about Krishna Consciousness. A 'Sunday School' for Asian children, has been started at which Krishna Consciousness philosophy is taught, and a prize is given to those who attend regularly. The theme of the plays held every Sunday comes either from the *Shrimad Bhagavatam* or from some aspect of Krishna Consciousness philosophy. The children listen intently and appear to delight in the devotees' garish and spangled costumes and the 'chamber of horrors' type sound-effects used.

ISKCON has also started youth clubs in Southall and Hounslow for Asian children. Entertainment at the youth clubs also includes puppet shows which are always an instant success. The puppets depict Asian characters. They are well made and of an exceptionally high artistic standard. They would not look out of place on a television puppet show. The dialogue dealing with Krishna and general Asian themes is exceptionally sophisticated and aimed at just the right level for obtaining the children's interest. In 1979, fortnight long summer camps were held for Asian children in the grounds of the Manor too. Some thirty Asian girls and some forty boys attended separate camps.

Traditionally in India at life cycle rituals such as death it is the custom for family members to make a financial donation to religious activities. ISKCON has now begun to receive an income from this source. Asians donate to ISKCON not only because they prefer the movement but because their temples are often more convenient for them to get to. Also because they have full time 'pujaris' and ascetics, unlike the traditional London *mandirs*, and it is the traditional custom to give to them rather than the mandir itself. One Sunday afternoon, for instance, an anglicised, trendily-dressed, young Asian couple with cockney accents came up to Dhananjaya, who was then the Manor temple president. Obviously having little knowledge of Asian culture they said that their father had died and they had been told it was the custom to make a donation. In broad cockney accents, they went on to say 'we want to give you some money, you know that custom, where you give money when your dad dies'. Dhananjaya, extremely knowledgeable about such customs after four years in India, interpreted Indian culture for them and replied, 'I think you mean *sraddha*'.

ISKCON has developed such complex involvement with the Asian community, that the latter is beginning to have a great effect on ISKCON's own institutional structure. It has forced the movement out of its inward-looking, contemplative isolation into active, in-depth, full-time involvement with the wider community. To impress the Asians and gain legitimacy in the wider society, ISKCON even invited the police and local notables to the opening of their youth club in Southall.

In fact, the Asian community have helped ISKCON mature by providing the movement with the means of transcending its original function as an essentially youth social-protest group. They have given ISKCON a rationale for existence well suited to a movement that is maturing and wishes to be accepted by the outside world. Despite themselves, and if they were to think about it, much to their chagrin, ISKCON devotees through their involvement with the Asian community are being brought back into the mainstream of conventional society. As such they are being forced to perform a socially useful role and are being turned into an institution of benefit to the wider 'karmi' society.

Asian involvement in ISKCON has kept the movement, and the British devotees in particular, on the 'straight and narrow'. After Prabhupad died, it would have seemed likely that the new gurus would begin to develop their own philosophies and perhaps deviate a great deal from his teachings. But this has not been the case, particularly in Britain. Fear of alienating the Asian community and losing their financial support has been a major reason why the movement, especially in Britain has continued to conform closely to the niceties of Gaudiya philosophy. It seems probable for this reason too that the movement in Britain will continue to adhere closely to traditional Gaudiya philosophy in the future. Thus it seems likely that devotees both in Britain and abroad will continue to base their symbolic world view on smybols drawn from within the framework of traditional body-focused Gaudiya thought and that the movement will continue to preach its 'I am not my body I am spirt-soul' body-focused world view in a basically similar form in the future.

CHAPTER EIGHTEEN

Brainwashing: Fact or Fiction—Conversion or Subversion?

> Srila Prabhupad said "The whole world is under a misconception, and we are giving them knowledge. And yet they say we are brainwashing. People in general do not know that the body is valuable only as long as the soul is there. Therefore, their brain is rubbish and must be washed, or human civilisation is lost."
>
> BTG, Vol. 12, No. 5, p. 17.

It is often assumed by outsiders that people who join the new religious fringe sects are individuals who have inadequate personalities and psychological problems and/or have been 'brainwashed'. In fact, ISKCON is frequently accused, particularly by upset, parents, of 'brainwashing' its members. Organisations have been set up in America by aggrieved parents and friends such as the Committee Engaged in Freeing Minds (CEFM) and the Citizens Engaged in Reuniting Families (CERF) and in Britain, the People's Organised Workshop Against Ersatz Religions (POWER). Their aim is to 'de-programme' young people who have become members of these new cults, such as ISKCON and the Moonies. Ted Patrick, nicknamed 'Black Lightning' and one of the most notorious 'de-programmers' in America, maintains 'The cults completely destroy the mind...they destroy your ability to question things and, in destroying your ability to think, they also destroy your ability to feel. You have no desires, no emotion, you feel no pain, no joy, no nothing.' (Conway and Seigelman 1978: 64).

As far as ISKCON is concerned, it might appear that there was some truth in the brainwashing criticism for so dogmatic and parrot-like are the majority of devotees, so uniform in their beliefs and practices and so uncritical are they of Praphupad's teachings, that they, more so than any other of the eastern religious groups, appear archetypal products of brainwashing. The majority of devotees are unwilling to listen to criticism of ISKCON philosophy and immediately reject any in a very intolerant manner. They erupt and lose their temper if disagreed with too much, especially if the other person is a better arguer. If this is the case, devotees tend to show anxiety and are often abusive and rude. If it takes place within the temple, the person is generally asked to leave—'You are stupid', 'You are a nonsense person', 'I don't want to talk to you, go away', are responses frequently used by devotees for dealing with critics. For outsiders, who had only superficial contact with the devotees it would be reasonable to conclude that they were programmed robots.

Yet, although devotees may appear brainwashed, the majority of them do not seem to have any more psychological problems than their peers in the outside world which might make them susceptible to brainwashing and manipulation by the movement. Nor are the uniformity of devotees' beliefs the product of overt forced indoctrination, as critics maintain. There is no evidence to suggest that devotees, either in Britain or America, are forced to stay in the movement against their will. Since the majority of ISKCON temples are in urban areas and there are always visitors at the temples. It would be impossible for there to be 'secret goings on' such as enforced incarceration, without the outside world soon learning about it. Moreover, devotees can leave at any time. It would be easy for a devotee to find an excuse for leaving—'sankirtan' for example—and just not come back. As the devotees themselves say 'We have nothing to hide, everything is open, anyone can come and see for themselves'.

Devotees often discuss quitting the movement with other devotees before they 'bloop'. The latter see it as their duty to 'preach' to them, to get them to change their minds. But if a devotee decides to leave, and many do, particularly those who have only recently joined, then he or she is free to do so.

Given that devotees' conversion to Krishna Consciousness and commitment to the movement appear to be voluntary, and they seem to be extremely individualstic in outlook, it would appear that if devotees are brainwashed, this must take a subtle form. Conway and Siegelman's (1978) recent work *Snapping: America's Epidemic of Sudden Personality Change* uses a 'mind control' type hypothesis to explain membership of cults and mass therapies. They lump all the new cults and mass therapies together and argue that they use similar methods to manipulate and control their members' minds. They maintain that by means of these techniques they induce in their members powerful, deep and intense emotional and physical experiences, which generate a phenomenon they refer to as 'snapping'. Ex-cult members, they maintain, told them that when they had these experiences, 'something snapped inside me' or 'I just snapped'. They argue that these snapping experiences lead to a complete transformation, not just in outward behaviour, but a total radical change in personality too.

Conway and Siegelman use a model of the human brain derived from Cybernetics, and Information Theory in particular. They argue that the brain is essentially a human information system, holographic in form. It is fed by everyday experience and as such is continuously changing according to the information it receives. Deep emotional and physical experiences which generate snapping, Conway and Siegelman argue, affect fundamental information processing capacities of the brain. They may have a deep and lasting effect on important information pathways of the human brain and may actually destroy fundamental pathways of thought and feelings and lead to a total change in personality.

They hold that the snapping experience leaves people vulnerable and susceptible to suggestion, indoctrination and command. They become emotionally dependent on cult leaders and rapidly accept the beliefs and practices of their cult. They maintain that in so doing cult members lose their individuality, freewill and freedom of thought and that their spontaneity and feeling for others disappear. Conway and Siegelman state that after the snapping process cult members are no longer capable of carrying on a genuine conversation, and are no longer responsible for their actions.

The technique and methods used by cult leaders to induce snapping and radical change of personality according to Conway and Siegelman, include physical stress, poor diet, sleep deprivation, control of the environment, attacks on the sense of self, death threats, charged mental conflict needing urgent resolution and fasting. They also include, they say, religious rituals such as singing, dancing and drumming, isolation and other forms of sensory deprivation, potent rhetorical plays, individual and group techniques, mass marketing skills, fervid lecturing and earnest personal confrontation, slickly packaged appeals, casual conversations, active role playing and guided phantasies, the cutting of ties with the outside world, as well as being taught daily rituals of chanting and meditation which, Conway and Siegelman maintain, effectively prevent the cult member from regaining control of his mind. They view ISKCON as 'perhaps the most practised at inducing the snapping moment that brings about sudden changes in personality' (1978: 37).

ISKCON devotees' parrot-like reeling off of Krishna Consciousness doctrine would tend to confirm Conway and Siegelman's theory. Many of the points they make about the techniques and methods used to obtain conversion seems to apply to the movement. On the surface, ISKCON would appear an extremely mindbending organisation indeed.

Not only Conway and Siegelman but behavioural psychologists in general, including Sargant (1957) in his seminal work *Battle for the Mind*, argue that sleep deprivation provides a good basis for brainwashing, as it weakens resistance and thus makes people more susceptible to indoctrination. ISKCON is frequently accused of using sleep deprivation to brainwash its members. By outside standards, devotees do have irregular sleep patterns. Most make do with six hours sleep or less a night. Also it is compulsory for all devotees to attend *mangala arati* which, although it varies from temple to temple, is usually between 3.30 and 4.30 a.m. Any devotee who misses *mangala arati* three days running is expelled from the temple. Often, devotees appear sleepy at this ceremony. Medical evidence tends to suggest that this is the period during the day when individual defences are lowest and people are most susceptible to indoctrination. Thus the Krishna focused *mangala arati* ceremony, and the *Bhagavad Gita* class which follows it, at which the same basic philosophical concepts are described and discussed every day might well be assumed to foster and sustain conversion.

But a number of other factors have to be taken into account when evaluating sleep deprivation. Although most devotees get relatively little sleep at night, the majority take extra 'cat-naps' during the day. Most long term devotees appear to be adept at sleeping anywhere at any time. Many devotees too had irregular sleeping patterns prior to joining the movement and often seem not to need a lot of sleep anyway. Thus the lack of sleep at night is not of itself an important factor. Besides medical evidence suggests that the body adapts itself to irregular and new sleeping patterns within three weeks. So if sleep deprivation itself is an important factor in brainwashing, it has to be influential in the first three weeks before devotees bodies have had time to adjust and adapt to new sleeping patterns. Anyway if devotees find lack of sleep a hardship, they can leave, and many new devotees do leave for this reason. Generally people who stay in the movement after the first few days, are those who can do with little sleep, or else they are people who are willing to put up with little sleep because the movement offers some attraction which they consider more important.

Siegelman and Conway maintain that cult-leaders initially use a 'soft sell' and that individuals are at first either taken in by the cult members 'overt' happiness and satisfaction with their lives or by the smooth talk of the leaders who present their philosophy in an attractive way. This however does not appear true of ISKCON. The movement reaches a vast audience. Eight to eleven thousand visitors, (not including visitors from the Asian community) visit ISKCON temples in Britain each year. The movement also actively goes out of its way to recruit members, visiting places where they think like-minded people will congregate, such as squats, pop festivals, colleges and such places as the Mind and Body Festivals, Nevertheless, only a small minority who visit become further involved with the movement in Britain generally, a handful move into the temple every week, but the majority of these soon leave. Thus ISKCON's 'soft sell' approach does not appear to be very successful and is only a contributory rather than decisive factor making a devotee join the movement.

Most people find devotees' dogmatism and ISKCON's pettifogging rules too much. Few can manage the regime either—getting up before dawn, having cold showers, sleeping on a hard floor and living a spartan community life without privacy or possessions as well as having to eat vegetarian food, and abstain from sex before marriage. Many too are unwilling to give up television, cinema, alcohol, drugs and smoking. A Piccadilly 'bum', who had been invited to stay at Bhaktivedanta Manor for the weekend by a chanting party he had met in London's West End remarked 'They drove me mad. I could not stand all the chanting'. Yet, for the small minority who do become further involved with ISKCON after the initial encounter, especially those who join and stay in the movement, what the devotees have to say initially, and their orientation to life are important understandably so, since ISKCON's philosophy and institutional structure are so highly relevant to their situation and provide a meaningful frame of reference for them. As, for instance, in the case of Puru Dasa, who said it was the devotees' initial encouragement of his desire to be a musician that attracted him to the movement.

It is also frequently argued that a poor diet softens people up for indoctrination. Like all cults, ISKCON is often accused of feeding its devotees badly. Outsiders remark that devotees look pallid and ill. Devotees do appear to have a higher than normal incidence of illness such as boils and lung infection and many do look pallid. But far from being underfed devotees are obsessed by food, and eat a great deal. In Britain, they eat three times a day. At about 8.30 a.m. they have cereal, milk or yoghurt and fruit. At 1 p.m. they have a large vegetarian lunch and sweet, and in the evening at 6.15 p.m. they have sweets, savouries and hot milk. Most devotees appear to eat between meals too. Many of the women overeat through boredom and put on weight. Devotees like food so much that feasting has become institutionalised in ISKCON. Feasts are held on any pretext, generally at least once or twice a week. The food at feasts is wholesome and varied. Devotees' liking for food is reflected in their attitude to fasting. Fasting is generally associated with asceticism. Although traditional Gaudiya ascetics fast frequently and the devotees have attempted to emulate them, because of their liking for food devotees fast only on important holy days and on *Ekadasi* days, which occur twice a month. Even then they only abstain from taking grains.

Nevertheless the diet in ISKCON is often poorly balanced. Some days it is so badly cooked as to be inedible. Occasionally, too, there is not enough of it, particularly in the evenings. But when this happens it is the product of inefficiency and ignorance (usually due to the cooks not turning up) rather than intention. Anyway, although devotees sometimes complain about the food in ISKCON, they would leave if they were not satisfied with it.

On the surface, however, the philosophy of Krishna Consciousness and its interrelationship to ISKCON temple social structure do appear to have all the ingredients necessary for mind-manipulation. Indeed, they foster both rapid conversion and strong commitment to the movement as well as extremism and dogmatism This is apparent from the differences in the beliefs and practices of the two types of devotees found in the movement, namely the regular visitors and those who join fulltime and live in ISKCON accommodation. In America, most temples, particularly those on the West Coast, have a fairly sizeable proportion of 'fringes'. These are people who, although often firm believers in Krishna Consciousness feel they are too 'into *maya*' to become full time devotees and move into the temple They prefer to enjoy a more comfortable existence and to lead their own lives out in the 'karmi' world. They only visit ISKCON temples. Usually they regularly attend the feast held on Sunday afternoons at most temples.

In Britain, those in the regular visitor category are much fewer in number than their American counterparts, perhaps 15-20 at any given time. For example, they include a middle-aged working-class housewife who lives alone and has a son fighting in Northern Ireland; Linda, an intelligent loner, a clerk and ex-polytechnic student in her early twenties; Eva, an ex-teacher training college student prone to mental illness, who tried living in the temple but could not take the life; Pete, a very remote and withdrawn lower-middle-class ex-engineering student with a Jesus Christ hairstyle who sleeps at night at a Salvation Army doss-house and often spends the day browsing in the British Museum. He visits most days, partly for the food, partly for the company, but also because he is interested in the spiritual life. Don is a middle-aged bachelor who lives with his father and is very upper-class in manner and appearance. He was born in India where his father was an army officer, though he himself when working, usually works in factories. Lastly, Steve, is an art college graduate from a working-class background who works as a postman.

In Britain, too, in general, people who visit regularly show no tendency to become full-time devotees or to move into the temple, while if they do, like Eva, they do not stay. Those that move into the temple and become full-time devotees usually initially come alone and only visit a few times, many only once or twice before they actually stay. 'I knew it was for me' said one devotee who moved into the temple on his second visit. It is not uncommon for a person to visit the temple and move in there and then.

Most new full-time living-in devotees therefore know very little about Krishna Consciousness when they join the movement. They may perhaps have read the *Bhagavad Gita* one or two issues of BTG, or talked to a few devotees about the philosophy. But, generally, that is all. Their ignorance therefore suggests that initially they join the movement for reasons other than the Krishna Consciousness beliefs themselves. Even so, within as short a space of time, often after only a few weeks or a couple of months, devotees get to know and assimilate the basic tenets of Krishna Consciousness philosophy, in particular to identify with the concept 'I am not my body, I am spirit-soul'.

It is not uncommon for a devotee to become a convert within a matter of weeks. Within a short space of time too, despite their ignorance of the intricacies of the philosophy, devotees act like old hands and are only too happy to preach to visitors and engage them in discussions about Krishna Consciousness. Also as the weeks go by neophyte devotees tend to develop an outwardly strong commitment to ISKCON. They become increasingly defensive and dogmatic about the movement and its beliefs. They appear to convert more rapidly and develop a stronger commitment to the movement than do the regular visitors who live outside and only attend the temple for religious activities. These generally retain a relaxed and 'mellow' attitude towards Krishna Consciousness and the movement. This suggests therefore that there is something in the nature of being a full-time, living-in member of ISKCON which fosters rapid conversion, dogmatism and extremism.

An examination of ISKCON's beliefs and practices supports this view. That it indoctrinates its members by means of constant repetition of the movement's philosophy would appear on the surface to be a reasonable criticism of ISKCON. ISKCON is an ideological movement par excellence and to join it is to totally embrace a system of belief and a highly symbolic one at that.

Full-time devotees who live in the temple are bombarded by Krishna Consciousness throughout the day at rituals and classes and as they talk to each other all the time about Krishna Consciousness it might well be argued that they 'brainwash' each other. Rapid conversion is also fostered in ISKCON because new devotees, seeing the great importance attached to belief by 'advanced' devotees, feel that there must be something important about the philosophy of Krishna Consciousness, and willingly accept it too.

The uniformity of Krishna Consciousness philosophy makes it easy for devotees to become and remain converts. A devotee does not have to reconcile the tenets of Krishna Consciousness with other conflicting beliefs which might undermine it, or to face arguments against Prabhupad's teachings most of which are totally untenable within the framework of western thought and scientific rationality. Too much criticism would make it difficult for devotees to sustain their belief in Krishna Consciousness.

Great emphasis is placed in general on uniformity and group harmony in the movement which also helps foster conversion. This uniformity is reflected in the devotees speech. Admiring Prabhupad so much, his early devotees attempted to copy his speech. Out of their attempts, ISKCON has developed its own 'dialect' which new devotees learn rapidly. It is a kind of Indian English of the Peter Sellers or 'Babu' variety. Among British devotees, those in particular with uneducated accents speak the most pronounced ISKCON English and are often mistaken for Americans because of their accents. In fact the institutional structure of ISKCON has developed so as to prevent any dissension, conflict or criticism developing which might threaten the unity of the group and so lead to the undermining and questioning of the belief-system as a whole. Because ISKCON's institutions are in practice flexible and allow devotees to pursue an 'individualistic' line within the movement, the potential for conflict and dissension is high. But the movement has controlled this by expecting strict conformity to the rules. Those that do not conform, or who cause trouble are expelled.

Reflecting ISKCON's emphasis on group harmony, the movement is selective of membership. A devotee is always posted at the door to prevent anybody from coming in who looks like causing trouble. Subtle pressure to leave is also put on devotees who conform to the rules but do not fit in and are not liked. Even visitors who argue and criticise too much are asked to leave. One of the main tenets of Krishna Consciousness is not to 'blaspheme' other devotees and this helps prevent dissension and conflict. Rarely, and generally only in an indirect manner, are devotees ever heard criticising one another.

Devotees who remain in ISKCON therefore, if not like-minded people, are individuals who are willing to abide by the rules and pay lip service at least, to the movement's system of belief. In sum, being in a harmonious group where all accept the same belief-system, think along the same lines and share the same goal of

'Back to Godhead', provides an ideal and congenial environment for conversion and clearly sustains the commitment of neophyte devotees.

The role of the belief system plays in ISKCON's power structure also fosters rapid and long-lasting conversion. One of the most important critieria for becoming a leader in the movement is to demonstrate a thorough knowledge of the scripture and to be a good preacher, for such people are highly respected in the movement and prestige is conferred on them. Most male, devotees, once they become committed to ISKCON, become motivated to obtain a good position in the movement. In consequence most devotees start reading avidly soon after joining the movement. Thus most long-term 'advanced' devotees and leaders have a good knowledge of the philosophy. Reading Krishna Consciousness literature in depth of course facilitates and fosters conversion. Moreover, after becoming leaders, devotees naturally become more closely committed to the belief-system, since it legitimates and sanctions their own positions.

The actual process of aquiring knowledge of Krishna Consciousness also provides a favourable milieu for developing commitment to the philosophy. Many of the British devotees were academic failures and lacked educational motivation. Most left school at 16 and, prior to joining the movement, were semi-literate. Some of the American devotees, too, including the college dropouts, are not much better.

Learning about Krishna Consciousness in ISKCON is voluntary unlike the state educational system. Although it is compulsory to attend the twice-daily *Bhagavad Gita* classes devotees are not forced to listen or take part in the discussion as they would have been at school. Any further learning they do is up to them. But the philosophy of Krishna Consciousness has such high status attached to it and there is such competition between devotees to demonstrate knowledge of it that a new devotee, surrounded by people who are book-and-learning-focused, feels impelled and wants to follow suit and learn about the philosophy too. Most devotees try to learn a *shloka* or two from the *Gita* a day. To show ignorance of Krishna Consciousness in ISKCON and to be unable to preach, is to imply that one is stupid, or worse, that one is not a sincere and genuine believer in Krishna. Thus even the least academic devotees and the most uninterested in Krishna Consciousness pay lip service to the philosophy and go through the motions of trying to learn at least the basics and peruse BTGs when they are available.

The initial learning process is made easy for devotees being bombarded with Krishna all day in conversation with other devotees and in ritual. Thus new devotees pick up the basic concepts of the philosophy without having to read through and digest the intricacies of the *Bhagavad Gita*, the *Shrimad Bhagavata* and Prabhupad's commentaries, which would initially be beyond their capabilities. In both the *Bhagavad Gita* classes and the Bhakta Induction programme (an intensive course in ISKCON philosophy for neophyte devotees) devotees are taught verbally, making it possible for the semi-literate neophytes to assimilate the philosophy. Some devotees have to learn to read in order to be able to understand BTGs, let alone the *Bhagavad Gita As It is*. However a devotee would lose such face were he seen to be unable to read ISKCON literature that illiterate devotees once they move into the temple, learn to read rapidly, at least enough to read the BTG.

Some highly motivated devotees, through the process of acquiring a thorough knowledge of the scriptures, make a great deal of educational advancement. In fact ISKCON, particularly the British movement, has a broad educative and embourgeoising role, which also helps sustain and reinforce conversion. For example, Krishna Bhakti is a devotee of Irish Catholic descent. He came from a working-class background and was born and brought up in Islington, where he attended a local comprehensive. A highly intelligent, thoughtful and articulate boy, he was, nevertheless, a failure at school, which he hated and was glad to leave. He joined the movement in 1974 when he was 17. After a year he decided that his future lay with ISKCON, and like most of the more motivated devotees, he proceded to carve himself out a niche in the movement. He determined to become a preacher and set about reading the scripture and Prabhupad's commentaries. Being semi-literate, he found book-learning difficult at first. Other devotees too made fun of him, particularly some of the American ex-college students. But he showed great determination and kept at it. Within a few months he had become literate enough to cope with the philosophy. Two years later he started studying Bengali and Sanskrit at night-school and even obtained membership of London University's Oriental Library. He then went to India to increase his knowledge of Bengali. His cockney accent rapidly gave way to classless ISKCON English.

Looking at Krishna Bhakti now, it would be easy to take him for a well-scrubbed, rather 'straight'-looking, theological college student. He has even started to teach some of the other devotees, and has been asked to teach at the English *gurukula* too, when it is opened. Justifying his dedication to learning, he said that those devotees who know the scriptures are treated with respect wherever they go. 'The temple authorities', he said, 'don't hassle you as they know you will be teaching their children and they want to remain in your good books'. In the process of studying the scriptures, Krishna Bhakti became increasingly committed to (Krishna Consciousness) and ISKCON. The transformation from a Cockney boy into a serious-minded adult with academic pretentions and a genuine and sincere belief in Krishna is an outstanding example, but it happens in some degree, to most of the young people who join the movement.

Devotees in general appear to undergo a transformation when they join the movement. They become not only dogmatic and antagonistic but rather innocent-looking, with a well-scrubbed, fresh-faced somewhat pallid mien which the devotees themselves say is due to the 'pure' lives they lead.

However this is a superficial change only. Whilst with its massive emphasis on indoctrination, would appear to have far greater influence over the thoughts and behaviour of its members than the institutions of the wider society has over its members, if devotees' actual behaviour, their individualism in particular is examined, it is clear that this influence is not total but varies in degree in the movement from belief to belief and institution to institution.

The devotees' own view of their beliefs confirms that ISKCON's hold over them is not total. They themselves are well aware of the fragility of their beliefs and the ease with which devotees may fall into '*maya*' and 'bloop'. Hence when devotees go out the movement insists they should always go in the company of other devotees, though in practice, reflecting their individualism and the superficiality of their beliefs, devotees often go out alone.

Devotees like people everywhere vary in the degree to which they are impressionable and easily influenced. Some devotees particularly those with psychological problems, appear to be easily impressionable and succumb to the influence of ISKCON's beliefs and institutions more than others. But by their nature, marginal fringe groups in general, and the more bizarre ones such as ISKCON in particular, attract people with psychological problems. The movement, with its 'open door' policy of accepting anyone who will conform to the rules, has its fair share of people with psychological problems. It is often this group which appears the most robotlike and brainwashed and creates a bad impression on outsiders. Only one devotee was encountered, however, who exhibited what has been called by brainwashing specialists a 'thousand miles' stare, which devotees themselves refer to as a 'spaced-out' look. She already had the look when she joined. She had a remote and withdrawn personality which has remained that way.

But devotees with psychological problems are not representative of ISKCON. In the three-year period in which ISKCON was studied, no devotee was encountered who appeared brainwashed or had lost control of his or her mind. No one came to light either who had undergone a radical personality change. The majority of mainstream devotees seem to be only superficially influenced by ISKCON's mindbending internal organisation, as their individualism bears witness. In ISKCON devotees' individualism counteracts and overrules the controlling influence of the movements internal organisation. Where basic issues are concerned, such as where devotees live, what sort of work they do, how hard they work and how long they stay in the movement, devotees are in control of their own minds and make their own decisions.

Devotees' freedom to choose in crucial matters is reflected in ISKCON marriage patterns. Since men outnumber women in the movement there are not enough marriage partners for all the men. Yet the majority of male devotees who joined the movement between the ages of 18-25 have married before their 28th birthday, which indicates that those who do not find wives in the movement leave of their own accord. Also there are very few long-term devotees who have not carved out a comfortable position for themselves in the movement, which suggests similarly that those who do not also leave; a fact which devotees themselves openly admit. Infact the movement retains devotees' allegiance precisely by pandering to devotees' unfettered individualism. The insensitivity and lack of feeling for others displayed by some devotees is not therefore a product, as Conway and Siegelman maintain, of 'mindlessness', but of egotism.

What immediately strikes anyone who has a great deal of contact with ISKCON is that the movement appears to attract a diversity of personality types, all of whom appear to be going their own way. The movement has survived and increased in numbers precisely because it has developed an innate flexibility which allows for this personality diversity, and is thus able to contain and control the inherent problems, in particular conflict, which are involved in having such variation in personality types in the movement.

Some devotees have strong personalities. They have become 'personalities' and 'characters' in their own right and are renowned throughout ISKCON, such as the huge wrestler Swami Brahmananda. A devotee motivated to become a leader can get to the top within a short time of joining the movement, on the strength of personality and ability to organise alone.

Conway and Siegelman's assumption that an intense emotional and physical experience acts as a catalyst to radical personality change in cult members is invalid as far as ISKCON is concerned, since not all devotees experience intense emotional and physical feelings. ISKCON can indeed provide an emotional experience par excellence. At the *arati* ceremonies and during 'kirtan' and 'japa' a proportion of devotees do sometimes have deep emotional experiences. But others appear to be immune to and uninterested in the emotional side of ISKCON, being more concerned with the movement's material and social benefits. Neither was the term 'snapping' ever heard used to describe devotees' emotional experiences in the movement. The deep emotional and physical experiences which some devotees experienced in 'kirtan' or during chanting did often confirm a devotees belief in Krishna and commitment to the movement, but there is no evidence to suggest that these experiences led to a radical personality change. Sarubhavana's experience at the airport was, to use Conway and Siegelman's terminology, a classic example of the snapping 'phenomenon'. Sarubhavana has been in the movement for some five years and is one of ISKCON's few intellectuals. Like all devotees, he is well aware of the power the new gurus have and the possibility of their abusing it. As a subtle hint to the new gurus to conform, he has collected together and had published by BBT in book form all Prabhupad's comments on the correct behaviour to be expected of a bone fide guru. This book has been made available to all temples and devotees. Such a book would indicate the mind of a person who is well aware of what is going on, and on his own initiative has tried to do something about it, rather than the work of a mindless person devoid of free will, as Conway and Siegelman would maintain cult members are after the snapping moment.

Conway and Siegelman, and critics of cults in general assume that cult leaders manipulate and control the minds of their followers. But there is no 'grey hand' behind the scenes manipulating ISKCON devotees. While Prabhupad had a great deal of influence, he had little to do with everyday affairs in most temples, especially the British temples, which he visited rarely. Nor, except in Vrindaban, did he have any middle-aged right-hand man strategically placed to do his manipulating for him. The devotees have always run things themselves. If the devotees are brainwashed than the same would apply to the leadership in ISKCON, since they have gone through the same processing as the rank and file. But the incessant manipulation, politicking and petit entrepreneurism of the leadership demonstrate their individualism and freedom of thought and control over their own lives. Moreover the new gurus do not control the devotees; rather their relationship is symbiotic and mutually supportive. Far from attempting to brainwash the devotees, the new gurus are having to tread carefully for fear of losing the devotees' support.

The ISKCON temple in Hawaii puts Conway and Siegelman's whole argument in perspective and demonstrates its inapplicability to ISKCON. Most devotees sit around enjoying the weather and facilities, including surfing and sunbathing on the beach, offered by Honolulu, the most relaxed temple in ISKCON. The not inconsiderable number of devotees who 'bloop' permanently in Hawaii generally remain on good terms with the movement and continue to visit on Sunday afternoons for the festivities held there. The Honolulu temple demonstrates how little real power the movement has over devotees. The temple authorities attempt to control the situation, but to little avail; the devotees go their own way, do little work, and drift off to the beach. Honolulu devotees manipulate the movement totally to their advantage and are an example of ISKCON individualism at its most extreme. In sum, devotees are as much exploiters as exploited.

The main influence that ISKCON has is in the realm of religion itself. But even within this sphere, the degree of influence varies.

Some devotees are more impressionable than others, some are more religiously minded than others. ISKCON devotees' tendency to be 'seeker' types and to have had some kind of religious interest background or connection prior to joining the movement are important factors determining the influence ISKCON's belief structure has on them. Also the majority of devotees are young, the age when religious conversions are most common. The social milieu of ISKCON, too, which bombards devotees all the time with Krishna, provides an ideal nurturing ground for the flowering and sustaining of devotees' latent, or not so latent, religious orientation. For many devotees becoming Krishna Conscious is not the product of brainwashing but is a genuine and sincere spiritual conversion. Barber (1978) interpreted membership of the Unification church similarly. But for the majority of devotees, it is a rational act to join and remain in the movement. Movement's offer of a spiritual life is a factor that devotees take into account when deciding to join and remain in the movement, and for many it is all-important. But they also take into account social and economic factors and, for some devotees, these outweigh the spiritual ones. From a social and economic point of view, if the pros and cons are weighed up, the majority of devotees' even the most spiritually inclined, are better off in the movement than outside, especially British devotees. It is a primary reason why British ISKCON is increasing in numbers and doing so well. For British devotees, compared to life on the dole or in boring, dead-end jobs, life in ISKCON is much more fun, much more varied and far more interesting.

The longer devotees remain in ISKCON the more difficult it is for them to leave. This is not just because they get in a rut and become institutionalised, but also because devotees have poor academic qualifications and those who have been in the movement several years, particularly those in their late twenties, would find it difficult to get a job if they left the movement. By then, too, they generally feel too old to go back to their studies, nor do they have the necessary money. Anyway, after the easy, and interesting and varied life they have in the movement, the alternatives, especially in Britain are not very attractive.

This is especially true of prominent devotees most of whom have been in the movement since its inception and the rest for at least five years. They could not hope to have such powerful and interesting positions in the outside world. Also long term devotees tend to have maintained few contacts with people in the outside world to whom they could return, especially American devotees who often have cut their ties with their families completely. The thought of having to 'go it alone' if they leave, they find particularly off-putting. One devotee when discussing why she did not 'bloop', remarked that her parents were dead, she had no friends in the outside world, and her brother was a Communist. There was no one outside she could go to.

In sum, ISKCON devotees' apparently uniform attitudes and hostility towards outsiders can be better explained in terms of ISKCON's beliefs and social structure themselves rather than as due to brainwashing. Any group that expresses its frustrations through total condemnation and rejection of society is obviously going to be dogmatic and extremist in its point of view. The regular visitors appear to be less dogmatic in their point of view and less uniform in their beliefs about Krishna Consciousness than the full-time living-in devotees, which would suggest that it is living together all the time in close association, eating, breathing, sleeping Krishna, which fosters the latter's extremism and uniformity of belief. Although this is a factor, full-time devotees' attitudes can better be explained in terms of 'role-playing' rather than mind-bending by ISKCON. Extremeness is inherent in the role of the celibates, particularly the 'heavies', and it is those temples where they exist in greatest numbers that are the most heavy and uniform in outlook. The atmosphere tends to be more liberal where many householders live within the temple confines and are able to control the heavy extremism of the celibates. Thus in ISKCON, behaviour is to a great degree determined by the type of role the individual performs. The flexibility and ease with which the most extreme 'heavy' and the most parrot-like *brahmacharin* changes overnight on marriage into an easygoing householder suggests that devotees are role-playing rather than brainwashed. If devotees were brainwashed they would not be able to change their roles so easily or act so flexibly. The devotees' control over their own lives is demonstrated by their manipulation of celibate and householders, the two basic and focal roles in the movement to serve their own ends and interests.

The radical change in behaviour of prominent devotees when they became gurus reflects the ease with which devotees change roles.

The new gurus changed their demeanour and way of expressing themselves. They copied Prabhupad's ways and mannerisms and tried to act in a humble and saintly way. Their personalities significantly did not change.

In fact, devotees are role-players par excellence. They enjoy playing roles of all kinds, as is apparent from the central role that amateur dramatics plays in the movement and the positive feedback devotees get from 'dressing up' in ISKCON costume. Indeed, in a sense ISKCON provides devotees with an 'act' and a 'stage' on which to perform their social protest against society.

Looked at from the point of view of 'role playing' any devotees who wish to remain full-time members of ISKCON, to be accepted as such have to perform their roles correctly and abide by and follow the movement's rules and regulations. If they do not, they will be asked to leave. The rules state 'uniformity of belief' and 'no criticism of it' and devotees have to abide by these rules to remain a living-in member of the movement. When discussing belief they must come out only with Prabhupad's beliefs, accept no criticism of them and be uncritical themselves. That is in the nature of playing ISKCON's 'belief game'. To an outsider it is a symptom of brainwashing. But to a devotee it is role-playing and just acting according to the rules. Neophyte devotees who have been in the movement only a few months, because they are inexperienced in handling a belief system which insists on towing the party line at all times tend to be clumsy and unsophisticated when interacting with and preaching to outsiders.

Long-term devotees appear in general less dogmatic and extremist on the surface than those neophytes. Conway and Siegelman themselves recognised that long-term members of the new cults appeared 'normal'. But they took this as a sign of totally successful brainwashing, that such people had totally assimilated the beliefs and practices of the cults. The apparent 'normality' of long-term devotees in ISKCON, however, reflects their sophisticated handling of their roles and their skilful adjustment over the years to the uniformity and unacceptability of criticism demanded by the Krishna Consciousness belief system. They have learnt to deal with and manipulate outsiders so as to pay lip service to uniformity of belief whilst at the same time not antagonising the outsiders. To conclude, it is easy to recognise when a full time living-in ISKCON devotee is about to 'bloop'. When they no longer feel any commitment to the movement they start criticising ISKCON.

CHAPTER NINETEEN

Conclusion

> In the Age of Kali (Quarrel and Hypocrisy) the chanting of the holy name is the best means of God-realization. There is no other alternative, no other alternative, no other alternative.
>
> BTG Vol. 12, No. 9, p. 10.

This examination, of what often appears to outsiders a collection of strange and esoteric foreign beliefs and practices, has revealed that beneath the overt bizarreness of ISKCON devotees have developed a world view that is redolent with symbolism and emotional content. Through eastern mysticism and symbolism they have rendered their world knowable and suffused it with meaning. Far from eastern mysticism and the modern youth phenomenon forming an unholy alliance and being incompatible bedfellows, there is a remarkable congruence and agreement between the teachings of Prabhupad and the needs of his devotees. In imputing new symbolic meaning to his teachings, too, and remodelling and adapting them to fit the social milieu of western society, devotees have provided themselves with a reconstruction of reality which has enabled them personally and collectively to create a more meaningful way of life in which they are able to deal with the social and existential problems that confront them in their everyday world, a lifestyle, moreover, that is just as meaningful to them as the outside world is to outsiders.

What is particularly of interest is the degree of order in the ISKCON world view. The Structuralists, and the doyen of structuralism in particular, Levi Strauss, have demonstrated the logical ordering of the human mind. Levi Strauss has shown how, beneath the apparent irrationality of the 'primitive mind' and customs of 'primitive society' such as totemism, there is a highly logical ordering and complex interrelationship between parts.

Conclusion

Using the concept of 'bricolage', he has shown how the primitive mind, using what appear to be random everyday objects and concepts in a culture, like a 'bricoleur', builds up a logical model of the universe which has an innate logic of its own. These symbolic models which are frequently expressed in myth, Levi-Strauss argues, convey hidden codes or messages about the society. They express inherent contradictions in the fabric of the culture and attempt to reconcile them. His findings would appear to be applicable to western youth groups too, and ISKCON in particular.

Whilst ISKCON appears to be a hotch-potch of beliefs and practices on the surface, the movement has developed around the concept 'I am not my body, I am spirit-soul', a highly structured and organised symbolic world view in which the parts are complexly organised and organically interrelated to form a total whole, like the pieces in a complex jigsaw puzzle. Like primitive myth, ISKCON's symbolic model of the world and social relations conveys a hidden message too. It expresses and attempts to reconcile symbolically fundamental contradictions faced by modern youth in their daily lives in western society. It is, perhaps, appropriate that a western movement such as ISKCON should use sexuality, the major symbol of western society, and one which embodies fundamental contradictions for present day westerners as the basic symbol and framework for its social organisation. Like the primitive mind, which also uses inversion and the reconciliation of opposites to express contradictions, so too, in ISKCON the devotees have inverted the beliefs and practices of western society.

In the mid 1960s, in the heady days of the youth phenomenon and the Counterculture in America, the middle and upper middle-class youth, and fringe movements such as ISKCON which were seen to embody the counterculture, were viewed by many, including Roszak (1969) in *The Making of a Counterculture*, and Slater (1970) in *The Pursuit of Loneliness* as the vanguard of a new and better society and a blueprint for the values and culture of the future. With the hindsight of the economic depression of the 1970s, and the disappearance of the American Counterculture during this decade, such a positive interpretation was seen as wishful thinking.

But the negative conclusions of Wills (1978) with regard to secular youth movements in Britain and Wilson (1976) with regard to the new religious cults which sprang up in the 1960s, do not give enough credit to these movements particularly to ISKCON.

Willis (1978) in *Profane Culture*, a study of Motorbike boys and hippies in Britain, acknowledges the ability of these groups to influence the wider economic and political spheres and to change society is limited. But nevertheless, he sees as a major political failing of hippies and Motorbike boys and youth groups in general, that although they had insight into the external world and exposed its contradictions they were themselves forms of retreat. They did not attempt to organise or change society for the better.

He maintains that, a dialectic should exist between cultural groups such as hippies and Motorbike boys and the wider economic and political spheres, and that a genuine cultural politics of the people should come up from such groups as these.

Willis' criticisms, of course, are applicable to the new eastern religious groups too, and especially ISKCON, which is particularly introverted, isolationist, and uninterested in actively changing society socially. But it is precisely because Motorbike boys and hippies and this is true of ISKCON devotees as well, were unable to change society and their everyday lives for the better, that they have identified with and joined such movements and retreated from the wider society in the first place. They were doing all they could in the circumstances to change their daily lives for the better.

Wilson, who sees modern society as becoming increasingly secular, in *Contemporary Transformations of Religion* (1976: 96) views the new religious movements as fads and leisure-time activities:

> I regard them as a confirmation of the process of secularization. They indicate the extent to which religion has become inconsequential for modern society. The cults represent, in the American phrase, the 'religion of your choice', the highly privatized preference that reduces religion to the significance of pushpin, poetry or popcorn. They have no real consequence for other social institutions, for political power structures, for technological reintegration of society, and contribute nothing towards the culture by which a society might live.

Of course, not all these new religious cults are youth focused, but, those that are, including ISKCON, when seen as part and parcel of the whole modern youth social protest movement, clearly do have a lot to offer. They do serve society and do have significant

Conclusion

social consequences for other social institutions, the political power structure in particular. They provide a kind of safety valve, a channel for youth to express their social protest and come to terms with the problems that confront them in their daily lives. Without channels such as the new eastern religious cults and secular youth movements, many more young people might have become nihilistic and resorted to the only other channels open to them, namely vandalism, crime, and soccer hooliganism. Without these movements destruction and greater havoc might have been wrought in the wider society. Indeed they are a conservative force in society, maintainers of the status quo, and at least by conservatives, should be viewed in a positive light. Infact the new religious groups reflect the failure of modern western society to meet the needs of a large percentage of the population, namely its youth. Modern society prides itself on being more socially conscious than in the past, and has attempted through the natural and social sciences to learn more about mankind, society and the universe, so as to change things for the better. Rather than dismissing the new religious groups out of hand, therefore, academics and the Establishment should attempt to learn from them and thus, perhaps, a better way of life, greater harmony and a greater integration of society might be achieved.

The new religious sects are not a confirmation of the process of secularisation either if ISKCON is anything to go by. The movement does teach something of the seriousness of eternal verities. A sincere ISKCON devotee's beliefs are as real and meaningful for him and as genuine and spiritual too as those of a genuine and sincere member of any of the established Christian churches. ISKCON frequently produces an ethical and social transformation in the individual devotee, similar to that undergone by individuals who joined sects which developed in the eighteenth and nineteenth centuries, such as the Methodists and Baptists. ISKCON's right to consider itself a genuine bona fide religion has, of course, been upheld by the Supreme Court in America. ISKCON represents, and is part of the resurgence of religious interest and spirituality among the masses that mushroomed during the 1960's. These new religious cults do as Wilson says, represent a 'highly privatized preference' and the 'religion of your choice', but that is exactly what religion should be. Man's search for personal salvation and his personal internalised private relationship with God have always been a major feature of the universal religions', a quest impossible to realise, however, within the monolithic bureaucratic structure of the modern Christian church devoid of emotional content and unable to cater for personal spirituality. The personal focus of some of the new religious cults such as ISKCON is an attempt to follow this path, of personal salvation.

It is because ISKCON and the other new cults are the 'religion of your choice' that they have a positive social function. It was precisely because the established Churches were superimposed from above and supported the ruling elite that they were unable to cater for individual needs. Modern youth, however, by choosing their own beliefs and practices, have developed religions closely related to and well suited to their needs, and as such they have a socially useful role. Movements such as ISKCON may well be described as the 'religion of the people' or 'folk religion', and have value as such.

Some of the new eastern religious movements could be characterised as 'fads' and 'leisure-time' activities, such as Transcendental Meditation. But, ISKCON is not only here to stay but, for many devotees, is not only a full time, but likely to be a permanent commitment. Membership of ISKCON leads to a reintegration of the individual devotee within the social order too, as the behaviour of householder devotees bears witness. The movement too as it becomes increasingly institutionalised, is gradually, adapting to and reintegrating into the wider society as the devotees' involvement with the Asian community in Britain evidences. For instance, ISKCON invites local dignatories to its functions, while to attain local goodwill in Letchmore Heath, it has started to give parties for the village children. To achieve reconciliation between devotees and their estranged parents, ISKCON, in 1979, invited all the parents to a Christmas 'Krishnatarian' dinner with all the traditional trappings. It turned out to be very successful and an excellent piece of public relations.

Like the Methodists and Quakers too in the eighteenth century, ISKCON in Britain provides a vehicle for social mobility since it offers lower-class devotees the means of embourgeoisement. The movement, especially in Britain, recruiting as it does from people who have suffered from some form of deprivation, fits in neatly with the general interpretation of new sects as 'the religion of the disinherited'. In fact, it fits in with Wilson's (1975: 12) own definition of sects as 'a self-distinguishing protest movement.'

Conclusion

Although ISKCON's future is sound, it is problematic, whether the movement will be able to obtain future members from devotees' children, even though these are increasing rapidly in numbers. At the *gurukulas*, devotees' children, are totally indoctrinated and get a concentrated diet of Krishna Consciousness. Although the aim of child-rearing practices in the movement is, to produce a 'pure soul' uncontaminated by materialism and *'maya'*. ISKCON seems to be having problems with the few adolescents it has produced so far particularly the boys. A number of them appear to be rebelling against the ISKCON lifestyle. Although devotees' children have been socialised to hate materialism and the 'karmi' world nevertheless most of the children have grown up in urban settings well aware of what is going on in the outside world. Brought up in a spartan manner and deprived of luxuries such as television, cinema and girlfriends that 'karmi' children take for granted, some devotees' children, on reaching adolesence, appear to be attracted to the 'karmi' way of life and to want the materialist luxuries that go with it. For example, Sura Surabir, a young adolescent of 15 who spent several years in the *gurukula* in Vrindaban, frequently stated how much he enjoyed visiting the luxurious Intercontinental Taj Mahal Hotel in Bombay, which he would describe with popping eyes. One or two of the young adolescent boys also appear to feel frustrated at their lack of academic qualifications, knowing that with their minimal formal education they cannot hope to get a good job in the 'karmi' world.

ISKCON has managed to cope with the potential rebellion of the adolescent girls more effectively, by introducing the traditional custom of early marriage. So far, two girls of 15-16 have had marriages arranged for them to devotee boys in their twenties. Whilst early marriage of the girls to devout devotee boys may, in the short-term, keep adolescent females in the movement, this may only be effective as a short-term measure, given the fragility of devotee marriages in general. On reaching adulthood, the girls may very likely leave both their marriages and the movement. In sum ISKCON may well have to rely primarily on outside recruitment for future members.

The movement has survived, consolidated its position and expanded, unlike many of the cults that developed during the 1960s primarily because it developed early on a sound financial basis based on a regular income through book distribution. In Britain, financial support given by the Asian community has put it in a particularly strong position. The development of ISKCON's economic organisation primarily around enterprises which need only an unskilled labour force has been a realistic and rational use of its labour force, and has contributed to its economic success. Also, the flexibility of the work-force, which has allowed for devotees' individualism, is a major reason for their remaining in the movement over the long-term and, as such, has also contributed to ISKCON's success.

The movement's highly regulated and strict control over devotees' sexual behaviour has also contributed to its survival and success. The majority of devotees are in their sexual prime. Since men outnumber women by more than two to one, if their sexual lives were not highly regulated and they were allowed free reign, conflict over women would soon arise. The movement would soon fall apart, as often happened to many hippy communes based on 'free love' during the 1960s.

Kanter's (1968:499-517) study of 'commitment mechanisms', used by Utopian Communities in America between the War of Independence and the American Civil War to retain the commitment of their followers, concluded that 'successful' Utopian communities, which survived for a long time, shared a number of common 'commitment mechanisms', which contributed to their success and long-term survival. Many of these features are also found in ISKCON.

'Sacrifice', she found, was a feature common to all the successful Utopian communities she examined, and a means by which they retained the commitment of their followers:

> Sacrifice involves the giving up of something considered valuable or pleasurable in order to belong to the organisation ; this stresses the importance of role of the member to the individual. Sacrifice means that membership becomes costly and is therefore not lightly regarded or likely to be given up easily ... The process of sacrifice asks members to give up something as a price of membership; once the members agree to make the sacrifices, their motivation to remain participants should increase. Membership should become more sacred; more valuable and meaningful ... those systems exacting sacrifice will survive longer because sacrifice is functional for their maintenance ...

Conclusion

sacrifice operates on the basis of a simple principle from the cognitive consistency theories: the more it 'costs' a person to do something, the more valuable he will have to consider it, in order to justify the psychic 'expense' and remain internally consistent.

Kanter saw as supporting sacrifice, organisational arrangements involving abstinence and austerity, including abstinence from tobacco, meat, alcohol, personal adornment, and going to dances and an emphasis on celibacy and the denial of sexual graification. They of course form the core of ISKCON's institutional structure, too, and understandably since they have so positive a function have continued to do so as the movement has developed and matured.

'Investment' Kanter also sees as a trait common to successful Utopian communities' long-term survival.

Investment is a process whereby the individual gains a stake in the organisation; commits current and future profits to it so that he must continue to participate if he is going to realise them.... The process of investment provides the individual with a stake in the fate of the organization, he commits his 'profit' to the organisation so that leaving it would be costly in terms of future gain from present involvement.

In ISKCON, the majority of devotees, contribute a great deal and have much invested in the movement, particularly those who obtain a large income from 'doing business', or have obtained powerful positions in the movement, or are 'sankirtan' devotees who make a great deal of money for the movement and are given perks and rewards by the movement. Because their futures, economically and politically, are tied up with the movement's future and success they are likely to retain their commitment to ISKCON over the long-term. Devotees long-term committment is further fostered because all devotees receive the profits from their 'investment' directly since all money made in ISKCON is ploughed back into the movement so as to benefit all devotees.

Kanter also concluded that a feature common to all successful Utopian communities was a strong allegiance to and emphasis on the group, where an 'individual's fund of effectivity and emotion' was attached to the group. Given ISKCON's emphasis on individualism, this point should not be over-emphasised, but the movement's strong group focus and the individual devotee's generally strong identification with the movement do appear to have contributed to the movement's survival.

Another common trait she found in successful communities was the renunciation of dyadic relations and the prevention of the development of ties both between individual members and between members and the outside world, which might conflict with an individual's allegiance to the community. The under-emphasis on dyadic relations is, of course, a major feature of ISKCON too, with its emphasis on individualism and the stress in *bhakti yoga* on the underplaying of all personal relations. The emphasis on individualism in ISKCON has led the individual devotee, being unable to rely on other devotees for his emotional and psychic needs. In consequence devotees turn instead to the movement itself for the fulfilment of these needs, as their strong identification with the group bears witness.

ISKCON has survived, and is in a strong position now, because the movement has had strong and capable leadership in both Prabhupad and the new American gurus. Their spiritually sanctioned guru roles have given them enormous power which they have been able to use to prevent disintegrative conflict and to hold the movement together. The leadership has also given firm and shrewd direction which has enabled the movement to consolidate and expand. ISKCON was lucky that Prabhupad, lived well into old age, for by the time he died, ISKCON had a whole stratum of leading 'advanced' devotees with proven management capabilities, whose abilities were demonstrated by the minimum of disruption caused when Prabhupad 'passed over'.

But, the very form of autocratic leadership embodied in the guru role, which has contributed so much to ISKCON's success, has also been looked on with increasing suspicion by the outside world since December 1978, when some 900 members of the Peoples Temple either committed suicide or were murdered at the behest of their alcoholic and psychopathic leader, in their retreat in the Guyana forest in South America. Autocratic leadership of the kind embodied in the guru role is, of course, potentially open to abuse. But it is invalid to lump all the cults together and assume that they are all potential Peoples Temples for often all they have in common

Conclusion

is that they are seeking an alternative life-style to that offered by Western society. Many are body-focused. But they vary considerably in ideology, social structure and the type of people they recruit. As such it is impossible to make any but the most superfical generalisations that are applicable to all the cults. This is particularly true of specific, behaviour patterns, such as leadership behaviour, or their potentiality for committing mass suicide or even their brainwashing potential. To determine how any cult is going to react to a specific situation, it is necessary to examine it individually.

In ISKCON, it would be unlikely that any psychopathic guru could get the devotees to commit suicide *en masse*, since suicide is considered, as in Hinduism generally, a sin and against the tenets of Krishna Consciousness. In fact, never once in three years was there a case of a devotee who committed suicide.

Those cults in the West which have Asian gurus at their head have little to fear that they will incite their followers to mass suicide. They may well be materialist in orientation and financially milk their followers, or find satisfaction in adulation as Prabhupad did, but Asian gurus would consider incitement to suicide a heinous sin. Moreover gurus are expected to play saintly roles by westerners, any Asian guru like 'Dad' Jones would not have attracted followers in the first place. Though, of course, ISKCON now has American gurus, and they may have the same western cultural potential for psychopathy built into them as 'Dad' Jones, as yet, though, whilst some of them appear to be revelling in their new found guru status and one or two seem to be developing delusions of grandeur, none, has begun to show psychopathic tendencies.

Even if ISKCON were to produce a leader with such tendencies, the movement has developed internal constraining mechanisms which would enable it to control his behaviour. The form of these internal constraints reflects ISKCON's uniqueness and emphasises the fact that cults', internal organisations differ so widely that it is difficult to make generalisations which are applicable to all of them. The decision on Prabhupad's death to make all the most powerful devotees GBCs and gurus rather than just selecting one of them to head the movement, was a wise decision. It has produced a balance of power and a constraining mechanism within the movement, for the gurus in terms of political power, balance each other out. If a guru or a leading devotee gets out of line, the other gurus either put pressure on him to conform or else push him out of the movement, as they did with Swami Govinda. This balance has been able to prevent any guru from becoming too extremist and manipulating devotees to their disadvantage.

The devotees themselves act as a check on the actions of the gurus and leaders. They are well aware of the gurus' potentiality for abusing their position, [and are sensitive to the fact that the new gurus were, until recently, their erstwhile peers. Any new guru who gave himself airs or who got 'too big for his boots', would soon lose the support of his new disciples. The new gurus themselves realise they tread a slippery path. To supplicate and not to offend the other devotees, they stress the ascetic, saintly, humble side of their guru roles. They spend all their time demonstrating their humbleness and humility. The other devotees, well aware why the gurus act in this manner respond in kind and play up to them. One of the most frequent comments made by a devotee about any of the new gurus (usually accompanied with a look of admiration) is 'Gee, the Maharaj is so humble!'

Anyway, devotees, being such individualists are their own bosses. It is unlikely that they could be made to do anything they did not want to. If a guru behaved in an unacceptable way, they would just leave and transfer their allegience to another guru a fact of which the gurus are well aware so that they are unlikely to do anything which would meet with the disapproval of the rank and file devotees.

Finaly it has become fashionable to view movements and cults such as hippies, 'beats' and new eastern religious groups such as ISKCON, which recruit primarily from young people, as constituting what Van Gennep has termed a *'rite de passage'*; that is, a liminal betwixt and between stage, in this case, between childhood and adulthood: a structureless period free from the responsibilities of adulthood.

Prince (1974), for instance, views the concern of contemporary middle-class youth with the mystical, and their search for altered states of consciousness, which he refers to as 'Neotranscendentalism', as 'cocoon work'. The Neotranscendental quest of modern youth he sees as a self-imposed *rite de passage* whose primary task is a psychological one. Movement from one stage of life to another, he maintains, presents the individual ego with a major problem of adaption. Contemporary youth, he claims,

Conclusion

has sought solutions to the problem of adapting to adulthood by regression through mystical states. He thus views 'Neotranscendentalism' as a kind of metamorphosis or 'cocoon work' which enables young people to break away from parental authority and emerge as adults ready to take up their position in adult society. Psychologists (p. 257), he states, interpret mysticism as 'regression in the service of the ego' and as 'de-automatisation of ego function'. He interprets modern youth's concern with mystical states similarly:

> The regression explanation holds that mystical states occur when an individual or group is confronted with a problem which seems insoluble by habitual means. The individual's (or group leader's) ego regresses to earlier levels of adaption in an attempt to discover an alternative solution. It is as though the ego has an elevator which can descend to several lower levels in which prior experience and earlier coping mechanisms are stored. The mystical descent is to the earliest level of experience, before the creation of the world as it were, in the primal chaos, long before self and other have become differentiated, before space and time, before language, when the coping mechanism, the panacea for all ills and discomforts, was sucking at the breast. The mystical state is a "flash back" of that primal experience. The mystic returns from his descent with the perennial mystical message: at the root of things all is one, all is good, the universe may be trusted; salvation lies in simplification, in de-institutionalization, and above all, in love.
>
> The de-automatization hypothesis is based upon the observation that in the early stages of the learning process a good deal of attention energy is required. But with practice, the motor and perceptual patterns become automatic with attendant energy conservation. Deikman (1966) believes that through the mystic's life of renunciation and in the process of meditation he is reinvesting attention energies in these automatic actions and returning them to awareness. The resulting relation with the world may be less efficient from a biological point of view but may permit the experience of aspects of the real world formerly ignored. The undoing of automatic structures permits a gain in sensory intensity and richness at the expense of abstract categorization and differentiation.

Price relates his hypothesis to Victor Turner's concept of, '*communitas*' which Turner, famous for his *rites de passage* studies expounds in detail in *The Ritual Process* (1969). Turner, uses a basically structural-functionalist model and derives his theory from his study of ritual among tribal people in East Africa and *rites de passage* in particular, i.e. rituals which accompany transitions from one status to another, generally from one stage of life to another. He conceptualises social life in terms of two alternating models of social relations, namely 'structure' and anti-structure or '*communitas*'. The latter he veiws as 'giving recognition to an essential and genuine human bond, without which there could be *no* society'. He sees it as emerging in liminality and the boundary period in *rites de passage* in particular; in the 'betwixt and between' period when an initiate has been detached from his previous role and status, but has not yet acquired his next.

> It is as though there are here two major 'models' for human inter-relatedness, juxtaposed and alternating. The first is of society as a structured, differentiated, and often hierarchial system of politico-legal-economic positions with many types of evaluation, separating men in terms of 'more' or 'less'. The second, which emerges recognizably in the liminal period, is of society as an unstructured or rudimentarily structured and relatively undifferentiated *comitatus*, community, or even communion of equal individuals (p. 96).

Turner noted that in the liminal 'betwixt and between' stage of puberty *rites de passage* when the initiate has been detached from his childhood status but not yet acquired adult status, that the initiate was stripped of symbols of both youth and adulthood and resumed the role of infant.

In our own society, Turner sees the 'beats' and hippies of the 1960s as an example of liminality and *communitas*. Hippies and 'beats', he says, not having the advantage of national *rites de passage*, have opted out of the constraints of the status-bound social order in order to experience a period of *communitas*. He also points out that the sacred properties often associated with '*communitas*' in primitive *rites de passage* are also seen in the hippy interest in the mystical.

Prince interprets 'Neotranscendentalism' similarly. He argues that by the age of eighteen, American youth are glutted with organi-

Conclusion

sation and structure. 'Neotranscendentalism', he claims, as well as providing 'cocoon work' enables young people to opt out of the constraints placed on them by the social structure, and answers the need for a period of *communitas*. Presumably, he says, after the communal need is satisfied for a few years, young people will happily return to the old world of structure and organisation.

Youth does have problems adapting psychologically to adulthood and this is reflected in mystical movements such as ISKCON, which focus on altered states of consciousness. ISKCON's beliefs and practices however would suggest that there is far more to youth's interest in the mystical than Prince's hypothesis would suggest. Indeed they throw doubt on it, particularly his attempt to focus his argument on the mystical states themselves and encapsulate them in a *rite de passage* framework.

Actual mystical states themselves, of course, such as meditation is intended to produce, play a relatively minor role in ISKCON and this is true of a number of the other new eastern religious cults too. Some devotees in ISKCON get very little out of meditation and for others, it plays no part at all. To account for youth's interest in 'Neotranscendentalism' in terms of the mystical states alone, therefore, only partly explains the phenomenon. It does not explain the development and structure of the movements themselves.

If ISKCON's beliefs and practices are viewed as providing young people with the means to come to terms with and control the existential and social problems that confront them in their everyday lives, then the movement's mystical focus is not so much a form of 'regression', or 'cocoon' work as a response to the 'here and now' for they are problems faced by adults in an adult world. Having broken away from their families and childhood, their interest in mystical states and eastern religions in general is an attempt and, is in many cases, a first attempt by devotees as adults, to deal with the adult world.

To see ISKCON as representing 'anti-structure', as a reaction to the overstructuring of western society, is also open to criticism, for ISKCON both in America and Britain, attracts its recruits generally from the most unstructured section of society. Moreover, rather than providing an unstructured undifferentiated fellowship or *communitas*, ISKCON is, of course, extremely structured, ritualistic and hierarchical, for ISKCON devotees are people who need structured relationships and have created ISKCON in their own image.

With hindsight, looking at the new religious cults and movements that developed out of the youth phenomenon of the 1960s, it is open to question that they should be viewed as *rites de passage* at all, especially ISKCON. Certainly, the majority of followers recruited into these movements, with the exception of a few movements, such as TM, are predominantly youthful. For some too they function as a *rite de passage*, for after a few weeks or years their members leave. But many of these new religious movements, including ISKCON, are here to stay. ISKCON, with its highly organised internal structure and the long-term membership of many of its devotees' bears little resemblance to a youthful *rite de passage*. In fact, it is precisely because it offers more than an adolescent *rite de passage*, because it provides a permanent full-time occupation, a life-long home and the possibility of a spouse and family within the movement that so many devotees have remained in the movement so long. Rather than being seen as a *rite de passage*, ISKCON should be viewed for what it is a new religious movement, increasing in maturity, that has a positive role to play in the wider society.

Because it is primarily young people who control the movement, its true nature should not be misconstrued. That movements such as ISKCON should be viewed as liminal stages, and periods of irresponsibility prior to the responsibilities of adulthood, sheds a great deal of light on western society's attitude to youth and their abilities. But ISKCON's rapid, successful development over the last decade demonstrates that young people are, if given their heads, just as capable of being leaders and holding responsible jobs as are the middle-aged. ISKCON indicates, with its stress on individualism, petit entrepreneurialism, capitalism as well as its focus around a theme basic to western civilisation, namely its emphasis on a body/soul dichotomy, that western youth, even those who exhibit so bizarre an exterior as ISKCON, are not so different from the parental generation which they claim to despise.

Bibliography

ARGYLE, M. (1958) *Religious Behaviour*. International Library of Sociology and Social Reconstruction. London : Routledge & Kegan Paul.
BARKER, D. (1978) *Living the Divine Principle*. Archives de Science Sociales des Religions, 75-93.
BELLAH, R. (1970) *Beyond Belief : Essays on Religion in a Post-Traditional World*. New York : Harper and Row.
—— (1976) 'New Religious Consciousness and the Crisis in Modernity' in Glock, C. and Bellah, R. (eds.) *The New Religious Consciousness*. Berkeley and Los Angeles : University of California Press, 333-352.
BENTHALL, J. (1976) *The Body Electric : Patterns of Western Industrial Culture*. London : Thames & Hudson.
BENTHALL, J. and POLHEMUS, T. (1975) *The Body as a Medium of Expression*. London : Allen Lane.
BERG, G. C. (1951) *The Unconscious Significance of Hair*. London : George Allen & Unwin.
BHAKTIVEDANTA BOOK TRUST, The

Bhagavad Gita As It Is: Srimad Bhagavatam (30 vols.); *Krsha the Supreme Personality of Godhead* (3 vols.) ; *Sri Caitanya Caritamtra* (17 vols.) ; *Teachings of Lord Kapila*; *Teachings of Queen Kunti*; *Teachings of Lord Caitanya*; *Science of Self-Realization*; *Handbook of Krsna Consciousness*; *Life Comes from life*; *Nectar of Devotion*; *Hare Krishna Diary*; *Sri Isopanisad*; *Nectar of Instruction*; *Perfect Questions—Perfect Answers*; *Beyond Birth and Death*; *Perfection of Yoga*; *Scientific Basis of Krsna Consciousness Easy Journey to Other Plants*; *Back to Godhead Magazine*; *Readings in Vedic Literature* (Swami Satsavarupa) ; *What is Matter and What is Life*; The Bhaktivedanta Institute Monograph Series No. 1 (Singh, T.D. and Thompson, R.L.) ; *Demonstration by Information Theory That Life Cannot Arise From Matter* (Thompson, R.) ; *Consciousess and the Law of Nature* (Thompson, R.).

BHANDARKAR, SRI RAMAKRISHNA GOPALA (1913) *Vaisnavism, Saivism and Minor Religious Systems*. Strasburg : R.J. Trubner.
BLACKING, J. (1977) *The Anthropology of the Body*. A.S.A. Monograph No. 15. London: Academic Press.
BON MAHARAJ B.H., SWAMI (1973) 'Sri Caitanya's Concept of Finite Self' in *Indian Philosophy and Culture*, 18: 47-69.
BROADBENT, J., (1975) 'The Image of God, or Two Yards of Skin' in Benthall

J. and Polhemus, T. (eds.) *The Body as a Medium of Expression*. London: Allen Lane, 303-326.

CHAKRAVARTI SUBHINDRA CHANDRA. (1969) *Philosophical Foundation of Bengal Vaisnavism* : *A Critical Exposition*. Calcutta : Academic Publishers.

CLARKE, J. (1976) 'The Skinheads and the Magical Recovery of Community' in Hall, S. and Jefferson, T. (eds.) *Resistance Through Rituals*: *Youth Subcultures in Post-war Britain*. London: Hutchinson of London in Association with the Centre for Contemporary Cultural Studies, University of Birmingham, 99-102.

COHEN, A. (1977) 'Symbolic Action as the Structure of the Self' in Lewis, I. (ed.) *Symbols and Sentiments in Cross Cultural Studies in Symbolism*. London: Academic Press, 117-128.

CONWAY, F. and SIEGELMAN, J. (1978) *Snapping*: *America's Epidemic of Sudden Personality Change*. Philadelphia & New York: J.B. Lippincott Company.

DANER, F.J. (1976) *The American Children of Krsna. A Study of the Hare Krsna Movement, Case Studies in Cultural Anthropology*. New York: Holt, Rinehart and Winston.

DASGUPTA, SURENDRANATH (1932-1955) *A History of Indian Philosophy*. Cambridge: Cambridge University Press. 5 vols.

DE, SUSHIL KUMAR (1961) *Early History of the Vaisnava Faith and Movement in Bengal*. Calcutta: Firma K.L. Mukhopadhyay. 2nd edition.

DIMOCK, E.C. Jr. (1966a) *The Place of the Hidden Moon*. Chicago: University of Chicago Press.

────── (1966b) 'Doctrine and Practice among the Vaisnavas of Bengal' in Singer, M. (ed.) *Krishna, Myths, Rites and Attitudes*. Honolulu: East-West Centre Press, 41-63.

DOUGLAS, M. (1966) *Purity and Danger. An Analysis of Concepts of Pollution and Taboo*. London: Routledge and Kegan Paul.

────── (1970) *Natural Symbols: Explorations in Cosmology*. London: Barrie & Rockcliff, The Cresset Press.

────── (1971) 'Do Dogs Laugh? A Cross-Cultural Approach to Body Symbolism,' *Journal of Psychosomatic Research*, *15*, 387-90.

DUTT, KANAI LAL (1963) *The Bengal Vaishnavism and Modern Life*. Calcutta: Sribhumi Publishing Company.

ERIKSON, E. H. (1963) *The Challenge of Youth*. New York : Anchor.

ERIKSON, E. G. (1968) *Identity* : *Youth and Crisis*. New York : Norton.

GLOCK, C. and BELLAH, R. (eds.) (1976) *The New Religious Consciousness*. University of California Press, Berkeley, Los Angeles and London.

GLOCK, C. (1964) 'The Role of Deprivation in the Origin and Evolution of Religious Groups,' in Lee, R. and Marty, M. E. (eds.) *Religion and Social Conflict*. New York: Oxford University Press. 24-36.

GOFFMAN, E. (1961) *Asylums* . New York : Anchor.

HALLPIKE, C. R. (1969) 'Social Hair,' *Man, 4 (N.S.)* 256-264.

HALL, S. and JEFFERSON, T. (eds.) (1976). *Resistance through Rituals* : *Youth Subcultures in Post-war Britain*. London : Hutchinson of London in

Bibliography

Association with the Centre for Contemporary Cultural Studies, University of Birmingham.

HEBDIGE, D. (1976) 'The Meaning of Mod' in Hall, S. and Jefferson, T. (eds.) *Resistance through Rituals : Youth Subcultures in Post-war Britain*. London : Hutchinson of London in Association with the Centre for Contemporary Cultural Studies, University of Birmingham, 87-96.

―――― (1979) *Subculture : The Meaning of Style*. London : Methuen & Co. Ltd. New Accent Series.

HERTZ, R. (1960) *Death and the Right Hand*. Translated by R. & C. Needham. London : Cohen and West.

JEFFERSON, T. (1976) 'Cultural Responses of the Teds : The Defence of Space and Status' in Hall, S. and Jefferson, T. (eds.) *Resistance through Rituals : Youth Subcultures in Post-war Britain*. London : Hutchinson of London in Association with the Centre for Contemparary Cultural Studies, University of Birmingham. 81-86.

JOHNSON, G. (1973) 'An Alternative Community in Microcosm.' Harvard : Ph. D. Thesis.

―――― (1976) 'The Hare Krishna in San Francisco' in Glock, C. and Bellah, R. (eds.) *The New Religious Consciousness*. Berkeley & Los Angeles : University of California Press.

JUDAH, J. S. (1974) 'The Hare Krishna Movement' in Zaretsky, I. & Leone M. P. (eds.) *Religious Movements in Contemporary America*. Princeton : Princeton University Press, 463-478.

KANTER, R. (1968) 'Commitment and Social Organization : A Study of Commitment Mechanisms in Utopian Communities' *American Sociological Review*, August, 499-517.

KENNEDY, M. T. (1925) *The Chaitanya Movement : A Study of Vaishnavism of Bengal*. Calcutta : Association Press, New York : Oxford University Press.

KURATH (1949) 'Dance : Folk and Primitive' in Leach M. and Fried, J. (eds.) *Dictionary of Folklore, Mythology and Legend*, New York: Funk and Wagnalls. *1*, 277-296.

LANGE, R. (1975) *The Nature of Dance : An Anthropologicial Perspective*. London : McDonald & Evans.

―――― (1975) *Dance Studies*, Centre for Dance Studies. Les Bois, St. Peter Jersey, Channel Islands. *1*.

―――― (1976) *Dance Studies*, Centre for Dance Studies. Les Bois, St. Peter Jersey, Channel Islands. *1*.

LEACH, E. (1958) 'Magical Hair' Curl Bequest Prize Essay, 1957. *Journal of the Royal Anthropological Institute of Great Britain and Ireland*, 88, 147-164.

LEARY, T. (1968) *The Politics of Ecstasy*. New York : G. P. Putnams & Sons.

LEECH, K. (1973) *Youthquake : The Growth of a Counter-culture through Two Decades*. London : Sheldon Press.

LEWIS, I. (1977) (eds.) *Symbols and Sentiments : Cross-cultural Studies in Symbolism*. London : Academic Press.

LOFLAND, J. and STARK, R. (1965) 'Becoming a World Saviour : A Theory of Conversion to a Deviant Perspective' *American Sociological Review*, 30, 862-875.

LOMAX, A. (1968) *Folk Song Style and Culture.* Washington D. C. : American Association for the Advancement of Science, Publication 88.

MAJUMDAR, A. K. (1965) *Bhakti Renaissance.* Bombay : Bharatiya Vidya Bhavan.

MAJUMDAR, B. (1969) *Krsna in History and Legend.* Calcutta : University of Calcutta Press.

MAUSS, M. (1936) 'Les Techniques du Corps.' *Journal de Psychologie Normale Et Pathologique,* 32. March-April.

MELLY, G. (1972) *Revolt into Style.* London : Harmondsworth : Penguin.

MINER, H. (1956) 'Body Ritual among the Nacirema' *American Anthropologist,* 58, 503-507.

MUKHERJEE, D. K. (1970) *Chaitanya.* New Delhi : National Book Trust (National Biography Series).

MUKHERJI, S. C. (1966) *A Study of Vaisnavism in Ancient and Medieval Bengal up to the Advent of Caitanya.* Calcutta : Punthi Pustak.

NEEDLEMAN, J. (1972) *The New Religions.* New York : Pocket Books.

POLHEMUS, T. (1978) (eds.) *The Body Reader : Social Aspects of the Human Body.* Pantheon Books, New York.

PRINCE, R.H. (1974) 'Cocoon Work : An Interpretation of the Concern of Contemporary Youth with the Mystical' in Zaretsky, I. and Leone, M. P. *Religious Movements in Contemporary America.* Princeton, N. J. : Princeton University Press, 255-271.

RAWSON, P. S. (1975) 'The Body in Tantra.' in Benthall, J. and Polhemus, T. *The Body as a Medium of Expression.* London : Allen Lane, 271-290.

REICH, C. A. (1970) *The Greening of America.* New York : Random House.

ROSZAK, T. (1969) *The Making of a Counterculture : Reflections of the Technocratic Society and Its Youthful Opposition.* Garden City : Doubleday.

ROYCE, A. P. (1977) *The Anthropology of Dance.* Bloomington/London : Indiana University Press.

SARGANT, W. (1957) *Battle for the Mind : A Physiology of Conversion and Brainwashing.* London : Heinemann.

SINGER, M. (1966) *Krshna, Myths, Rites and Attitudes.* Chicago : University of Chicago Press.

SLATER, P. E. (1970) *The Pursuit of Lonelines: American Culture at the Breaking Point.* Boston : Beacon Press.

SNELLING, C. H. and Whitley, O. R. (1974) 'Problem-solving Behaviour in Religious and Para-religious Groups : An Initial Report' in Eisetr A. (ed.) *Changing Perspectives in the Scientific Study of Religion.* New York: John Wiley and Sons, 315-334.

TURNER, V. (1964) 'Betwixt and Between : The Liminal Period in 'Rites de Passage'' in Helm, J. (ed.) *Symposium on New Approaches to the Study of Religion.* Seattle : American Ethnological Society.

――― (1967) *Forest of Symbols.* Ithaca and London : Cornell University Press.

――― (1969) *The Ritual Process : Structure and Anti-Structure.* London : Routledge & Kegan Paul.

WESTHUES, K. (1972) *Society's Shadow : Studies in the Sociology of Counter-*

cultures. Toronto : McGraw-Hill Ryerson Ltd.

WILLIS, P.E. (1976) The Cultural Meaning of Drug Use' in Hall, S. and Jefferson, T. (eds.) *Resistance through Rituals : Youth Subcultures in Post-war Britain*. London : Hutchinson of London in Association with the Centre for Contemporary Cultral Studies, University of Birmingham.

WILLIS, P. (1978) *Profane Culture*. London : Routledge & Kegan Paul.

WILSON, B. (1975) *Magic and the Millenium*. St. Albans : Paladin.

——— (1976) *Contemporary Transformations of Religion*. Oxford University: University of Newcastle-upon-Tyne Publications.

ZABLOCKI, B, (1971) *The Joyful Community*. Baltimore : Penguin Books.

ZAEHNER, R. C. (1968) *Hinduism*. New York : Oxford University Press.

Index

Acyutananda (Swami), 122
Adikesvara (Swami), 127
Advaita, 51
Amburisha, 129
American Counterculture, 29, 163, 277
American devotees, 68; and drugs, 16-19
American gurus, 284
Amish Mennonites, 7
Anandadasa, 107
Anandalila, 95
Aquinas, St. Thomas, 142
Art Department, 103, 107-8, 196
Asceticism, power and politics of, 115-32
Asian Community, and ISKCON, 239-40, 246, 247, 251
Association of Social Anthropologists, 151

Back to Godhead, 4, 137, 140, 142, 144, 173, 226
Beaton, Cecil, 25
Benthall, Jonathan, 155
Berg, G. C., 217
Bhagavad Gita, the, 49, 109, 136-37, 142, 260, 264, 267
Bhagavata Purana, 52
Bhaja Hari, 130
Bhaktisiddhanta Saraswati Thakura, see Thakur
Bhaktivedanta Book Trust, 93, 103, 118, 138, 267, 270; Travelling Sankirtan Party, 182
Bhaktivedanta Institute, 138, 178
Bhaktivedanta Manor, 80, 90, 101, 102, 193, 199, 211, 239, 245-46, 248-49; young children and, 248

Bhaktivedanta (Swami), 45, 118-19, 121-23, 125, 128, 143
Bhaktiyoga, 44-45, 49, 50, 90, 207, 240, 284; ideology of, 77
Black Lightning see Ted Patrick
Body symbolism, 151, 172, 178; and women, 200; Bodily Liberationists and, 150
Boston temple, 80
Bothes, 272
Brahmacharin, 206,
Brahmananda (Swami), 143, 207, 270
Brainwashing, 261; and ISKCON, 271
Britain, religions and cults in, 7; youth culture of, 25
British Charity Commission, 91
British devotees, 19-21, 130; and drugs, 36
British host society, 240
British Ministry of Education, 249
British Museum, 263
British Temples, 78, 271
British working class, culture of, 24-25
Brown, Norman, 150
Burghart, 218
Burr, Angela, 45, 161, 198, 199

Caine, Michael, 24
Caste system, spiritual order of, 178; vedic interpretation of, 116
Chaitanya Mahaprabhu, 3, 50, 63, 66, 198, 229, 240, 250; and Krishna bhakti, 50-51; verses and philosophy of, 51
Christianity, 13
Cohen, 165
Committee Engaged in Freeing Minds (CEFM), 257

Conway, F., 259-61, 270-71, 274
Courtney, Tom, 24
Cybernetics, 259
Coward, Noel, 24
Dalrymple, Richard, 173
Dance, ISKCON and, 224, 228; a form of self expression, 226; a language of communication, 226
Daner, Francine, 16, 34, 50, 163-64
Danielou, Cardinal, 142
Detroit Temple, 109, 129
Deikman, 287
Devotees, behaviour of prominent, 273-74; business of 111-12; customs of, 31-33; female, income of 94-95; and Indians, 235, attitude of, towards their bodies, 173-76; attitude to food, 180; and Prabhupad's body, 182-84; modern youth and, leadership of, 115; long-term, 274; manipulation of, 97-98; materialism of, 113; projects of, 117-18; Muslim villagers and, 234; problems of, 31-33; rejection of their bodies by, 176; sexual renunciation and, 193-95; social patterns of, 227; in Vrindaban, 234-35
Dhananjaya, 111, 114, 126, 229, 254-55
Divine Light Mission 1, 46, 67
Douglas, Mary, 151, 173, 227, 228

East African Gujaratis, 240, 241, 247, 251
Emanuel, 33, 133
Entrepreneurism, 111
Eva, 263

Fate, 103, 109; devotees, 129; studios, 109, 110, 210
Freudian theory of the unconscious, 217
Finney, Albert, 24
First American Theistic, Exhibition, the, 109
Ford, Henry, 129

Ganga, 177
Gaudiya, Matha, 46, 140, 172, 204; mission, 92; philosophy, 255; sect, 46, 47, 50, 52, 240; scriptures, 46
Gennep, Von, 286
Glock, 17, 78
Goalen, Barbara, 25
Gopalabhatta, 243
Governing Body Commission, 79, 112, 117, 118, 122, 126, 127, 131, 202, 219, 236, 285; Gurus and, 123, 127; zones of, 123
Govinda (Swami), 112, 114, 116, 120, 122, 125, 203, 209
Graham, Billy, 43
Guru Maharaj Ji, 67, 100

Haight Ashbury, 34, 91, 132; drug culture of, 35
Haight Ashbury temple, 45, 134, 194; devotees in, 80, 164
Hair symbolism, 215-21
Hallpike, 216
Hamsaduta (Swami) 118, 121-23, 128
Hare Krishna Mantra, meaning of, 60-62
Hari Bhakti Vilasa, 243
Harikesa (Swami) 119
Harrison, George, 3, 20, 21, 29, 95
Hawaii temple, 220
Heavies, 199, 200-2, 206, 238
Hebdige, Dick, 153
Hertz, Robert, 151
Hindu Asian Communities, 240, 242
Hinduism, 113, 172, 248
Hobbes, 154-55
Human Potential movement, 150
Huxley, Aldous, 23

'I am not my body, I am spirit-soul,' concept of, 160-62, 227-28, 236, 242, 277; devotees responses to, 161; meaning of, 145-147
Information Theory, 259
Institute of Contemporary Art, 151
International Guest House, 51, 234

Index

International Society for Krishna Consciousness (ISKCON), accused of brain washing, 257; administrative control of, 79; and adolescent girls, 281; aim of, 81, 207; in America and Britain 10-40; anti-materialism of, 89; art of, 64; artists in, 107-8; asceticism in, 121-22; Asians' involvement in, 244-46; attitude of, to sex, 191-92; attitude of, towards women, 196-97; belief and practices of, 264, 289; belief system of, 57, 138-40, 165, 266, 273; bodily movement and dance in, 222-30; bodily ritual in, 172-84; in Britain, 20-23, 280; celibate ideal of, 206; centres of, in India, 231-32; concept of, 8-9; criticism of, 99; and devotees, 277, 279, 283; countercultural youth and, 16; development of, 208; diet in, 262; economic projects set up by, 102-7; economic structure of, 90-93; enterprises of, 113; exploitation in, 101; features of, 62; festivals held by, 99; financial solvency of, 91; focus of, on body, 185; future of, 131, 281; goal of, 42; group harmony and, 265; and gurus, 284-85; householders in, 211-13; ideology of, 198; impersonalism in, 54-55; importance to dress in, 196-98; and India, 231-38; institutional structure of, 283; influence of, 271-72; internal politics of, 117; literary output of, 93-95; male domination in, 20; marriages in, 201-2; membership of, 280; modern youth and, 27-29; new cults and, 280; philosophy of, 3, 45, 47, 100, 144-45, 163, 205, 258; philosophy and Hinduism, 46; politics, 133; political system of, 124; preaching centres of, 3; rational bureaucratic norms in, 103-4; religious leadership in, 120; rituals in, 79; role of Gurus in, 66-76; role of, in India, 143; secular pattern of, 204-5; sexual rites of, 191-213; sources of income of, 140; symbolism in, 133-34; Temples, 78; 120, 239, 240, 252-53, 262, 271; and Western Society, 7; young children and, 248-49; youth club started by, 254; zones of, 78-79

Isherwood, Christopher, 23
Jagannatha (Swami), 122
Jayatirtha Maharaj, 74, 104, 117, 119, 123, 128-31, 197, 203 243-44; appearance day of, 130; Governing Body Commission and, 130
Jefferson, Tony, 153
Jnana Dasa, 21, 64
Johnson, 16, 34-35, 80
Judah, Stillson, 16, 34, 78

Kanter, 282-83
Karmi Society, 90, 132, 211, 212, 255; and ISKCON; 115
Kennedy, John, 15
Kirtanananda (Swami), 118, 125-26, 131
Krishna, 47-49; form of, devotees views regarding, 53-54, 56, 60, 61; in Vaishnava writings, 48
Krishna Balaram Mandir, 51, 231
Krishna Bhakti, 267-68
Krishna Consciousness, 68, 92-94, 178, 208, 213, 242, 258, 285; acquiring knowledge of, process of, 266; aim of, 58; ISKCON and, 266; philosophy of, 53, 55, 58, 134, 137, 262-64, 273
Krsna, 236
Kulasekhara, 13, 21

Lange, R., 223
Leach, E., 221
Leary, Timothy, 34
Levi-Strauss 276-77
Lewis, I., 133
Life Membership Scheme, 103, 233, 251, 252; members of, facilities to, 234
Lomax, A., 224
London ICA Conference, 153

London University Oriental Library, 267
Los Angeles Herald Examiner, the, 173

Mahabharata, 49
Malati 20
Manjvali, 74, 197, 203
Martin Luther King, 15
Mayapur, devotees in, 234-35; ISKCON School in, 237
Mind and Body Festivals, 145, 152, 261
Miner, Horace, 150
Moonies, 91, 257
Morarji, Sumati, 111
Motorbike boys and Hippies in Britain, study of, 278
Mukanda, 54
Muktananda (Swami), 152

Nacirema culture, 150
Ndembu, 151
Neotranscendentalism, 288, 289
New York temple, 210, 219
Nityananda, 51

Patrick, Ted, 257
People's Organised Workshop Against Estate Religions, 257
Permissive Society, 6, 116, 194-95, 216, 228, 276; equalitarianism of, 195; symbol of, 205
Plato, 142
Prabhupad, 12, 14, 17, 20, 46, 48, 51, 57, 66, 67, 75, 76, 79, 110, 113, 117, 119-28, 130, 132, 142-43, 147, 158, 172, 174, 178-79, 181, 192-93, 196-98, 231-33, 237, 255, 257, 265, 267, 270-71, 284-85; behaviour of, 111; birth of, 2; books of, and ISKCON, 135-38; death of, 3; devotees, feelings towards, 69; mission of, 92; philosophy of, 5; relation of, with devotees, 73; speeches in praise of, 70-71; teachings of, 3, 138, 276; Vaishnava belief and, 46; view of, on women, 195-96; will, of 129; writings of, 68

Prince, R.H., 286, 288; views of, regarding middle class youth, 286-87
Purangana, 113

Radha, 47, 52, 181
Radhadamodara temple, 51
Radha Damodara Travelling Sankirtan Party, 118
Rajneesh Meditation Group, 152
Ramanuja, 50
Ramesvara (Swami), 75, 118, 121, 131
Rathyatra Festival, 140
Rattigan, Terence, 24
Reich, Wilhelm, 150
Rishi, Atreya, 117, 118, 126, 182
Roszak, T., 15, 277
Royce, A.P., 223

San Francisco temple, 80
Sanatana Dharma, 47, 51
Sankirtan devotees, 99
Sannyasins, 120-22, 202-4, 206-219; bodily symbolism and, 204; power of, 122; role of, 120-21, 208-9; way of life of, 209-10
Sargent, 260
Satsvarup (Swami), 4, 68, 123, 125-28, 131, 138
Schopenhauer, 142
Science of Self Realisation, 163, 166
Sexual renunciation and *Sannyasa*, 203-4
Shankaracharya, 54-55
Shrimad Bhagavata, 13, 109, 137, 267
Shri Vaishnava Sect, 50
Shyamsundara, 20
Siegelman, 258-61, 271, 274
Sidh Yoga Group, 152
Slater, 15, 77, 277
Sleep deprivation, 260-61
Spirit soul, concept of, 141; devotees identification with, 163; traditional Vaishnava's views regarding, 141
Spock, Dr, 25
Sri Vyasa Puja, books, 69, 73, 75, 128, 182

Steve, 145
Structuralists, 276
Swinging Sixties, 23, 43, 66, 224; function of, 27
Symbolic system, 160-62

Thakura, Bhaktisiddhanta Saraswati, 2, 4, 51
Transcendental Meditation, 1, 91, 280, 290
Transcendental nature, 45
Turner, Victor, 151, 288

Utopian communities, 282-83

Vaishnava, Gaudiya sect, 2; Gaudiya Matha, 47; philosophy of 56, 61, 161; sects, 50, 70;
Varma, Raja Ravi, 64
Vedic culture, 48, 237-38

Vedic system, 203
Vietnam War, 22
Vijitravirya, 103
Visakha, 108, 145
Vrindavan International Guest House, 115
Vrindavan (Swami), 114
Vrindavan temple, 122, 126

Watts, Alan, 23
Wesker, Arnold, 24
Western society, awakening in, 10-14; love in, 53; role of body in, 149-59
Whitelow, Billie, 25
Wills, 277-78

Yadhubhara Dasa, 108, 145
Yadurani, 16, 108, 196, 199
Yamuna, 177